D1087573

Miscarriage of Justice

Justice

The Jonathan Pollard Story

Books By Mark Shaw

Testament To Courage
Larry Legend
Forever Flying
Bury Me In A Pot Bunker
The Perfect Yankee
Diamonds In The Rough
Nicklaus, A Biography
Down For The Count

Miscarriage of Justice

The Jonathan Pollard Story

by
Mark Shaw

PARAGON HOUSE
St. Paul Minnesota

First Edition, 2001

Published in the United States by
Paragon House
2700 University Avenue West
St. Paul, MN 55114

Library of Congress Cataloging-in-Publishing data

Shaw, Mark, 1945-
    Miscarriage of justice : the Jonathan Pollard story / by Mark Shaw.—1 st ed.
    p. cm.
    Includes bibliographical references and index.
    ISBN 1-55778-803-0 (cloth)
        1. Pollard, Jonathan Jay, 1954-—Trials, litigation, etc. 2. Trials (Espionage)—United
States. 3. Espionage, Israeli—United States. 1. Title.

KF224.P58 S53 2001
345.73'0231—dc21
                                                                        2001033134

10 9 8 7 6 5 4 3 2 1

For current information about all releases from Paragon House,
visit the web site at http://www.paragonhouse.com

No person shall be held to answer for a capital, or otherwise infamous crime…nor be deprived of life, liberty, or property, without due process of law….

—Fifth Amendment, *United States Constitution*

In spite of the fact that I have been greatly troubled over how this affair has been mishandled by both the Israeli and American governments, I am nevertheless confident that what I did, however ill-advised it was in retrospect, will make a significant contribution to Israel's military capabilities. From my perspective, if this results in the saving of Jewish lives either during a war or by the prevention of one through the strengthening of Israel's deterrent capacity, then at least something good will come from this tragedy.

—Jonathan Pollard, letter to Elie Wiesel, January 27, 1987

The government's breach of the plea agreement was a fundamental miscarriage of justice.

—Judge Stephen Williams, United States Court of Appeals

[Marc] Rich's former wife contributed over $1 million to democratic campaigns, while Rich's direction of some ill-gotten gains to charities induced Israel's Ehud Barak to use up his one big pardon favor with [President] Clinton, dooming the unrich Jonathan Pollard to a life in jail.

—William Safire, *New York Times,* February 1, 2001

If the truth is buried underground, it swells and grows and becomes so explosive that the day it bursts, it blows everything wide open along with it.

—French novelist Émile Zola, *J'Accuse*, January 13, 1898

CONTENTS

ACKNOWLEDGMENTS

Each book I write is like a child to me; off into the world to entertain, provide information, educate, or make people stop and think. The process is the joint effort of many who assist me with their expertise, knowledge, and faith.

This book's family of contributors begins with my wife Chris, a fine editor and a loving partner who supports my efforts. She and my stepchildren, Kimberly, Kyle, Kevin, and Kent, all share in the completion of this task as do my canine buddies, Shadow and Peanut Butter, and the dear departed White Sox, Reggie Miller, Bach, and Snickers.

Providing editorial assistance were two dear friends Donna Stouder and Becky Howard, and consultant Paul McCarthy, whose sharp pen improved the book with each draft. I also thank University of Baltimore law professor Kenneth Lasson and University of Notre Dame law professor Charles Rice for perusing the manuscript to confirm that my legal observations were appropriate.

Most helpful were Morris and Mollie Pollard and daughter Carol who spoke to me about Jonathan. They are a loving family who continue their support of efforts to free him. Former United States Attorney Joseph diGenova cooperated by providing an exclusive interview regarding the case.

Others who contributed to the evolution of this book are Tom Peterson, a former key business executive with the Jack Nicklaus company, Jack Lupton, a special friend, Jerry Bales, a state legislator and radio talk show host whose strong sense for accuracy aided the consistency of the text, and Nancy Baxter, whose editing skills and friendship assisted me with completion of the book. Pastor Tim Bond provided insight regarding biblical quotes in the book. Cherished friends Beverly and Larry Newman were an inspiration for my interest in the Pollard case, reviewed the manuscript providing valuable comments, and aided in contacting Paragon House. Syndicated columnist and television talk show host Arlene Peck assisted my efforts.

At the pubishing company, I thank Laureen Enright, a dedicated professional whose assistance was invaluable, Gordon L. Anderson, and Dean Curtis. I will be forever grateful for their belief, and that of literary agents Andrew Stuart and Kimberly Cameron, in the book.

Above all, of course, I thank the Good Lord for permitting me to complete *Miscarriage of Justice*. Unquestionably, I am the most blessed man on the face of the earth.

AUTHOR'S NOTE

For the United States of America to remain a great Republic, the Constitution must protect the worst of us in order to protect the best of us. Under that standard, even those who violate the law in a manner so despicable as to turn our stomachs and inflame our souls must be treated like every other citizen.

During the past decade, the government and the courts have gone to great lengths to ensure that ruthless individuals like Ted Bundy, Timothy McVeigh, Unabomber Ted Kaczynski, and those charged with racial and sexual preference hate crimes in Jasper, Texas, and Laramie, Wyoming, have been protected by the Constitution. No matter how offensive the alleged crimes, their Fifth Amendment rights to due process were protected.

While those cases have progressed in the courts and advanced through the appeal process, one man, former Naval Intelligence Service (NIS) junior analyst Jonathan Jay Pollard, who violated his loyalty oath to the United States by spying for Israel, has been incarcerated since 1985. That despite the fact that, according to millions of his supporters, a dark cloud hovers over the case like none before it or since.

This belief is based on their allegation that Pollard, dubbed a traitor by many, was denied *his* Fifth Amendment rights to due process. Supporters charge that he was railroaded into prison by a government determined to hide the truth.

The contradictory state of affairs regarding the Pollard case has been apparent to me ever since I prepped for an interview with Jonathan's father, Dr. Morris Pollard, for a radio talk show I hosted in 1999. To prepare, I read portions of three books published about the case: *Territory of Lies* (1989) by former *Jerusalem Post* journalist and future CNN White House correspondent Wolf Blitzer, *The Spy Who Knew Too Much* (1993) by journalist Elliot Goldenberg, and *Pollard, The Spy's Story* (1988) by Bernard Henderson, father of Anne, Jonathan's ex-wife. Each book addressed issues in the Pollard case based on a personal agenda; two were written by members of the Jewish faith while Henderson was a non-Jew whose wife was Jewish.

After reading the material, I asked a perplexing question: what was so exceptional about the Pollard case that had frozen it in controversy for more than a decade? Having been a criminal defense attorney, I knew prisons were full of inmates who shouted their innocence, believed they were represented by incompetent attorneys, or pleaded that their constitutional rights had been violated. Was Pollard just another whiner, or had he indeed been wronged by a government and a judicial system bent on persecuting him no matter the unethical or illegal means employed?

My first inclination was to believe that Pollard was the former, a man who cried foul, but had no one but himself to blame for the life imprisonment sentence imposed by Federal Court Judge Aubrey Robinson. Having admitted he violated the law, Pollard deserved to be severely punished, especially since he violated the NIS loyalty oath that prevented him from disclosing secret, classified information crucial to the security of the United States.

That frame of mind triggered combative questions when Dr. Pollard appeared on the radio show. As the interview continued, however, I recognized that the most critical aspect of the case had not been fully researched: whether Jonathan Pollard's constitutional rights to due process had indeed been jeopardized. Doing so meant, among other factors, evaluating the charges against Pollard, his representation, the conduct of government prosecutors, and the appropriateness of the life sentence.

Believing that an independent analysis by an individual outside the Jewish community who possessed both an impartial perspective of the case and the legal and journalistic credentials to accurately present the facts was missing, I decided a book was in order. Most importantly, I felt that there appeared to be considerable misunderstanding of the facts that led to Pollard's arrest and imprisonment. That point was reemphasized during a fall, 2000 trip to New York City where I conversed with the owner of a prestigious publishing company. During our conversation, I mentioned the Pollard book. He said, "Pollard's right where he should be because of all the money he made spying." When I asked, "Just how much do you think Pollard earned?" the publisher replied, "A couple of hundred thousand dollars," a figure that was excessive.

Earlier, I had attempted to interest my friend in publishing the book, only to have him say, "Pollard's guilty as hell." At that time, I tried to explain that the book wasn't intended to debate guilt or innocence, but to examine the concepts of equal justice and whether Pollard was denied his. My friend stated that Pollard was a "traitor" and his punishment just. Since he had never been charged with that crime, defined as aiding the enemy in time of war, I debated the issue, but to no avail.

Due to misconceptions, the key to researching the case was separating fact from fiction. To evaluate whether Pollard had been denied his rights to due process, I investigated the "whys" behind the spy's actions and examined the conduct of the media in reporting the case. Those issues had continued to cause heated debate between Pollard supporters and those who believed he should have been shot.

As my research progressed, I became curious as to why the majority of Jewish community leaders had turned their backs on Pollard once he was arrested. That seemed illogical since the spy was an Orthodox Jew aiding Israel, the spiritual homeland for millions of that faith.

Jewish conduct toward Pollard was considered in lieu of observations I had gathered throughout my life. My parents taught me to treat everyone on an equal basis regardless of his or her race or religious faith. Some years ago, a friend mentioned that he could easily tell whether someone was Jewish by their last name. He was surprised when I told him I had never considered the stereotype.

Predicting how people of any faith or ethnicity will react to circumstances affecting that faith or culture is difficult. I'd often questioned the behavior of Jewish leaders toward issues affecting their brethren as well as non-Jews' attitudes toward those of the Jewish faith. The former was most apparent when some members of the Jewish community criticized my book, *Testament To Courage,* the memoir of Holocaust survivor Cecelia Rexin.

In one chapter, Cecelia related the story of two German prison guards at Ravensbrueck who assisted her in saving the life of a young Russian girl named Laddie. Condemnation by Jewish leaders of her account was based on the belief that *no* German could have *ever* exhibited such kindness. To them, they informed me, Cecelia's story was akin to blasphemy.

After probing the Jewish issue, I pondered the stern criticism of the spy by such national leaders as Secretary of State Madeleine Albright, CIA Director George Tenet, and Senator Joseph Lieberman, an Orthodox Jew who was the unsuccessful candidate for vice president of the United States in 2000. Journalist and author Seymour Hersh's badgering of Pollard drew my attention since his writings were notably venomous in nature.

Analyzing media accounts and extensive legal documents filed in the case permitted use of legal experience garnered as a practicing lawyer in California and Indiana. My work as an investigative reporter and commentator for ABC, CNN, ESPN, and the BBC on the Mike Tyson, O. J. Simpson, and Claudine Longet cases proved invaluable. The research on the Tyson case resulted in a *USA Today* column during the trial and *Down For The Count*, my book which examined the legal and societal issues in the boxer's case and whether he was afforded his constitutional rights to due process.

In order to provide a thorough analysis of the Pollard case, I examined every legal document filed, including the indictment, guilty plea agreements, and appellate briefs. I also reviewed at length the portions made public of the explosive Pollard memorandum and letter produced for the sentencing judge by former Secretary of Defense Caspar Weinberger. Personal letters written by Pollard to his father and others added to the mix.

To gain further insight into a case that continued to provide fiction-like drama, I attempted to interview all of the principals. Two men I *most* wanted to speak with were Judge Robinson and Jonathan Pollard. Unfortunately, the judge died in the early months of 2000, and Pollard, awaiting a court ruling on a motion for resentencing, declined through his representatives to be interviewed.

Interviewing Dr. Morris Pollard and Joseph diGenova, Jonathan's fiery prosecutor was most revealing. Eighty-four years old, Dr. Pollard, a revered scientist, was best known for his research efforts to cure prostate cancer. His experimental study was conducted at the University of Notre Dame where the kindly man operated out of a small, nondescript building dubbed affectionately, "the Outhouse." It was adjacent to the coal yards on the outskirts of the campus.

Despite the obvious heartache caused by his son's case, Dr. Pollard, a wise man who flattered me with never-before-revealed personal details about his life and his son's upbringing, approached each day with renewed vigor. He and his effervescent wife, Mollie, whose health deteriorated over concern for her son, remained steadfast in their support of Jonathan despite his refusal in recent years to communicate with them and his devoted sister, Carol, an embattled woman who has devoted herself to Jonathan's release.

When I interviewed Joseph diGenova, who uttered the famous line "It is unlikely that Pollard will ever see the light of day" after the sentencing, the prosecutor attempted to debunk Pollard supporters' allegations of impropriety on the part of the government and the court. In an impassioned tone, diGenova, a man who appeared to have enjoyed the celebrity status the Pollard case has afforded him, provided another side to the story, one that portrays his view that Pollard and his loyalists have time and time again distorted the truth. His revelations made me stop, think, and reconsider many of the opinions I had formed about Pollard's actions, especially since Appellate Court Judge Stephen Williams, in a dissenting opinion, had called the case, "A fundamental miscarriage of justice."

DiGenova's proclamations stirred my interest in researching another aspect of the Pollard case. Since research confirmed that he had spied in an attempt to aid the ally Israel in pursuit of personal beliefs that United States conduct toward Israel was immoral, if not illegal, I questioned how his mission compared with others in history who had been of like mind. That led me to read *Bombshell: The Secret Story of America's Unknown Atomic Spy Conspiracy*, by noted authors Joseph Albright and Marcia Kunstel. They chronicled the betrayal of Theodore Hall, the young Los Alamos scientist who leaked secrets about the atom bomb to the Soviets, then an ally of the United States.

I believe my search for the truth presents a fresh approach to a confusing case filled with lies, half-truths, innuendo, speculation, and deception. That done, I decided to compare Pollard's case to the historical saga involving Alfred Dreyfus, the Jewish French captain railroaded by the military into prison for spying in the late 1800s. I read *The Dreyfus Affair* by Émile Zola, the renowned French novelist and author of *J'Accuse*, which detailed disturbing facts behind accusations that Dreyfus was a spy for the Germans.

Observations gained from that publication were helpful when I assessed the circumstances surrounding why Pollard was not released by President Clinton during his final days in office. Similar to the chaotic nature of the Dreyfus case, I discovered that Pollard's chances for freedom were entwined in a cesspool of political chicanery, distressing conflicts of interest, and basic greed. When the clock struck 12:00 A.M. on January 20, 2001, fugitive American financier Marc Rich had been pardoned, while Pollard remained incarcerated.

Besides analysis of that scenario, comparisons of the Pollard case with those involving Alfred Dreyfus and Ted Hall, information garnered from extensive interviews, and insight gained through various articles, books, and legal documents permitted me a more detailed picture of the lonely spy incarcerated in a North Carolina prison cell. Though I condemn his breaking of the law, I gained a clearer understanding as to how Pollard catapulted himself into a position where opponents labeled him a traitor while supporters believed he was an Israeli patriot who caused no harm to the United States. By respecting those positions, and considering the arguments presented by both sides, I trust I have accurately portrayed the life and times of America's most controversial spy, Jonathan Jay Pollard.

PROLOGUE

To spy or not to spy, that was the agonizing decision facing Jonathan Pollard during the winter months of 1983. Over the course of the four-plus years he had been employed as an intelligence research specialist by the Field Operational Intelligence Office of the United States Navy (NIS), Pollard had come face to face with an inescapable conclusion: the powerful elite in the US intelligence community were violating the edict of the 1983 US-Israel Exchange of Information Agreement by deliberately withholding classified material vital to the national security of one of America's strongest allies. In effect, he believed that certain government officials, spearheaded by Secretary of Defense Caspar Weinberger, were imposing their own brand of foreign policy.

Day after day, Pollard's thoughts reflected conflicting loyalties to the United States, his birthplace, and to Israel, the country he had adopted as his spiritual homeland during his teenage years. Each second of every minute, he wrestled with his conscience as to whether he would betray the United States in order to save Israel from potential extinction, since he believed that the classified information being withheld was vital to Israel's very existence.

While weighing his options, Pollard, a junior analyst with access to strategic military information concerning the Middle East, presented his concerns to superiors at the NIS, but no one responded to his desperate and repeated attempts to alter policy. Worse, Pollard was shocked by the anti-Semitic tone that pervaded the office. A colleague, in response to Jonathan's question about Israel's need for intelligence information regarding Iraqi poison gas research, turned to him, according to Pollard, laughed, and said "Jews are overly sensitive about gas due to their experiences during World War II." He then suggested that "they should calm down a bit."

To Pollard, that comment was akin to stabbing his heart with a dagger. Following an NIS headquarters meeting between US intelligence personnel and their Israeli counterparts, he approached one of their officials and said, "I am Jewish and I want to help you." The Israeli thanked him, but no channel of communication was established.

Pollard's protocol to complain about both the anti-Semitism and the failure of the NIS to provide Israel with critical security information was through the Navy's inspector general. Whether Jonathan considered that option was unclear, but records indicate that he never contacted the proper officials.

In 1984, Pollard's ability to rein in his passionate desire to single-handedly rescue Israel by providing classified documents affecting its security grew weaker. Devastated by what he felt was a continuing pattern of disturbing conduct by NIS officials, he began considering no longer *whether* to spy, but *how* he would do so.

Pollard's only ally during this turbulent time of indecision was his live-in girlfriend, Anne Henderson, who shared his belief that Israel was sacred ground and must be defended at all costs. Nevertheless, Pollard, a committed Zionist, had no way to approach the Israelis without compromising his position.

When Pollard's frustration peaked, he considered resigning his post at the NIS and fleeing to Israel. As he debated that notion, the idealist engaged in a telephone conversation with Steven Stern, a wealthy New York-based stockbroker and family friend of the Pollards. During their discussion in December 1983, Stern mentioned a speech he had just attended.

"I have just returned from the most fascinating lecture I have ever heard in my life," Stern said. "Colonel Sella is a spellbinding speaker."

Pollard snapped to attention, for Colonel Aviem Sella was a soldier he highly respected. Through heroic missions for the Israeli Air Force, the colonel had served his country as a true patriot.

When Pollard asked whether he might meet Colonel Sella, his friend said that was possible. Several days later, on May 29, 1984, Jonathan Jay Pollard, desperately seeking someone to listen, and Colonel Aviem Sella, eager to do just that, sat in a corner booth in the crowded coffee shop of the Washington, DC, Hilton Hotel. Five sentences into their conversation, Pollard had voluntarily crossed the line, violating the NIS loyalty oath he had sworn to uphold, and became a spy.

BOOK I

Chapter 1

COLONEL SELLA

Jonathan Pollard's clandestine meeting with Colonel Aviem Sella was indirectly related to a relationship established between Jonathan's father, Dr. Morris Pollard, and Gustav Stern, president of the Hartz Mountain Company, famous for bird food products. In the 1950s, Stern, interested in science, conceived the idea for a symposium in New York City that would include one hundred scientists discussing "New Developments In Virology." Dr. Pollard, a noted expert in the field, was invited, and during one conference he discussed with Stern the cause and cures for psittacosis, parrot fever. Stern was impressed with Dr. Pollard's knowledge and requested that he coordinate future meetings and assist in selecting the participants.

The symposiums were held in February, when adverse weather conditions prevented attendees from sightseeing. Stern provided perks such as opera tickets and lodging at the ritzy Waldorf Astoria. That caused one observer to dub the gatherings the "Mink Coat Meetings." One hundred scientists were selected each year, one-third of whom were young researchers. Findings at what were known as International Symposiums on Virology (viruses) were published by Harper and Row. Dr. Pollard edited the text.

The volumes, titled *Perspectives in Virology,* featured insert photos of Nobel Prize winners including John Franklin Enders, Peyton Rous, and Wendell Stanley. The books are still regarded as excellent research guides today.

Dr. Pollard's association with Gustav Stern led to the introduction of Stern's son Steven, a graduate of Cornell who became a successful stockbroker in New York City. He met Jonathan at the scientific conference and they became friends. From time to time they discussed Jonathan's frustration with events occurring at the NIS.

Steven Stern's acquaintance with Israeli colonel Aviem Sella had occurred when the colonel mesmerized an audience of Jewish stockbrokers and financial wizards meeting in New York City to learn about the advantages of purchasing Israeli bonds. The meeting was held at Stern's office on Broadway, near the Wall Street district.

Colonel Aviem Sella was as devout a defender of Israel as Jonathan Pollard had become. The colonel's grandparents had been killed in Nazi death camps, and he was disheartened with the lack of worldwide Jewish resistance to Hitler's madness.

Growing up, Colonel Sella was determined to serve in the memory of the fallen loved ones. His name Aviem was a tribute to them, "avi" in Hebrew meant father, "em" mother.

Colonel Sella was born in Haifa in 1946. Fifty years later, use of the Freedom of Information Act provided access to his United States Defense Intelligence Agency (DIA) dossier. According to the report, he had entered the Air Force when he was eighteen. During the 1967 Six-Day War, he had flown Mystere aircraft in combat.

The Colonel, a fighter pilot in the 1970 War of Attrition with Egypt, flew Mirage aircraft during the 1973 war. In 1976, he commanded the celebrated 201st Fighter-Bomber Squadron.

A highly educated man, Colonel Sella was thirty-eight years old when he met Pollard. He earned a bachelor's degree in economics from Jerusalem University. In 1979, the colonel was awarded a master's degree in business from Tel Aviv University.

Colonel Sella was promoted to chief of Air Force Operations in 1980. A year later, as lead pilot, he planned and participated in Israel's bombing of Iraq's nuclear reactor at Osirak. In 1982, the colonel was credited with planning the air campaign that resulted in the destruction of more than ninety Syrian MiGs.

Colonel Sella's personal characteristics were listed in the DIA report. It stated: "Sella possesses a good sense of humour and is considered highly creative. An energetic individual, he is a scuba diving enthusiast and an avid tennis player." The report also outlined that the colonel had met his wife, Yehudit, while she was an officer in the Air Force. The Sellas had two sons, five and twelve years old.

By late 1983, Colonel Sella requested leave from the Israeli Air Force to pursue a doctorate in computer science at New York University. Advances in technology employed by the Israeli military required the Colonel to further his study in that area.

Colonel Sella's ninety minute speech to the Jewish group detailed his operation over Lebanon with sweeping drama. The audience cheered him with rousing applause when he concluded.

To Jonathan Pollard, the colonel was a true legend, a man to venerate, a man he admired for his courage in defending Israel at all costs. In the days that followed the speech it was unclear whether Pollard attended another given by Sella or spoke to him on the telephone. Regardless, Pollard knew that Sella was the perfect person to assist him in aiding his beloved Israel.

Before a meeting could occur, Colonel Sella, a lanky, handsome man whose chiseled cheekbones, deep-set eyes, and pointed nose complemented his receding hairline, required approval from Israeli officials. He first contacted the Mossad, the Israeli equivalent of the American CIA. They rejected any involvement with Pollard due to a continuing relationship with that branch of US intelligence.

Colonel Sella's second attempt at approval involved a telephone call to Yosef Yagur, a fireplug of a man who was serving as science counselor at the Israeli consulate in New York City. Yagur reported directly to Rafael "Rafi" Eitan, whose prowess as a spymaster elevated him to head of the Office of Scientific Liaison, an intelligence branch of the Israeli Defense Ministry. It was known by its Hebrew acronym LAKAM (Lishka le Kishrey Mada).

Eitan, an unattractive, bold sort who wore black horn-rimmed glasses, was an expert in covert operations. He was given credit for the 1960 Argentine apprehension of Nazi war criminal Adolf Eichmann.

Despite that feat, Eitan, who suffered from poor eyesight and hearing, was considered an outcast within the Israeli government. His lack of discipline and social skills led to the nickname, "Rafi Hamasriach," or "Rafi the Stinker."

When Colonel Sella informed Eitan, who had long doubted that the American government was providing Israel with first-rate classified intelligence information, of Pollard's interest in aiding Israel, Eitan was aware of the potential to surmount the Americans through one of their own. After a quick background check that confirmed Pollard's position at NIS and his affinity for Israel, and the gaining of written permission from Major General Amos Lapidot, commander of the Israeli Air Force for Colonel Sella to perform a "special assignment," Eitan authorized a meeting through Yagur for Sella with Pollard.

On May 24, 1984, Pollard's heart was pounding so fast it almost exploded. Colonel Sella had called to schedule a meeting over coffee in the restaurant at the Washington Hilton Hotel, just blocks from Pollard's apartment. As the minutes ticked by until the fateful rendezvous, one that ultimately caused scandal to spread throughout two of the most influential governments in the world, Pollard fretted over which of two ties to wear for the rendezvous chat with his hero.

That morning Pollard arrived at the Hilton and awaited Colonel Sella as unsuspecting businesspeople milled by. Moments later the colonel arrived dressed in civilian clothes. Pollard, his palms moist, greeted his idol with a hearty handshake. Small talk about the colonel's flight from New York City to Washington, where he was to speak that evening, filled the first few minutes. Both men were nervous.

If anyone noticed the unlikely twosome, there was no record. Meeting in broad daylight bothered neither man. Such blatant conduct characterized the mission on which Pollard was embarking, one that should have been exposed several times over.

Believing it important to be direct, Pollard told Colonel Sella, "You have no idea how much vital information the US is denying Israel. I know I can help you."

As the conversation continued, Pollard shocked Sella, who spoke English with a noticeable accent, by bombarding him with the prospect of providing classified information of such a sensitive nature that the colonel must have felt he was being set up and that his companion was a CIA operative. He shouldn't have worried; Pollard was doing what he had always done as a youngster in South Bend, Indiana, during college days at Stanford, and during his six years at NIS—attempting to impress people with his vast intellect, one enhanced by a photographic mind.

By the time the men parted, Sella was convinced that Pollard was a sincere, dedicated Zionist whose loyalties were to Israel. When Jonathan informed the colonel that he intended to provide classified documents to Israel and then emigrate there to live his life in peace and continue fighting for the preservation of his spiritual homeland, Colonel Sella was convinced.

Later, Pollard swore that he made it clear to the colonel that he would be spying *for* Israel and *not against* the United States. Federal prosecutors would dispute that claim.

Regardless, the spy game was on. First, Pollard, who had planned ahead, produced a list of several pay telephone numbers near his apartment where contact could be made. To each he had assigned a Hebrew letter (aleph, bet, daled, gimmel, etc.) as a code. When Colonel Sella telephoned Jonathan's apartment, he was to mention the Hebrew letter and Jonathan would scamper to the proper location for a conversation with his designated "handler."

Encouraged by Sella's report of his initial meeting with Pollard, Eitan and Yagur prepped the inexperienced Sella for a second. It occurred on July 7, 1984, a sweltering hot day in the nation's capital.

Colonel Sella and Pollard once again met at the Hilton, where Sella was staying, before walking to the hotel garage where the colonel's car was parked. They drove to Dumbarton Oaks, a historic park in Georgetown. There they sat, both complaining about the heat.

Anxious to impress Colonel Sella, Pollard, dabbing his neck with a hankerchief, reemphasized his access to classified documents and satellite photographs. Then he withdrew several sheets of paper from a worn leather briefcase. One included a photograph that Pollard knew was dear to Colonel Sella's heart.

Days earlier, Pollard had discovered a photo of the Iraqi Osirak nuclear reactor bombed into oblivion three years earlier by the Israeli Air Force. He knew that the photo would bring a smile to his handler's face, since the commander of that raid was none other than Colonel Sella.

Despite his pleasure at viewing the photo, Colonel Sella, under orders from Eitan and Yagur, deferred possession of it and 48 other classified documents during the half-hour meeting. Instead, the colonel, per instructions, discussed with Pollard potential compensation for his spying duties. That was crucial since Yosef Yagur realized one thing: that Jonathan Pollard, dubbed a "walk-in" since he solicited interest from

Israel, had to be corrupted into becoming a dependable spy, one who wouldn't walk away on a whim. Paying him a salary would guarantee a change in lifestyle, permitting Jonathan and Anne Henderson to experience the better things in life. They would grow dependent on the extra income so that Jonathan would never be tempted to quit spying.

In effect, the money would serve as an insurance policy for the Israelis. The only questions left unanswered were the amount of compensation and when it would begin.

Regarding his decision to spy, Pollard later told the *St. Louis Jewish Light*, "I came to the conclusion that the choice I faced was between my belief in Israel's right to continued security and my legal obligation to uphold Mr. Weinberger's betrayal of the Jewish state. Having thus identified my options, I acted accordingly." Little did he know that one day in the future, that same "Mr. Weinberger" would be in a position to punish him for his perceived treachery.

Chapter 2

BLOOD MONEY

As Jonathan Pollard, briefcase of stolen documents at his side, left his meeting with Colonel Sella at Dumbarton Oaks, he was living out his childhood fantasy. Since his teenage years he had dreamed of serving his beloved Israel, and now it was a reality. The glamour of being a spy had overridden any realization that his efforts were illegal, since he was violating the NIS loyalty oath by exposing classified secrets. To cap off his adventure, his handler was a war hero who was treating him with respect as a fellow comrade and defender of Israel.

Unconcerned about detection, a third meeting between Pollard and Colonel Sella occurred on 21 July at the Four Ways French Restaurant near Pollard's apartment. For the first time, Anne Henderson was present. Colonel Sella escorted his wife, Yehudit, a lawyer in Israel, who was anxious to meet the American spy.

Anne swore later that she had little knowledge of Jonathan's illegal operation (Sella was introduced as a "potential business partner"), but that was questionable. Colonel Sella discouraged Pollard from informing Anne of his activities, but Jonathan shared everything with her. She approved of Pollard's decision to spy for Israel; there is little evidence to the contrary.

Any thoughts of turning back ended when Pollard met with Colonel Sella on 28 July. Using the telephone code, the budding spy was directed to a pay telephone at the corner of Florida and Connecticut Avenues. Instructions were then provided for delivery of the stolen documents to an elite, secluded, wooded neighborhood filled with quarter-acre lots featuring million-dollar-plus homes in Potomac, Maryland, an hour's drive from Washington, DC.

To effectuate his spy mission at NIS headquarters, Pollard had devised a clever plan. After securing the sensitive documents, he removed them from their brown "Top Secret" envelopes. Displaying a rare maturity for one so inexperienced in the world of espionage, he then transferred the documents into similar envelopes marked "Secret." If guards stopped him as he exited, he could explain that he was taking less-sensitive documents home to review them.

After exiting the building, Pollard relaxed during his drive to Potomac, but tension filled the air when he was welcomed into the spacious home of Ilan Ravid, the science counselor to the Israeli embassy. Colonel Sella welcomed Pollard with a vigorous handshake in the smoke-filled room and the two men then viewed his cache, which included several photographs and classified documents.

Accessing the sensitive documents had been child's play for Pollard, since he possessed the required clearances to obtain what he needed from NIS files dealing with Middle East matters. Colonel Sella commended the spy for his effort while Israeli embassy secretary Irit Erb copied the material.

Colonel Sella knew that Pollard's security clearance only permitted him to secure certain high-level documents. Despite that fact, later the spy would be accused of stealing information that he never had access to.

To up the stakes, and reel his minion in, Colonel Sella informed Pollard that he would be required to meet "a higher-up" in Israeli intelligence whom he dubbed "the old man." The reference was to Rafi Eitan, who though delighted at receiving the classified information, remained cautious of the Pollard scheme for two distinct reasons: 1) Colonel Sella was inexperienced in matters of intelligence, which increased the chances of disclosure; and 2) Eitan was still not convinced that Pollard wasn't part of an undercover operation to entrap the Israelis.

Like Yagur, Eitan, of whom Sella had informed Pollard "never trust him," knew that until Jonathan was corrupted with money, he couldn't be trusted. Colonel Sella was thus ordered to convey to Pollard that when "the old man" and he met, matters of compensation and questions regarding the specificity of documents requested would be further discussed. The confab was to take place in Paris, where detection of the meeting with the well-known Israeli figure would draw little attention.

To Pollard's disappointment, Colonel Sella informed him that their partnership was coming to an end. "'The old man' will explain everything and you will be well taken care of," explained Sella, who was returning to Israel to begin a new command. On the way home Pollard brooded, since a major portion of the excitement of spying for Israel included association with the famous Colonel Sella.

* * *

When Pollard returned to his apartment, there was Anne to comfort him. They were inseparable and deeply in love.

Anne Louise Henderson was nearly born in Chuquicamata, Chile, where her father Bernard, a gentleman of Scottish ancestry, labored as a foreman at a copper mine owned by the American-based Anaconda Company. When wife Elaine became pregnant, she began to worry about whether the child should be born at the ten-thousand-foot altitude. This prompted relocation to New York City, where Bernard assumed the position of editor for *Engineering and Mining Journal.*

During her early years, Anne was influenced by her mother's Orthodox Jewish heritage. Like Jonathan Pollard, she traveled extensively with her family, visiting California, Montana, Washington, Mexico, and the Caribbean.

An extrovert who spoke fluent French, Anne was a feisty young woman with flashing emerald eyes and fiery red hair. She lit up any room she entered. During her grandfather's birthday at the famous Copacabana Nightclub, romantic Italian opera legend Sergio Franchi asked Anne, a natural actor, to perform a Romeo and Juliet duet with him. According to her father, the audience gave them a standing ovation.

Home for Anne was a predominately Jewish neighborhood in White Meadow Lake, New Jersey. She was active in Jewish affairs, though not outspoken in her views. Later, in a letter sent to the appellate attorney Leon Charney, she outlined her Jewish beliefs. "As Diaspora Jews," she wrote, "our families instilled in us the vital importance of preserving human life through the deterrence of war. Their convictions stemmed largely from their recent memory of World War II, in which six million Jews were systematically massacred during the Holocaust. As a result of our upbringing, our perceived moral and racial obligations dictate that we should do everything in our power to prevent another systematic slaughter of mankind [especially Jews] from ever occurring again whether it is directed against a nation or a person. Human life is too precious to sacrifice. It is because of this rationale that Jay [the Pollard family called Jonathan "Jay"] and I felt compelled to take certain actions which have ultimately resulted in our personal Holocaust."

In 1976, Anne's parents moved to Bethlehem, Pennsylvania, where she discovered her Jewish faith to be in the minority. Crushed by the separation of her parents when she was eighteen, Anne moved to Washington, DC to reside with her father, press secretary for the Teamsters Union. She graduated from Emerson Preparatory School in 1979, the same year Jonathan Pollard accepted his job with the Naval Intelligence Service. Her parents now divorced, Anne remained in Washington after her father departed, and she began working while taking journalism classes at night at the University of Maryland.

Anne's love affair with Jonathan began in 1981, when her roommate introduced the twenty-one-year-old to Pollard. At the time she was employed at the American Institute of Architects.

Jonathan and Anne were inseparable from that first moment. Even though Jonathan had experienced at least two other serious relationships through the years, he was smitten with Anne's intelligence and, more important, her willingness to share his feelings about Jewish heritage and the precarious state of Israel.

For Anne, the new love in her life was a gateway to the world. Day by day Jonathan imparted new information, exciting information about subjects she had never considered. His deep knowledge of Jewish history impressed her, and she felt more of a kinship with her heritage. Jonathan shared his deep desire to help Israel and his plan that one day they would live together in his spiritual homeland.

In 1999, Anne Pollard told Leslie Katz of the *Jewish Bulletin of Northern California* about her feelings toward Jonathan. "I really loved my husband…because I saw something in him I didn't see in many people in Washington." Katz said Anne was referring to Pollard's "passionate love for Judaism and Israel."

Syndicated columnist and television talk show host Arlene Peck said she witnessed the strong bond between Jonathan and Anne through letters written between the two. "Every letter [to Anne] contained deep love," Peck said, "and appreciation for the loyalty and concern that she without fail showed Jonathan.…They were beautiful and sensitive letters written from a man who loved his wife deeply."

From day one Anne became Jonathan's sounding board for his frustrations at NIS. Soon they were cohabiting, with marriage on the horizon. Turbulent times prevailed, as with any relationship, but the couple survived their differences.

In the letter to attorney Leon Charney, Anne revealed her inner thoughts about Jonathan and Israel. "My only crime was that of being a loyal and devoted wife and ardent supporter of Israel…knowing what I know today, would I again attempt to help my husband in his hour of need? Would I ultimately sacrifice my life to save the lives of essential Israeli officials and their respective spouses, including one general who was known for his heroic exploits and is considered to be a future leader of the state? The answer to both questions is an emphatic yes."

After Jonathan and Anne married, she became an instant Pollard, a true member of the family. She marveled at the "storybook" love between Morris and Mollie, and how they cherished their children, especially Jonathan.

"She fit in with us right away," Dr. Pollard said. "We visited them quite often in Washington, and she was a lovely girl."

As a term of affection the family called her Annie. "I was living in New Haven, Connecticut, and it was my birthday," Jonathan's sister Carol recalled. "Jay called and asked what I was doing. I told him I was going to do one of my favorite things—take a hot bath and read a good book. Next thing I knew the doorbell rang, and when I opened it, there stood Jay and Annie holding balloons and wishing me happy birthday. Later, Jay told me in the kitchen, 'Sis, this is the girl I'm going to marry.'"

When asked about her brother's relationship with Anne, Carol described him as a "complex person few really knew." She added, "He was really sweet, and gave himself totally to those he cared about. Perhaps he did so to a fault, for he was also somewhat immature and certainly not streetwise. People took advantage of that."

Prior to marriage, Jonathan and Anne lived together just a few blocks from DuPont Circle in the Nelson Building at 1733 20th Street NW in central Washington, DC. Furnishings were scarce at the $750-a-month apartment, but it was comfortable. Shelves were stacked with books that Jonathan, an avid reader, collected. A third occupant infiltrated the apartment when Dusty, a cat possessing no vocal cords, took up residence.

If Anne's feelings were based on blind love, he loved her unconditionally knowing that her health was fragile. A rare stomach disorder caused her to have difficulty digesting food. Living in excruciating pain produced instances where she cried out in anguish.

Anne's fear of her stomach disorder was understandable. She was twenty-one and knew that a similar illness had caused the death of her grandmother at the tender age of thirty.

Despite the medical problems, Anne worked for both the Chemical Specialties Manufacturers Association and the National Rifle Association. There she directed the press office, furnishing media information for the National Rifle Championships, the United States Olympic team, and various firearms safety programs. Both organizations praised Anne's work ethic and strong-willed dedication to her jobs.

* * *

On the steamy Washington, DC evening of July 25, 1984, days after the dinner meeting Anne attended, Jonathan Pollard made the biggest mistake of his spying escapades—he accepted money when Colonel Sella passed him a white envelope containing two thousand dollars in cash. Their spy now corrupted, the Israelis continued to suck as much information out of Pollard as possible.

The final meeting with Sella featured the passing of more classified documents and, according to the colonel, another payment of two thousand dollars. Shortly thereafter, copies of the contraband were whisked across the Atlantic to Eitan and his LAKAM brethren, who in turn dispersed the information piecemeal into selected defense department outlets throughout the Israeli government. Later Pollard learned he was known by the code name "Hunting Horse," a translation from Hebrew depicting one who gathers information and then forwards it to superiors who use it to their advantage.

The documents Pollard provided to Colonel Sella had been stolen during Pollard's 6 A.M. to 6 P.M. shift at the NIS Anti-Terrorist Alert Center (ATAC). In the fall of 1984, he had been promoted by his boss, Commander Jerry Agee, who had no idea that his new intelligence research specialist at ATAC was a spy. Commander Agee later acknowledged that he was aware Pollard had a compelling interest in Middle East matters, even though he was assigned the Caribbean and continental United States desk.

Access to certain documents was even easier for Pollard during his new daytime watch. As his scheme intensified he requested sensitive material early in the week in order to secure its possession by Friday. After collecting the material he transported it to an Israeli go-between's Watergate apartment for copying purposes. On Sunday evening he retrieved the material and then returned it to the NIS files early Monday morning when he reported for work.

From time to time Pollard and his colleagues were submitted to routine security clearance examinations, though none involved polygraph tests. Safe from detection, Jonathan Pollard continued his duties as an Israeli operative, rationalizing his acceptance of money by convincing himself that he was providing a means of salvation for his beloved homeland.

* * *

Prior to the scheduled trip to Paris, Pollard told Colonel Sella that he could not afford to purchase the round-trip tickets. The colonel was sympathetic, but instead of assisting, he suggested that Pollard borrow money from the Navy Credit Union.

After doing so, Anne and Jonathan flew coach to Paris where they used their American Express card at the Paris Hilton Hotel. Sella had promised that the Israelis would reimburse all expenses once the meeting with the "old man" was completed.

En route to the rendezvous on a beautiful Paris day, Jonathan was reminded by Colonel Sella that he wanted to continue being his handler. Apparently the colonel, despite his anticipated command in Israel, enjoyed the duty and the generous expense account accompanying it.

Arriving at the "safe house," Pollard was escorted by Colonel Sella into a modest home where he met the remaining two-thirds of the Israeli triumvirate responsible for him. Introductions to Rafi Eitan and to Yosef Yagur were cordial, both men complimenting the insecure Pollard for his efforts in behalf of Israel. That reinforced Jonathan's belief that he was only providing Israel the intelligence data it had a right to under the US-Israel Exchange of Information Agreement, which required US intelligence to share security information with Israel.

Pollard later disclosed that he became uncomfortable when the conversation turned to continued compensation for his spy mission. Nevertheless, a monthly stipend of fifteen hundred dollars was agreed upon with the promise of more to come.

"I suspect the best way of characterizing the way I felt at the time [about the money]," Pollard told journalist Wolf Blitzer in his book, *Territory of Lies*, "was extremely dirty, which was not how I envisioned feeling as a result of helping the Israelis. This was an ideological operation that was slowly being turned into a banking expedition by Eitan."

Discussions with Eitan and Yagur included the procedure by which Pollard would be rescued if disclosure of his spying efforts occurred. He was informed that the Israelis would protect him and that a plan was being finalized guaranteeing his safe passage to Israel.

A point of disagreement during the conversation concerned the exact makeup of the classified information that Pollard was to steal. That discussion, he said, focused on his determination to be a spy *for* Israel, but *not against* the United States.

Whether or not the ideology Pollard professed was heartfelt is subject to conjecture. From his perspective, Pollard was dead-solid sure of his intentions. He said he would not compromise US national security or provide any critical national defense information that could fall into the hands of an enemy. The low-level junior analyst later swore that he never compromised the identity of any overseas US agents and did not reveal, as he summarized it, "Any US ciphers, codes, encipherment devices, classified military technology, the disposition and orders of US forces, war fighting plans, secret diplomatic initiatives and obligations, classified organizational writing diagrams or phone books, vulnerabilities of nuclear stockpiles or communications security procedures."

In essence, Pollard believed that his actions did not constitute betrayal of the United States. Months later, government prosecutors and a federal judge named Aubrey Robinson strongly disagreed.

Chapter 3

SUSPICIOUS MINDS

Once the Paris meeting with Eitan and Yagur was concluded, Jonathan and Anne were treated to a luxurious European holiday. Convinced that a first-class spy deserved first-class treatment, the Israelis allocated ten thousand dollars, one-fifth of what Anne and Jonathan earned each year, to their trip.

From "gay Paree" the couple traveled to Saint-Tropez, Cannes, Nice, Monte Carlo, Florence, Rome, Innsbruck, and Munich. Though government prosecutors later emphasized their affluence, the couple ran out of money and were forced to spend some nights sleeping in their car.

While in Paris, Anne and Jonathan walked along the Champs-Élysées, two young people in love in the midst of the whirlwind world of international intrigue. Israeli praise for his work had dissipated any doubts Jonathan had concerning his illegal activities, and there was no talk of terminating the relationship.

Confident that the seduction of Anne Henderson secured the loyalty of Jonathan, the Israelis made certain Anne enjoyed herself in the French capital. To that end, Colonel Sella, a charmer extraordinaire, told Jonathan to visit the prestigious Mappin and Webb jewelry store on Place Vendome.

There, a friendly Algerian-born Jewish salesman suggested that a diamond and sapphire ring might be a perfect gift, compliments of the Israelis. If someone inquired as to how the Pollards could afford such luxury, the explanation was to attribute the ten-thousand-dollar ring (discounted price, seven thousand dollars) to the generosity of a rich "Uncle Joe Fisher," a fictitious benefactor.

Despite Jonathan Pollard's denials, the truth appeared to be that he savored the Israeli gifts and compensation, viewing them as some sort of badge of courage. He knew that Anne, who proudly wore the ring upon their return to Washington, DC enjoyed their improved lifestyle.

To be certain, opulence was an opiate that affected both Anne and Jonathan. When Dr. Pollard straightened up their DC apartment after the couple was arrested, he found among other items several bottles of very expensive French perfume.

* * *

During the months following the Paris trip, Jonathan Pollard, now immersed in his world of spy intrigue, removed, then had copied, document after document from NIS headquarters. At least three times a week, he retrieved information from either the libraries at the Defense Intelligence Agency or the Naval Intelligence Support Center.

Without apparent suspicion, Pollard's routine consisted of transporting files containing classified documents to his car. As before, he transferred them into a briefcase, delivered it to the proper location, left the documents, and then retrieved them before returning to work.

Like every good employee, Pollard was rewarded with a salary increase. By the Spring of 1985, to be known infamously as the "year of the spy" when at least fifteen others, including the John Walker Jr. family, were exposed as infidels, he was earning two thousand dollars a month. Later Pollard professed of the money, "I felt like a prostitute." After his arrest, government prosecutors disagreed, labeling him a "simple mercenary."

The extent of Pollard's delivery of documents to Israel was debatable but the government alleged that the documents passed by the spy could be spread "six feet wide, six feet long, and ten feet high." Skeptics labeled those figures pure fantasy, but there was no question that Pollard was an able spy.

When copies of the documents arrived in Israel, members of the LAKAM assembled the material, dissected it, and then continued to pass it along to defense experts. Enthusiasm with the material turned to outrage when critical documents already forwarded from US official government sources were compared with those stolen by Pollard. Discrepancies existed, prompting the Israelis to question whether certain sensitive documents provided by American intelligence were "doctored."

When Jonathan had embarked on the sabbatical to Paris, Dr. Morris Pollard suspected nothing out of the ordinary. He knew little of Jonathan and Anne's financial status, only that his son seemed content with his life and his job. "During that time," Dr. Pollard said, "for all I could tell he was enjoying himself. He loved Anne, and they seemed a happy couple. Of course, I had no idea as to what he was doing, that he was working for Israel."

News that his son was departing on another European holiday, during which he intended to be married, triggered mixed emotions for the Pollard family. "We were pleased they were getting married," Dr. Pollard recalled, "but disappointed that the wedding wasn't going to be here so we could attend. Nevertheless, Jay wasn't going to change his mind."

To his boss, Commander Jerry Agee, Pollard told a whopper: Rich "Uncle Joe" was financing the trip, which included travel in France and Italy with the marriage to be performed in romantic Venice. He never mentioned that the true purpose for the trip was to meet Rafi Eitan in Israel.

Despite Commander Agee's apprehensions about Pollard's conduct the administrator believed Jonathan's story. Either he was too busy or thought Pollard was a strange bird and sloughed off the trip explanation and the "rich uncle" explanation to his strangeness. Regardless, when Jonathan Pollard departed on his trip in the summer of 1985, the commander didn't have a clue that he had been spying for almost a year.

Anne Henderson was ecstatic about the honeymoon as they traveled across the Atlantic to Tel Aviv. The festive mood enjoyed in Paris continued, but more important was Pollard's introduction to a mysterious man known as "Uzi." He was assigned as Pollard's new "handler," replacing Yagur.

To sweeten the pot for their redoubtable spy, the Israelis provided a prewedding gift for Pollard and his bride. According to prosecutors, Eitan informed him that the Israelis would open a Swiss bank account in the name of Danny Cohen, significant for two reasons: 1) the name Cohen was a reference to a heroic spy for Israel in the 1960s who was hung in Syria, and 2) it was to be Pollard's new name when he "retired" to Israel once his spying days were over.

Into the account was to flow the sum of thirty thousand dollars a year for a period of ten years. Pollard acknowledged existence of the promise by the Israelis, but said he believed they never intended to deposit funds into the account. Based on disclosures by Colonel Sella and other Israeli officials, Pollard's claim appeared to be true.

While in Israel, Jonathan and Anne visited Jerusalem. "When I walked through Yad Vashem, the memorial to the Holocaust in Jerusalem," he stated, "I was able to look at those countless lost faces staring out of the faded pictures and know, for once, that I had kept faith with them."

Once the Israeli meetings were completed, Anne and Jonathan celebrated their marriage, which occurred on August 9, in Venice. They drank red wine and enjoyed gondola rides along the scenic waterway canals as a starry sky brightened the horizon.

The Pollards then spent three weeks touring Europe. First-rate hotels, a seven-hundred-dollar-per-night compartment on the Orient Express, and restaurants in Jerusalem, Venice, Paris, London, and Zurich made possible by a ten-thousand-dollar payment from the Israelis to cover all expenses, provided once again a life of elegant upper-class indulgence, all courtesy of "Uncle Joe."

* * *

"I think Jay knew he was going to be caught," Dr. Pollard later admitted. "I should have known something was going on."

Whether he or anyone else could have recognized Jonathan's misadventures, the spy and his handlers realized that the longer the mission continued, the greater was the chance of exposure. They no longer worried that Pollard would attempt to leave their service, since they believed he was hopelessly hooked on the glamour of his venture and the money he was receiving, with the promise of more in the future.

FBI and government prosecutors alleged that money was Jonathan's ultimate motive. They produced American Express receipts for luxurious restaurant dining and expensive jewelry purchased for Anne. That despite the fact that, no matter what the Israelis promised in the future, Pollard, in addition to money spent on the two European holidays and Anne's ring, was being paid only two thousand dollars per month, hardly a king's ransom. The truth was that Jonathan and Anne were so extravagant that they ended up deeply in debt. In fact, Morris and Mollie Pollard later paid in full a significant outstanding balance owed to the Navy Credit Union in order to clear their son's record.

Jonathan Pollard alleged that the bulk of the money secured from the Israelis was used to influence several important Saudis he had met during his days at the Fletcher School of Law and Diplomacy at Tufts University. According to Pollard, he was attempting to lure them in and then report all security information garnered to his Israeli handlers. "I spent a lot of money on one particular contact," Pollard stated. "Money on expensive dinners, hotel rooms, theater tickets, jewelry, the works. Also some on what I would call 'companionship.'" Government prosecutors later doubted the accuracy of Pollard's claims, claiming he was neurotic.

Anticipating disclosure, the Israelis had assured Pollard that he would be "taken care of," but the plan to do so was vague and incomplete. Pollard said it was more of a fly-by-the-seat-of-your-pants approach than a well-organized plan featuring various options. Believing he was invincible to exposure, Pollard never pressed for specific details.

Meanwhile, Commander Jerry Agee at the ATAC had begun to suspect his subordinate of wrongdoing. Remarkably, the spy's propensity to tell tall stories had provided the perfect cover for his clandestine activities. Commander Agee and others just assumed the erratic behavior was part of the stupefying Jonathan Pollard persona.

When Pollard's detection occurred, its simplistic nature revealed how he could have been exposed months earlier. In essence, all Commander Agee did was to do what he should have been doing all along: monitor an employee's work performance.

At the time, Pollard later told journalist Elliot Goldenberg, he had completed ATAC assignments concerning "appraisals of the Grenadian Communist Party's support network in the United States, the Venezuelan Intelligence Service's Caribbean apparatus, and a report on the intelligence services of the eastern Caribbean, including Trinidad, Barbados, and the Dominican Republic." He said he had refused to complete an assignment, one detailing national organizations opposed to US involvement in Central America.

To substantiate that claim, Pollard told Goldenberg, "What I was actually supposed to do involved identifying which groups should be targeted for 'black bag' operations—in other words, breaking, electronic bugging, and harassment. Now, I may be conservative, but I don't believe in this kind of action by the government…and I am not ashamed to say that I consciously sabotaged the project by refusing to compile a list of groups that would have been subjected to this kind of treatment."

While attempting to understand Pollard's defiant conduct, Commander Agee realized his employee was spending considerable time away from the office during his shift. Puzzled, he began to chronicle Pollard's actions, and while doing so noticed several irregularities that caused concern.

Commander Agee's initial inquiry focused on investigating the type of documents that Pollard checked out from the research department. He discovered that the analyst gained possession of material dealing with Soviet threats to Arab countries. Commander Agee knew that was not included in Jonathan's area of expertise. Seeking answers, the commander confronted Pollard, but was stymied when the spy explained that the documents were background research for a report he was preparing on Caribbean territories.

Later, Pollard denied Commander Agee's statement, saying, "I would never have made up such a statement.…How could I plausibly claim that a new generation of Soviet main battle tanks would be used by groups like the Martinique Liberation Front?"

Commander Agee's suspicions about Pollard lingered and he continued to monitor his activities. The commander did not realize that time was limited, since Pollard had informed his Israel handlers that within a few months he was going to resign his post. Eitan, who had told Sella, "I can't stand agents with morals," and Yagur were furious, but the spy was steadfast in his determination to leave NIS.

As Pollard expedited his spy efforts with the end in sight, two events recharged his pro-Israeli batteries. On September 25, 1985, tragedy occurred when a band of PLO (Palestine Liberation Organization) terrorists aligned with Yasser Arafat's deadly Force 17 group boarded a yacht anchored in the harbor off the Cypriot port of Larnaca and ruthlessly murdered three Israelis. According to Pollard, coworkers at ATAC made fun of the incident at his expense. He reported that a bloody wire service photograph depicting the body of the female victim (Esther Paltzur) slumped over the bow of the yacht like a grotesque figurehead was posted on a Bunn coffee maker adjacent to his office. Imprinted next to the photo were the handwritten words: "Force 17–Mossad 0." To Pollard the reactionary, the joke was a reminder of a past nightmare. He told journalist Goldenberg, "The scene of that poor woman hanging over the end of a ship with the bullet in her head reminded me of the Holocaust when many of our European cousins were disposed of like so many sheep."

Event number two, five days later, brought great satisfaction to Pollard. On October 1, 1985, eight Israeli Air Force F-16 fighters bombed the headquarters and personal residence of Arafat located at Hammam Plage, a beach outside of Tunis. Mohammed Natour, commander of Force 17, was killed.

Though Arafat was uninjured, Pollard beamed with pride, for he believed he had been responsible for passing along classified documents that pinpointed the location of the PLO hideouts. The same President (Reagan), whose Secretary of Defense (Caspar Weinberger) would later condemn Pollard for having committed "treason," called the Israeli raid "justifiable."

The first puncture wound in Pollard's cloak of security occurred when Commander Agee caught him in a lie. The incident involved Pollard's absence from the ATAC office in September. Commander Agee confronted his employee when he returned and was told that he had been conducting intelligence research at a nearby library. After some discussion, Pollard admitted that he wasn't at the library, but had interviewed for a new job. Commander Agee bought the story, but his suspicions were mounting.

Suspicions peaked in October when a subordinate noticed Pollard exiting the ATAC center with several classified folders under his arm. Based on that information, Commander Agee redoubled his surveillance of the spy to determine if there was a pattern to his daily routine.

Later Agee told journalist Wolf Blitzer, "What I found was that he was picking up packages periodically. It looked like he was picking them up every Friday, and maybe sometimes twice a week, but at least once a week on Fridays. That caused me to say, 'Why on Fridays?' And that right there told me something was wrong. There was a pattern....'Something's not right here,' I said to myself."

When files unrelated to any project Pollard was assigned were requested, Commander Agee acted. His forehead damp with perspiration, he called Lanny McCullah, the Navy's senior counterintelligence officer. Outlining his suspicions in a face-to-face meeting, Agee, his face as red as his hair, shouted, according to Wolf Blitzer, "I've got a f_____ spy here!" Minutes later, after hearing more of the facts, a stunned McCullah agreed, telling Agee, "The guy's a g__-damn spy."

Believing Pollard to be a spy, and securing enough evidence to arrest and convict him, were two different things. Meetings between Commander Agee, McCullah, counterintelligence officers, and an FBI agent were unproductive. At Agee's insistence, the FBI agreed to enter the case, albeit a *week* later since they needed to wrap up another investigation.

Meanwhile, Agee and McCullah installed a surveillance camera near Pollard's desk and monitored his activities. When Agee learned that Jonathan had requested yet another set of classified documents from the computer center, he made them unavailable. Pollard was upset, but it never occurred to him that vultures were circling and that he was the prey.

Chapter 4

EXPOSURE

While Commander Jerry Agee and his cohorts attempted to devise a scheme to snare the spy, Jonathan and Anne Pollard dined out on a chilly Friday, 15 November. Their dinner guest at the dimly lit Marrakesh Restaurant in Washington was, according to Pollard, a "Saudi contact." Dom Perignon was purported to be the drink of choice; it was the last bottle of the bubbly Jonathan would enjoy.

On Sunday night, 17 November, the Pollards met Colonel Sella for dinner at the exclusive La Marée restaurant in Washington. As he laughed and joked about politics and enjoyed the rendezvous with his friend, Pollard didn't realize that not only were the Americans suspicious of his activities, but that Colonel Sella had been ordered to evaluate him as well.

Returning from a trip to Toronto, Canada, where he had sought Canadian assistance for building a synagogue on an Israeli air base, Colonel Sella was instructed to report on Pollard's present state of mind in light of recent demands he had made to his handlers, Rafi Eitan and Yosef Yagur. Those included a new apartment, since Pollard apparently felt escape routes from his current one would be few if detection occurred.

Sella knew that Pollard's relationship with Eitan was unstable. Pollard was upset when Eitan hinted at the use of the apartment as a "safe house" for Israeli agents. To Pollard, being a spy was one thing; harboring them quite another.

To determine Pollard's mental state and discover if the request for a new apartment was genuine or if the spy was simply seeking additional compensation, Sella, no longer officially Pollard's handler, but operating at the request of Eitan, made an appointment to see the apartment. That was scheduled for Monday, 18 November.

On that fateful day, Colonel Sella wasn't aware that when Pollard arrived at NIS headquarters, more than twenty sets of eyes were watching his every move. Tightening the noose, Agee and his cohorts possessed the perfect bait to lure Pollard—the classified documents requested the previous Friday.

Overkill nearly caused the ruse to fail. If Pollard had been alert, he would have realized that when three different clerks called to inform him that the documents were ready, something was amiss. Overconfident, he failed to notice the obvious: NIS and FBI agents were strategically positioned to make an arrest.

A few minutes after four o'clock, Pollard returned to his desk after retrieving the classified documents. Agents watched as he opened the outer folder, sorted through the documents, and discarded several into his "burn bag." He then crumpled up small pieces of paper and stuffed them into the rear of a file drawer. The FBI alleged that those papers contained lists of documents to be stolen.

Agents suspected that the lists were compiled by a person they dubbed, "Mr. X," a higher-up who controlled Pollard and pinpointed documents to be copied. If "Mr. X" did exist, he or she was never exposed. Pollard's comment regarding that matter was intriguing. Later, he said, "If I had known the identity of a Mr. X, don't you think I would have traded it in for Anne's freedom?"

Pollard informed journalist Goldenberg that the FBI made too much of what was a simple process. "Say the Israelis had officially been given a document with the identification number DIAM/433-72TS," he explained. "This translated out to a 1972 Top Secret-level study by the Defense Intelligence Agency [DIA] of a particular missile system. If the Israelis needed the latest Top Secret assessment of the missile, all they had to do was ask me to collect a copy of a DIAM/433-85TS. It was as easy as that."

Nevertheless, as dusk began to settle over Washington, DC on a cold and windy day, Pollard waved good-bye to the night security guard and exited possessing nearly sixty classified documents. He intended to drop them at the home of Irit Erb, the secretary at the Israeli embassy, after stopping at the car wash on Connecticut Avenue. There Pollard's procedure was to transfer the documents from his briefcase into one provided by the Israelis while giving his green 1980 Mustang a bath.

All seemed normal as Pollard stepped out of NIS headquarters. Over-confident, he was proud of the documents he carried. They included information regarding a missile guidance system that the Syrians were implementing, and more important, the specs for the MiG-29 cockpit. Both would be welcomed by the Israelis.

Anticipating dinner with the Sellas, Pollard rubbed his mustache and walked with a brisk gait toward his car, the briefcase tight in his right hand. He was unaware that less than a hundred yards away FBI and NIS agents were poised and ready to intercept him.

The moment Jonathan Pollard sat in his Mustang, a boisterous agent approached (Pollard later said he brandished a shotgun; the FBI denied it), flipped a silver badge in his face, and demanded that he return to the building for questioning. Pollard's face froze. The unthinkable had occurred: his spy scheme had been uncovered.

* * *

Several miles away, Anne Pollard dressed for dinner with Colonel Sella and his wife. Anne thought ahead about a media training seminar scheduled with the Campbell Soup Company on 25 November. After selecting a modest evening dress, she added the jewelry Jonathan had purchased for her.

Prior to exiting the NIS building, Pollard telephoned to inform her he was on his way home. As the minutes ticked by, Anne became anxious since it was unlike Jonathan to be late, or, if he was going to be, not to call.

At 7:15 the ringing of the telephone broke the silence in the apartment. Anne grabbed the receiver and was relieved to hear Jonathan's voice, but his stern tone warned her that something was wrong. She listened carefully, but her eyebrows arched when he said that while he was delayed by working late, she should join the Sellas. He added, "Don't forget the wedding album, and the cactus."

Mention of that final word caused Anne's heart to skip a beat, for it was the code word they had agreed upon the previous evening after Jonathan was spooked when he encountered a mix-up during the drop-off of documents to secretary Erb's apartment. He had arrived at the appointed time only to discover that she was not home. Pollard even opened the unlocked door, but could not enter due to the chain bolt being engaged. He left, concerned that perhaps she had been detained. Erb later told Pollard that she did not answer the door since she was having sex with a boyfriend.

When Jonathan told Anne of the incident at Erb's apartment, she was concerned. Setting in front of them was a prized cactus they owned, and Jonathan quickly settled on that word as the code for trouble. "If I ever mention cactus in a conversation," he told her, "that means I'm in danger."

The word having been spoken, Anne, who had earlier that day paid their delinquent American Express bill with the two thousand dollars Yagur had given Jonathan, sat transfixed on the couch after his telephone call. Attempting to think rationally was difficult, but she located the wedding album as instructed. Twenty-plus classified documents, some of which referenced China, were hidden within. Anne removed them, and hid them in a suitcase in a hall closet.

Anne had studied the Chinese information in hopes of securing production of a media training film project through the Chinese embassy for her new employer, CommCore, a New York-based public relations firm. An interview with the Chinese ambassador had been secured by Dr. Pollard. Later, due to Anne's connection to the Chinese, she was labeled a "suspected Chinese communist spy" by the *New York Times*, adding to the misinformed media frenzy that followed the Pollards' arrest.

What Anne had access to were documents marked "Secret" that revealed Chinese diplomats and their operations in the United States. Later investigations disclosed the mild nature of the material as well as the fact that Anne did not disclose any classified information to the Chinese. CommCore was cleared as well even though they were not awarded the contract they sought.

While Anne rushed around the apartment collecting other classified documents and readying herself to meet Colonel Sella and his wife, Jonathan incurred intense questioning from NIS and FBI agents. His ability as an actor with an instinct for exaggeration permitted him to dodge their inquiries and initiate dead-end discussions that revealed nothing.

To his credit, Pollard, who telephoned his wife twice to make certain she realized the importance of clearing the apartment of classified documents, realized that while the agents had apprehended him with the NIS documents, they had no idea who was receiving them. That provided an advantage for the spy as the investigation continued.

The cat-and-mouse game between Pollard and his interrogators lasted five hours. "Unfortunately, I had no idea what the government knew about my activities," Pollard later said. "The only thing I kept telling myself was that the longer the attention was on me, the easier it would be for Avi [Sella] to escape and perhaps take Anne with him, though I wasn't sure she would go."

After discrediting Pollard's statement that the documents were being given to a Naval Intelligence Service analyst named Andy Anderson, Pollard introduced the name Kurt Lohbeck, the journalist whom the spy had illegally provided business documents in the past. Since Lohbeck had spent considerable time in Afghanistan and was known to have connections in the Far East, Pollard concocted a wild story. "I told them point-blank that Lohbeck was a confidant of Brigadier Hamza, the Pakistani military attaché in Washington," Pollard proclaimed later. "That afternoon, I took the plunge by finally 'admitting' that I was supplying intelligence to the Pakastanis."

Hours later, Pollard continued the ruse by accompanying agents to Lohbeck's home. He toyed with their emotions by mentioning that he had once seen an East German agent there. "That really got them going," Pollard said.

To be certain, the accused spy was not going to expose the Israelis, since he was convinced they would rescue him. He knew intelligence information that he passed along had proven quite worthy, prompting Pollard to later proclaim, "Perhaps the most direct role I played in helping to eradicate the terrorist threat to humanity occurred in the fall of 1985 when the Israelis decided to raid Yasser Arafat's headquarters outside Tunis. I spent two hectic weeks collecting information pertaining to [Tunisia's] air defense reporting system and the PLO's disposition of antiaircraft weapons, which evidently contributed significantly to the mission's success....As far as I was concerned this constituted a perfect example of when I thought my actions were of service to both Israel and the United States, which at the time seemed unable or unwilling to protect its own citizens overseas. By having helped Israel, I assumed they were going to help me."

Pollard's mind-set at that time was debatable, but the fact remains that he did not betray the Israelis. As the months passed, he had every opportunity to do so. If he had, he may have received a lighter sentence. At the very least, Anne would have been spared heavy punishment. Despite the temptation, however, Pollard was not a rat, something never acknowledged. He kept his mouth shut, and was judged accordingly.

* * *

When the NIS and FBI agents failed to break Pollard, it was Commander Agee's turn. Upset over his inability to ferret out the spy, he inflicted his own anger on Pollard, who still had not been arrested. After two hours of badgering his employee, demanding answers, Agee became so belligerent he had to be removed from the room.

While Pollard endured an increasingly hostile interrogation, Anne, her hands trembling in fear, attempted to rid the apartment of damaging evidence. After packing the suitcase with the documents, she realized it was too heavy for her to carry. Nevertheless, she left the apartment, but then noticed several unmarked cars double-parked on the street.

Frenzied, she knocked on the door of next-door neighbors Christian and Babek Esfandiari. Anne told them Jonathan was in trouble, and that she needed the suitcase delivered to her at the Four Seasons Hotel in Georgetown. That was where Colonel Sella was staying.

Babek Esfandiari was suspicious of Anne's story, but agreed to transport the suitcase. When he did, miscommunications occurred and he and Anne never met. Later, the Esfandiaris called the FBI and turned the suitcase over to them.

Unaware that Jonathan Pollard had been detained, Colonel Sella dressed for dinner while watching television. Not hearing from the Pollards to confirm their meeting at Mr. K's Chinese restaurant caused the colonel concern. By 9:30 he was perplexed, and then the telephone rang. Anne, her voice subdued, said, "Colonel Sella, we have a problem."

Tears welled in Anne's eyes as she pleaded with the colonel to meet her at O'Donnell's Fish Restaurant near the Four Seasons. When she arrived, the anxious colonel waited in a corner booth.

A chain-smoker like her husband, Anne explained the details of Jonathan's phone call as she puffed away. Then she began to cry. Colonel Sella, realizing her panic, sat arms-crossed, listening intently. He knew the risks that Jonathan's arrest might trigger.

As she spoke, Anne noticed that the brave war hero's face was flushed. Flying fighter planes into combat was one thing, being exposed in a spy scandal quite another. His stomach felt hollow as he tried to comprehend the unanticipated turn of events.

Colonel Sella was troubled since he was traveling without a diplomatic passport. He realized that if he were arrested, his chances of being immune from prosecution were doubtful.

Without consoling Anne, Colonel Sella excused himself and called Yagur in New York. The startled handler was furious that Pollard had been detained and certain of only one other thing—Sella had to flee. Colonel Sella, in turn, was shocked to learn that there was no contingency rescue plan. That meant it was every man or woman for themselves, including him. Colonel Sella returned in a stupor and asked Anne whether she wanted to leave the country. She refused, professing love for Jonathan, after which Colonel Sella stunned her by asking her to disavow that she had ever even met him. He then walked away as Anne stood alone, her legs rubbery.

When Colonel Sella returned to his hotel, he informed his wife of the danger. They decided to flee Washington, DC, and travel to New York's JFK airport by rental car. At the airport he and Yehudit boarded a flight for London. Colonel Sella would never again return to the United States.

At the same time the colonel was bidding good-bye to Anne, Jonathan Pollard was being accompanied by the NIS and FBI agents to his apartment. There he acquiesced to a search, believing that Anne had cleared out all incriminating evidence of spy activities. To his regret, and hers, she had not. Agents confiscated nearly sixty documents, many with "Top Secret" designation. Prosecutors could now prove that Pollard had confiscated NIS files. They just didn't know for whom they were intended.

At this point several "ifs" emerged, any one of which could have led to the government's inability to prove spy charges against the Pollards. *If* Anne had cleaned out the apartment, *if* Sella had remained calm and not rushed with his wife to the airport in panic and instead stayed and helped Jonathan and Anne stitch together a believable story, or *if* there had been a viable plan ready to whisk Anne and Jonathan away into the night and out of the country, then the Jonathan Pollard case might very well have ended right then. Instead, in view of the lack of planning and foresight, agents discovered incriminating evidence at the apartment, Sella abandoned Pollard, and Jonathan and Anne were left to fend for themselves.

Another "if" might have saved Pollard as well. *If* he had called an attorney and kept his mouth shut, he might very well have never been charged with a crime. Removing classified documents from NIS head-quarters without permission would have cost him his job, but criminal charges could have been avoided. Further investigation by the FBI and NIS might have turned up evidence as to the recipient of the docu-ments, but in all likelihood they would not have done so. In that event a scandal could have been avoided, and Israel would have never been exposed.

* * *

Anne, who returned to the apartment as investigators conducted the search, and Jonathan were not arrested that evening. Agents left after midnight, still shaking their heads while asking one important question: who was Pollard spying for? Some, like Commander Agee, suspected the Israelis because of Pollard's heritage, but there was no proof.

After several attempts, a desperate Jonathan Pollard spoke with Yosef Yagur in New York. He assured the frightened spy, "We will take care of you." Despite the words of comfort Sella, Yagur, and his Israeli compa-triots were abandoning Pollard. He just didn't know it yet.

Though flight might have been an option, early the next morning, Jonathan, as ordered, entered NIS headquarters to take a polygraph test and answer more questions. He still did not seek legal counsel, believ-ing that he could con his way through the crisis.

When government agents refused to reconsider ordering Pollard to submit to the polygraph, the suspected spy's demeanor was transformed. Realizing that the lie detector test would uncover untruths in a split second, a nervous Pollard made a fatal error by informing the agents what they may not have been able to prove otherwise: that he had passed along a few classified documents to a "friend."

Aware that a crime had been committed, the agents read Pollard his rights. Still believing he could talk his way out of anything, he waived them. Once he had signed the form, he continued talking, though most of it was mumbo-jumbo conceived in an effort to convince his inquisitors that he was aligned with Pakistan.

When Jonathan Pollard realized that the Israelis would no longer assist him remains unclear. It may have been after he was once again permitted to return to his apartment after eight excruciating hours of interrogation. From a nearby all-night coffee shop he and Anne had frequented in the past, he attempted to contact Yagur at a pay telephone while under surveillance by the agents. First, the New York number rang many times with no answer before Pollard hung up. Then a secret Washington number he had been given was out of service, causing him to slam the receiver down.

Pollard's disillusion over the Israelis' abandonment was surprising. In the world of spying, all spies realized that once exposure occurred, they were on their own. For Pollard to believe that the Israelis would save him was naive; he should have known better.

But he didn't. On that very Tuesday, 19 November, he asked Anne to walk the streets surrounding their apartment building. His hope was that a representative of the Israeli government, according to a plan that had been discussed, would "accidentally" bump into her and either whisper instructions as to how the Pollards were to leave the country or slip those instructions into Anne's pocket. Anne would duplicate the effort the next day as well but to no avail.

The following day, November 20, 1985, after several more hours of pointed questions, Jonathan's nerves were frayed. Lack of sleep, worry over what was going to happen to Anne, and awareness that his every move was being observed pushed him to the breaking point. Worse, he knew that Israel, and for that matter his hero Sella, had forsaken him.

In fact, all of the Israelis who had aided in the spying scheme were ordered out of the country. Realizing that Pollard was going to be arrested and interrogated, Rafi Eitan ordered Irit Erb, Yosef Yagur, and Ilan Ravid, the science counselor at the Israeli embassy whose house had been used to copy stolen documents, to pack their bags and leave. All did so.

Left to his own fate, Pollard paced back and forth in the apartment while considering a frenzied plan of escape. After much debate, a solution appeared: he and Anne would seek protection at the Israeli embassy.

Believing a resolution to be close at hand, Pollard called the embassy from a phone booth and was questioned about who he was and why he needed help. According to Jonathan, the duty officer offered assistance, telling the beleaguered spy, "Jerusalem wants you to 'come in.'" Pollard, unaware of what that meant, asked, "Come in where?"

Told to telephone the next morning, 21 November, Pollard said he'd do so. He then provided the make and model of his car. He later said he was instructed that after entering the Israeli compound, he should drive the length of the driveway and park adjacent to the parking garage.

After a sleepless night, Jonathan and Anne Pollard hurried into their Mustang, carrying with them a bagful of clothes, birth certificates, passports, their wedding album full of photos of the Venice honeymoon, and their precious cat, Dusty. The first stop was a hospital visit for Anne, still suffering from stomach disorders.

Aware of the suspect's movements and hoping he would lead them to his coconspirators, FBI agents followed the car at a close distance in standard-issue Chrysler K cars. They were equipped with black-sidewall tires and HF antennas on the trunk.

Following the hospital visit, Pollard drove around several thoroughfares and streets in an attempt to lose his pursuers. Despite his efforts, government-issue cars were positioned in front of him, to the side, and behind. A communications van lurked nearby.

Minutes later, Anne saw the blue-and-white Star of David flag of Israel waving in a brisk wind atop a flagpole at the Van Ness Street NW embassy. Two-way traffic enabled Pollard to lose the cars that were beside him, and at 10:10 A.M. he maneuvered the Mustang toward the electronically controlled, black, ribbed-steel gated entrance.

Gripping the steering wheel as if it were a lifeline, Pollard's face brightened when he discovered that his timing was superb. An embassy-owned car reserved for Elyakim Rubinstein, the Israeli #2 in command, had pulled up to the gate, prompting it to open. After the black car slipped into the narrow driveway, Pollard jerked the Mustang in behind before the gate closed. Accelerating, he drove down the ramp and parked directly in front of two rust-colored dumpsters set against a white concrete wall.

Agents in the unmarked cars realized that the spy named Jonathan Pollard was seeking asylum from the Israelis, whom they surmised to be his partner in the spying scheme. They realized that the spy they were pursuing had slipped into a dark hole and safety behind the closed gates of the embassy, perhaps never to be seen again.

The disgruntled agents radioed headquarters with news of Pollard's entry into the embassy. Their instructions were to remain in position outside the gates and monitor what transpired. If the Pollards were permitted to stay inside the compound, diplomatic efforts would begin at the highest levels of government for return of the spy. If, on the other hand, the Israelis rejected Pollard's plea for safety, the agents were instructed to take him into custody even though no concrete evidence existed that could tie him to a conspiracy with the Israelis.

Inside the embassy compound the action was frenzied. Anne, woozy from the medication administered during her hospital visit, and Jonathan, sweating profusely, sat wide-eyed inside the Mustang waiting for instructions. Two armed guards approached and Pollard breathed a bit easier when one, according to him, said, "Welcome home." Whether that was a standard greeting or meant to ease the tension wasn't clear, but Jonathan and Anne felt secure enough to exit the car.

During the next five minutes the Pollards' world stood still as they awaited their fate. Jonathan realized this was it, the final moment of truth. Either Israel would save him, or fail him in his hour of need.

Wiping away beaded perspiration from his forehead, and speaking at a fast pace, Jonathan spilled out his plight in both English and Hebrew, telling the guards of Eitan and Yagur, and his mission, and his need to invoke the "right of return," which guaranteed the right of Jews to seek asylum in Israel. When the guards appeared confused, Pollard repeated his plea for help, gasping for breath while Anne listened.

When Jonathan finished speaking, one guard stood by his side. The other, gazing at the bevy of unmarked cars surrounding the compound, stepped inside to a telephone in search of orders.

They came from Rubinstein, in charge in the absence of Meir Rosenne, Israel's ambassador to the United States. Rubinstein, who later became Israeli attorney general, was confused and instead of pursuing instructions from Rosenne or other officials in Israel, decided to handle the matter himself.

Outside the gate the agents sat poised as a perplexed Pollard stood beside the car. Inside was a nervous Anne holding a sleeping Dusty in her arms. Several minutes passed before the agents noticed that the guard, a tall man with a gruff expression, had returned and that whatever he was telling Pollard was not at all what the spy wanted to hear.

Later accounts confirmed that the disconcerting words were: "You must leave," and they entered Pollard's brain like a spear. Instead of attempting to reason with the guard, or ask to speak to someone of authority, or even refuse to leave in spite of the potential for being subdued, he screamed in Hebrew words detailing who he was, what he had done for Israel, and who his handlers were.

Anne's crying and Pollard's words of protest failed to deter the guard, who shoved Jonathan into his car. As he slammed the door behind him, the spy filed one final protest, only to hear the words, "Get Out."

BOOK II

Chapter 5

THE ANALYST

Jonathan Pollard's journey toward becoming a spy had begun in September 1979. The previous year United States President Jimmy Carter, Israeli Prime Minister Menachem Begin, and Egyptian President Anwar Sadat had signed the famous Camp David Peace Treaty.

The year 1979 featured a crisis for the Carter administration on 4 November, when Iranian revolutionaries in Tehran invaded the American embassy and captured 52 American hostages. When President Carter's attempts to negotiate their release through diplomatic channels failed, he authorized an ill-fated rescue mission. His failure to win release, among other factors, cost him the presidential election the next year. Ronald Reagan's regime took over, and developments regarding its efforts to win release for the hostages would have a foreboding effect on Jonathan Pollard five years later.

The hiring of the twenty-five-year-old Pollard, who had reported to the Suitland, Maryland, NIS offices as a junior analyst, was surprising. His background security check (Navy Defense Investigative Services interviewed Dr. Morris Pollard and ten others) was so slipshod that it missed critical information regarding the prospective employee's obsession with Israel and his duty to defend her "at all costs." Assessing the NIS employment of Pollard, Peter Perl of *Washington Post Magazine* later characterized it by writing, "The hiring and [later] promotion of Jonathan Pollard surely rank among the monumental blunders in the history of US Intelligence."

For the bespectacled, slightly overweight man with soft hands and a curious smile whose official security badge photo portrayed him wearing a vested green sweater, blue dress shirt, and navy-and-red striped tie, joining the NIS caused him to celebrate. But not everyone in the Pollard family shared his enthusiasm. When Dr. Morris Pollard learned the specifics of the job, he wondered whether an idealist like his son could deal with the harsh realities of the intelligence world.

A thorough background check could have revealed much about Dr. Pollard as well as Jonathan's upbringing that impacted his mind-set when he joined NIS. Like his sister Carol and older brother Harvey, Jonathan was very close to his father during his early years. "For some reason, Jay always thought of me as invincible," Dr. Pollard stated. "Even when he got in trouble, he expected me to get him out of it. I butted my head against a lot of walls, but there are times when no one can fight back."

For Dr. Pollard, "butting his head" was nothing new to a man whose Jewish heritage had often proven a sizable challenge.

"We were the only Jewish family in a village called Columbiaville, New York, near Kinderhook, not far from Albany," Dr. Pollard recalled. "It was so small no mention of it ever appeared on maps."

Morris Pollard attended school in Hudson, six miles away. He walked through the red light district to get to class. Prostitutes waved and giggled as he passed.

One of Dr. Pollard's teachers was Ms. VanAuldstein, who never attended college. Her favorite book was *101 Best Songs*. Morris remembered her as being "absolutely incompetent, confused to a great extent," but he did the best he could to learn as much as possible.

Morris was a devoted student since he realized the potential rewards. "When someone asks me what kind of student I was," he offered, "I say 'desperate' since I knew the only way to escape my environment was through education."

Later, Dr. Pollard explained to son Jonathan how difficult the Depression years were for his family since Morris's father Harry was killed in an industrial accident when Morris was five years old. "From the beginning, I let Jay know that I had to bite and scratch for everything," Dr. Pollard said. "You do what you have to do to survive."

Harry, a Russian immigrant, had been killed in a freak accident in Hartford, Connecticut, where Morris was born on May 24, 1916. Harry's death occurred when a concrete tower being built for the Fuller Brush Company collapsed. All Morris remembered was seeing his father's crushed body lying on the floor in a house, not a funeral home, with a sheet covering him.

Jonathan learned that his grandfather's death had affected Morris's psyche. "As the years passed, I missed him more and more," Dr. Pollard recalled. "I learned all about what growing up without a father meant. It made me tougher, but I knew that if I ever had children, I would work hard at being a good father for them."

Morris Pollard would never have been born if not for a quirk of fate involving his mother. In 1911, she was employed at a garment factory at the Triangle Shirtwaist Company on the corner of Greene Street and Washington Place near Washington Square in Greenwich Village. On Saturday, March 25, a raging fire swept through the factory where more than five hundred women were working.

Twenty minutes after the fire erupted, 146 women were dead, many of them teenage Jewish immigrants who had departed Europe for a better life. Outrage over the deaths (blamed on poor safety conditions and chained doors intended to prevent stealing), triggered a revolution in the garment industry. Trade unions protested, organized members into the thousands, and called for a strike, which proved to be successful in securing reforms from manufacturers.

One of the survivors of that tragic fire was a young Jewish immigrant named Sarah Hoffman. By the grace of God she had called in sick that morning.

"My brother Henry and I were blessed with a mother who cared," Dr. Pollard related. "Despite our lack of money, she told us something during the Depression years I will never forget. 'Boys,' she said, 'if anyone comes to the door asking for food, feed them.' And we did. That was a philosophy, help others, that I thought was fantastic. Mother taught us that you always had enough to share. I passed that along to Carol, Harvey, and Jay."

Lessons learned by Dr. Pollard included understanding that truth should prevail. "I told all the kids that I remember being arrested, actually arrested, by a policeman for driving our old tractor across the highway. He said he had to ticket me because I didn't have a driver's license. Well, I didn't have one because I was too young to drive. I said, 'You can't do that.' About that time, Mother came along and said, 'Morris, tell him the truth, tell him you are sorry.' And so I did, and that was that."

Morris's mother stressed to her son the importance of standing on your own. She was a woman who did what she had to do to survive, selling eggs and butter to earn money. Morris and his brother pitched in as well. They grew their own food, and not by using mechanical devices but by plowing with horses. The crops they raised placed food on the table. The two boys learned an important lesson: Nothing would be given to them in life; they had to earn it.

Young Morris's decision to pursue education intensified when his mother employed reverse psychology to encourage him. "She attempted to inspire me by saying, 'Why don't you just stay here and work on the farm?' That was meant to make me stop and think about expanding my horizons. To do that, I had to escape Columbiaville."

Morris Pollard entered high school at age eleven. Records were not kept in elementary school, so no one knew of his scholastic excellence. As the Depression continued, jobs became scarce, and high schools attracted the best teachers. Morris's physics teacher was a graduate of MIT and his French teacher had completed her studies at the Sorbonne.

A scholarship and funds from an insurance trust permitted fifteen-year-old Morris Pollard to attend New York University. His goal was to complete the one-year requirements of arts and sciences for entry into veterinary school.

"When I went to New York, Mom pinned money to my undershirt and told me to swear I wouldn't do two things," Dr. Pollard recalled. "She said *don't* sign anything and *don't* join anything."

Morris kept his word, but New York City didn't appeal to the small-town boy from Columbiaville. He discovered the world of museums, opera, and the symphony, but the culture shock was too dramatic. For two weeks he experienced migraine headaches.

In New York City, Morris Pollard learned firsthand about the persecution of minorities. Later he recounted shocking stories to his children about the inequities of being a Jew and about other minorities that were being abused. He informed them about Polish immigrants being corralled in industrial areas, and the Irish and Chinese being forced to work on the railroad tracks and then being abandoned.

Morris's mother influenced his mind-set concerning minorities. "My mother had no formal education," he said. "She came to the United States an orphan at age fourteen, leaving a village on the border of Austria and Poland. She used to tell me about how people were scorned if they had TB. They were banished to caves in isolation to accelerate their demise. Little food was provided, none had any future."

Reminders of Morris's heritage were everywhere. His instructors told the Jewish students, "Don't study engineering, because industry does not hire Jews." He learned that medical schools had quotas, and that in many cities, including Atlantic City, hotels wouldn't permit Jews to register, and they couldn't purchase real estate. He told Jonathan about those inequities and noted the boy's distress.

Jonathan Pollard learned that being Jewish was such a burden that his uncle Henry, at age eighteen, persuaded a court to change their last name from Polansky to Pollard. Morris was displeased with the decision, but Henry, who became a dentist, believed the name change was necessary for "business reasons."

* * *

While bright-eyed Jonathan Pollard was growing up, he learned of a great story—one featuring love at first sight.

The romance occurred at Ohio State University which Morris Pollard attended with the benefit of a scholarship. That after being turned away from Cornell, which rejected him for not having enough "farm experience."

"It happened the very first night I was at college," the former Mildred Kahn (Mollie) recalled for her son. "My trunk hadn't arrived and I had no clothing. Some friends of mine took me to the Hillel, a Jewish social organization on campus. All at once, the director said, 'There's a nice young boy I want you to meet. He's from your neck of the woods.' Well, I was from Pittsfield, Massachusetts, and the 'nice boy' turned out to be from New York, but when I walked down the staircase, there was this handsome guy. Later, he walked me back to the dorm and asked, 'What are you doing Tuesday night? How about going to the military prom?' I asked to think about it, but when I returned to the dorm, all the girls told me I should go. And so I did. And we were never apart much after that."

That pleasant experience for Morris Pollard in 1934 reminded him of a fact of life that wasn't so pleasant. He informed Jonathan that the reason he appeared at the Hillel the evening he met Mollie was due to Jews being unable to join fraternities, sororities, or social clubs. It was just one more example of how segregated he and other Jews felt.

Following his graduation from Ohio State with a degree in veterinary science, Dr. Pollard ventured to Virginia Polytechnical Institute where he earned a master's degree in one year. That proved worthy, though he told Jonathan about learning firsthand the dangers of anti-Semitism. It occurred when a job was offered to him at the agricultural experiment station and then withdrawn the next day. An official informed him that he couldn't be hired because he was a Jew. Upset, he protested, but the decision was final.

From VPI, Morris Pollard ventured first to North Carolina to study epidemiology before tackling research on leukemia in Beltsville, Maryland. Activated by the Army in 1942, Morris was ordered to the Brooke Army Medical Center at Fort Sam Houston, Texas, where he studied exotic diseases afflicting troops in the Southwest Pacific. His efforts earned him the Army Commendation Medal and a presidential citation.

By then, the Morris Pollard family numbered five. Jonathan was the latest addition, having been born on August 7, 1954 in Galveston.

If not for a telephone call in 1961, Jonathan's teenage years would have been spent in the Lone Star State where his father was entrenched in a prestigious faculty position at the University of Texas. That all changed for the seven-year-old when an administrator from the University of Notre Dame asked Dr. Pollard if he had interest in joining their faculty. Little did all those concerned realize that Jonathan was about to embark on a journey that would confront him with the very discrimination of his religion that Dr. Pollard had witnessed during the early stages of his life.

Chapter 6

THE BUDDING ZIONIST

Early in life Dr. Morris Pollard impressed upon his son the simple yet poignant message: "Jews have to be twice as good to get half as far." Nowhere would that be more true than in the unlikely city of South Bend, Indiana.

Jonathan's sojourn was guaranteed when Dr. Pollard visited the Notre Dame campus and met Father Theodore Hesburgh, the noted author, educator, and theologian who was president. "He asked me if I was interested in relocating to South Bend, and my ears immediately perked up," Dr. Pollard recalled. "I remember asking him at lunch what it would be like to be a Jew at a Catholic school and he said jokingly, 'Morris, we are all trying to get out of our ghettos.'"

Hesburgh's humor aside, Dr. Pollard leaped at the opportunity to join the Notre Dame faculty. In 1961, the year John Fitzgerald Kennedy was inaugurated as the youngest President in United States history, Cuban exiles were left for dead in their Bay of Pigs quest, and the spy trials of Gordon Lonsdale, George Blake, and the Krogers (Morris and Lona Cohen) were held in London, the Pollards became "Hoosiers."

"Father Hesburgh's invitation was simply too great to turn down," Dr. Pollard recalled. "The opportunity to head up the Lobund Laboratory, a very prestigious research facility, was the chance of a lifetime."

While Dr. Pollard's research duties at the university earned him international acclaim as an experimental oncologist, his son's formative years featured several incidents that shaped his mind-set as a teenager.

"When I look back at the early days we lived in South Bend," Dr. Pollard admitted, "I recall that it was a good city, but it wasn't hard to understand how my son got a chip on his shoulder when it came to the rights of Jews. I'm sure he felt that it was the world against the Jews and that their ancestral country, Israel, was especially vulnerable to those who hated our people."

Just as Morris Pollard was a member of the only Jewish family in Columbiaville, New York, his son was the only Jewish student at his neighborhood public school. For a year and a half he was taunted and bullied so much he was afraid to walk to and from school.

Adding to Jonathan's misery, he was a short, thin child with a reputation as a "mama's boy." Since his brother and sister were considerably older, Jonathan, named after an uncle of Mollie's mother, was essentially raised as an only child. His sister Carol cared for him when she was home, but Jonathan spent a great deal of time alone.

The seven-year-old who accompanied his parents to South Bend was more worldly in nature than his peers. By an early age he could brag about a travel log that included trips to England, Mexico, Sweden, Germany, Japan, and France. All with a family that was never reticent about discussing world affairs and the importance of Jewish pride.

Jonathan's early birthdays were memorable. His fifth was celebrated in Stockholm, where Dr. Pollard was attending a microbiology congress. Young Jonathan was serenaded with "Happy Birthday" by a dozen Nobel Prize winners and senior scientists, all friends of his father. Among the celebrants were Jonas Salk, discoverer of the polio vaccine, Selman Waxman, who developed streptomycin, Albert Sabin, a pioneer in polio vaccine research, John Enders, a Harvard Medical School researcher and pioneer in polio research, and Richard Shope, an early researcher studying the causes of cancer. Either their voices were off key or Jonathan was bored by their musical rendition since he began crying and wouldn't stop. Later, the precocious youngster asked his father, "What were all those old men doing at my party?"

Despite his tender age, Jonathan exhibited a bravado that foreshadowed later conduct. "Jay was always pretty headstrong," Dr. Pollard recalled. "He was never afraid to do or say what he felt and stand up for what he believed. After that fifth birthday party of his, I walked into a television room where a number of dignitaries were gathered. Jay had been sitting in a special kids' chair but when he left for the bathroom, a Russian member of their delegation decided the chair fit him all right. That is until Jay came back. He strutted up to the huge fellow and firmly said, 'That's my chair.' The mustachioed Russian, embarrassed, looked around and then got up. That avoided what I thought might be an international incident."

When the family traveled to West Germany, little Jonathan had the audacity to ask the rector of a German university if he was a Nazi. He was. More important in terms of understanding his future actions, the boy at an early age had an appreciation for what the Holocaust was and what it meant. "Jay asked me one time, 'Are we in Germany?' I said, 'Yes, we are,' whereupon he formed his hand and finger into the shape of a gun and shouted, 'Bang, bang, you're all dead.'"

* * *

If one trait characterized Jonathan Pollard more than any other, it was an unquenchable curiosity. He shared an interest with his sister in music (he became quite gifted on the cello) and archaeology. She introduced him to the outdoors by taking him hiking. In many respects a "second mother," Carol treated Jonathan with extra love.

Young Pollard's curiosity was most evident when the subject was books. His collection included a wide array of subjects (*Characters and Events in Roman History, A Panorama of Life in the Second Millennium, B.C.*), but even as a youngster, he focused on two distinct areas: Jewish history (one was called *Pictorial History of the Jewish People*) and military history. Aware that more than seventy members of his mother's family, the Kahns of Vilna in Lithuania, had been exterminated during the Holocaust, he read every book describing the horror of those dark days.

Based on Jonathan's readings, the impressionable boy developed an obsessive passion for Israel. At one point Pollard had collected more than one thousand books, the bulk of which related to Jewish history.

Pollard's deep-rooted devotion to Israel surpassed the depths of his parents. They had attempted to instill in their son a dedication to preserving Israel while still upholding allegiance to the home of their birth, the United States. "We tried to present a balanced picture of what the responsibility of an American Jew was," Dr. Pollard explained. "But Jonathan took it several steps farther."

Jonathan's parents knew his interest in Israel was strong, but they believed their son was an idle dreamer, a young boy fantasizing. "And we saw no problem with that," Dr. Pollard said. "Dreaming is good.

The dreams of young determined people are the ones that come true."

That attitude was commendable, except that mother and father hadn't realized that Jonathan had become *too* obsessive, that he wasn't a child whose passion for Israel would lessen as he grew older. His heroes were not television or movie stars or sports icons, but Jewish military officers and political leaders, all bound by a single purpose, the survival of Israel.

"Could we have toned down the rhetoric about Israel when Jay was young?" Dr. Pollard wondered later. "Yes, I suppose, but we felt so strongly about the need for Israel to remain strong. We wanted our son to feel that way, too."

Later, Jonathan Pollard echoed his father's feelings in a memorandum he submitted to the federal court. He wrote, "My parents never ceased in their efforts to portray this land [United States] as a Godsend for Jews, who throughout the course of our long, often tortuous history in the Diaspora, had never experienced a country so full of opportunities and constitutionally enshrined guarantee of religious toleration. It was constantly stressed by every responsible Zionist I encountered that Israel would simply cease to exist in the absence of a democratically secure and geopolitically ascendant United States, which was therefore in the collective self-interest of the various Jewish Diasporic communities to ensure."

Those thoughts pervaded later, but the mind-set developed earlier appeared to set the tone that whatever means were necessary to ensure Israel's survival were acceptable. Set as a shining example for the youngster as one who served these principles was a family member, an uncle (Mollie's brother) named Eliher Kahn, who served in the United States Medical Corps in France during World War II. He collected surplus field shoes, medical supplies, and equipment and diverted them to the Israelis. Nevertheless, Kahn became a hero to Jonathan as did others who supported Israel.

Another soldier Jonathan admired was an American, Colonel David "Mickey" Marcus, a decorated West Point graduate whom Dr. Pollard labeled an assimilationist. After Marcus retired from the Army, he emigrated to Israel as an adviser to their military. He was of great assistance to them, though in the end it cost him his life due to his tendency to visit off-limits areas and talk with the soldiers, many of whom were nervous about roving saboteurs. One evening, several soldiers, not realizing who Marcus was, accosted him, and when he couldn't speak Hebrew and explain his mission, they shot him.

A third hero in Pollard's mind was Vladimir Jabotinsky, a revisionist Zionist and nationalist who believed that Israel was destined by God to be a Hebrew nation. A spellbinding speaker, he also advocated the use of force to achieve results. And that every Jew's responsibility was to his homeland regardless of where that Jew lived in the world.

Unlike his parents, who believed their first allegiance was to the United States, son Jonathan saw it as Israel first, then the United States. The subject of duty to Israel was discussed in the interview he permitted with Wolf Blitzer, the bearded journalist for the *Jerusalem Post*. After pointing out that he admired those who had stood up for Israel, "whether it meant shotgunning a trainload of illegal dynamite through San Antonio, stevedoring a covert Israeli arms shipment at night out of Galveston, or spiriting a stripped-down aircraft out of an Air Force Reserve parked in the desert," Pollard was quoted in Blitzer's book *Territory of Lies* as saying, "I was brought up with the notion that this kind of service was not breaking the law but was the discharge…of a racial obligation. Certainly, it was made easier by the fact that as far as I was concerned—the way I was brought up—there were no differences between being a good American and good Zionist…"

* * *

Intensifying Jonathan Pollard's continuing passion for a foreign power and his agitation for the country of his birth was the treatment he experienced in South Bend, a two-hour drive east of Chicago. For two years, classmates made his life miserable, based on their dislike for what they perceived as a short, nerdy kid who was arrogant and, worst of all, Jewish.

Jonathan Pollard attributed the scornful treatment to a single factor: anti-Semitism. He had only to walk out the front door of the modest ranch-style home his parents owned at the end of a cul-de-sac on Hanover Court to witness how Jews were treated.

Pollard later described those days as requiring a "daily fight," one carried out on the streets and in the schools that he attended. The neighborhood where he grew up may not have been symbolic of the racial atmosphere of South Bend, which had encountered economic woes with the closing of a job-producing Studebaker automotive plant. Nonetheless, Jonathan said he knew where the prejudice originated.

"When you have an economic dislocation of that magnitude [the Studebaker closing], there is a need on the part of the community for certain elements of that community to become a scapegoat," Pollard later told Wolf Blitzer. He then added, "And there's always one around when you've got Jews, always," emphatic words that pinpointed the exact mind-set of a troubled young man who was intent on blaming the conduct of anyone who disagreed with him on one consistent factor—anti-Semitism.

"Was I surprised when I heard Jay's strong words about the problems encountered when he was growing up?" Dr. Pollard queried. "I have to say no, but I thought he would grow out of having such harsh feelings as time went along."

Jonathan Pollard also pointed to another factor that led to his belief that an atmosphere of persecution existed during his teenage years—the presence of the Ku Klux Klan in South Bend. Time and time again Jonathan learned of racial incidents by those who hated all minorities, ones bent on their destruction.

According to Pollard, verbal assaults and then later physical attacks took place the moment his head popped over the hill behind his house. Dr. Pollard knew Jonathan "felt" he was being persecuted, to the extent of kids punching him for no reason. "Jay was having a tough time," Dr. Pollard said, "so we decided it was time to remove him from the Marshall Elementary School, where most of the taunting took place."

Realizing the extent of their son's frustration and anger at the taunting, both parents attempted to talk to him. An exasperated Mollie told her son, "Jay, you must remember, this is a Christian country, perhaps the only way you will be happy is in Israel." Little did she know how much her son would take that thought to heart.

To avoid the persecution, Jonathan was enrolled at a private institution, the Clark School. There he flourished. He played the cello, became a distance runner, and participated in soccer. More important, at least in Dr. Pollard's memory, was Jonathan's continued fascination with books. "I used to tell him, 'Listen, Jay, all those bullies are out there, but books are your friends, and they are at home waiting for you.'"

If Jonathan Pollard discovered some sense of tranquillity at the Clark School, the nightmarish treatment reappeared when he attended South Bend Riley High School, where sentiment against all minorities was evident. While many of the kids chastised Pollard, he made friends with those who were scorned. "When Jonathan discovered a black classmate couldn't afford a dictionary," Dr. Pollard recalled, "Jonathan found him one. The boy told him, 'When it comes time to burn all the houses down, we'll skip yours.'"

Later Jonathan Pollard recalled more incidents of persecution tied to his heritage, and to blunt the effects the sixteen-year-old boy spent much of his time at the Sinai Synagogue Hebrew School. There he met a teacher named Mrs. Brown who shared his one significant passion in life: an unparalleled devotion to Israel.

"Mrs. Brown became Jay's window to everything he wanted to know about Israel," Dr. Pollard said. "She especially taught him the importance of the homeland and the allegiance expected that Jews had the obligation to make 'Aliyah' [live] in Israel." Mollie Pollard remembered Mrs. Brown as well, "She was a wonderful person. She had been to Israel several times and encouraged Jay to go. When the opportunity presented itself for him to visit for the summer, and he was chosen, he was as excited as I ever saw him."

One story that Mrs. Brown told Jonathan, and that he loved to retell, concerned the Jewish defense of Masada, the mountain top fortress located in the Negev. In 73 B.C., according to lore, more than two thousand Jews committed suicide rather than wave the white flag and surrender to a Roman legion.

"Mrs. Brown impressed Jay," Dr. Pollard admitted. "And he was *very* impressionable in those days."

Emphasizing disdain for his early years in South Bend, Jonathan Pollard later penned a memorandum which was filed with the Federal Court. He explained, "I was never able to establish friendships in my neighborhoods and was compelled to spend most of my time around the city's Hebrew Day School where I at least felt physically safe and emotionally protected. The association lasted six days a week for ten years and involved a highly concentrated curriculum of religious and Zionist indoctrination that regularly stressed the advisability of *aliya*, or emigration to Israel." Of his friends, Pollard wrote, "Jewish children I saw grew up angry and alienated, wishing only to leave and never return."

A turning point for Jonathan Pollard occurred in 1967, when the Six-Day War threatened Israel's very existence. During a time when he should have been enjoying a recent Bar Mitzvah, his pain and stress over what was occurring thousands of miles across the world was so intense that it bordered on being frightening. The thirteen-year-old boy became upset over the potential devastation of Israel. Mollie Pollard recalled that during a visit to her mother's home in Massachusetts, Jonathan shouted "Israel is going to be destroyed, I will never get to see my homeland. When the Israeli Air Force won out, Jay jumped for joy."

Jonathan Pollard affirmed his mother's thoughts about the Six-Day War later in a memorandum to the court. "...I saw for the first time a strong Jewish state successfully defending itself and not simply playing the role of victim. During the days preceeding the onset of hostilities, though, our small community was in the grip of depression, fearful that this time Israel's luck, like that of so many other Diasporic groups, had finally run its course. Yet poised on the brink of annihilation, Israel had suddenly exploded across her threatened borders in what appeared to us to be a blinding flash of biblical decisiveness."

"Should we have seen Jay's intense reaction to the Six-Day War as a warning that he was too caught up in the affairs of Israel?" Dr. Pollard later asked himself. "Perhaps, but we saw it as a sign that he was a compassionate boy, one who cared deeply for his homeland. We always thought that as he matured, his attitude would be tempered."

The Pollards, perhaps to a fault, were determined to make their son happy. They switched their synagogue affiliation when Jonathan decided he didn't like the reform rabbi. "Jay wrote a Bar Mitzvah speech that was very pro-Israel, that called for it to be a leader of the world," Dr. Pollard recalled. "The rabbi, who was not a Zionist, shortened it considerably. I canceled it and moved to the conservative synagogue."

Jonathan Pollard later characterized his childhood as an "unhappy one." Though there was a strong basis for that generalization, Dr. Pollard, who believed that his son needed to be tough and stand up for himself, disagreed with those who chastised him for submitting Jonathan to the ridicule in South Bend. "It would have happened anywhere," he explained.

In defense of South Bend, Dr. Pollard pointed to the good graces of many of the city's residents regarding Israel. "Planes ferried across the ocean, arms were collected and so forth," he explained. "They saw Israel as I did, as a bastion of democracy in the Middle East. Its existence was crucial, never to be forgotten."

Whether the Pollards realized it or not, their headstrong son had become a Zionist, a word much misinterpreted. It is a derivation of the word Zion and has several meanings, among them: the Jewish people, Israel as the Jewish homeland and symbol of Judaism, and heaven as the final gathering place of true believers. In Jonathan's mind a Zionist was one who believed in Zionism, defined as a "worldwide Jewish movement for the establishment and development of the State of Israel."

To many, a Zionist was a fanatic, one who supported radical measures, and that any means necessary was appropriate to achieve the desired end result of a unified homeland. That label, which produced the image of a troublemaker, was attached to Jonathan as a teenager and followed him into his adult life.

The writings of Louis Brandeis, the first Jewish member of the United States Supreme Court, reflected the thoughts that were going through Pollard's mind. The youngest child of Jewish parents born in Prague, Brandeis blazed through Harvard, earning the highest grades ever recorded. After several years as a noted attorney he ascended to the Supreme Court while being recognized as the "leading US Zionist." His quote, "To be a good American, we must be better Jews, and to be better Jews we must become Zionists," fit with Jonathan Pollard's budding ideals.

Pollard didn't require any more fire in his belly to accentuate his view that Jews must survive at all costs, but fuel was added in 1968. During a European trip, his parents took the impressionable fourteen-year-old to Dachau, the notorious concentration camp where hundreds of thousands of Jews were exterminated. Pollard roamed Dachau by himself, experiencing the horror of the crematoria and the sight of the smokestacks that belched the ashes of Jews into the air. In the museum, gut-wrenching photos of the victims, many of them children subjected to Nazi "experiments," made a lasting impression on a young boy whose heart was already filled with Jewish nationalism.

Pollard never forgot the experience. In a memorandum filed in Federal Court, he wrote, "As I walked through the camp all I kept thinking about was the similarity of the German Jewish community which all but vanished in the ovens of that facility, with that of my own back in the United States....All the books I had read on the Holocaust...by such writers as Elie Wiesel, Andre Schwartzbar, Hannah Arendt, and Primo Levi were equally pessimistic about man's ability to refrain from such barbaric behavior in the future. As I stood in the ruins of the crematoria, it slowly dawned on me that every Jew had a responsibility, an obligation, if you will, to ensure that his nightmare would end."

In a letter released later, he emphasized those feelings. "Everyone I respected in my adolescence emphasized that American Jews had a special obligation to provide Israel with help," he wrote, "because it represented insurance against a repetition of the Holocaust in which so many European Jews were trapped without a refuge that would accept them."

Dr. Pollard knew that a side trip to Czechoslovakia, where his son witnessed the destruction that had occurred to an occupied country, added another dimension to his realization of what would happen if Israel ever fell prey to its enemies. Obsessed with his fears regarding Israel's survival, Jonathan knew the timing was perfect for a trip to his spiritual homeland.

Jonathan Pollard first stepped on Israeli soil in 1970 at age sixteen. Months prior, he had returned home from school to inform his parents of an announcement on the bulletin board. It invited students to apply to study at the famous Weizmann Institute of Science at Rehovot. Later, when Jonathan opened the acceptance letter, his war-whoop could be heard all the way to Chicago.

Though the visit was beneficial in many ways, Pollard's time spent in Israel proved that his rebellious nature could produce a firestorm of trouble. When his parents visited him, they discovered that he had earned a reputation as a child who was in constant conflict with other students.

One educator at the Weizmann Institute of Science, Dr. Harry Lipkin, later told the *Jerusalem Post* that, among other things, Jonathan Pollard was an "unstable troublemaker." Always the defender, Dr. Pollard said the reputation was undeserved, pointing out that "Jay and a non-Jewish kid from England got into a fight and Jay had to be taken to the infirmary. That was all there was to it."

The Pollards had hoped that the trip to Israel would quench their son's thirst to become one with Israel, but they were sadly mistaken. Later, when they rehashed their son's disturbing actions, they concluded that the trip to Israel had finalized Jonathan's decision that he was an Israeli first and an American second. No clearer indication of that could have presented itself as Jonathan informed his parents, at the ripe young age of sixteen, that he wanted to remain in Israel for the rest of his life.

Chapter 7

COLLEGE BOY

For a revolutionary in the making whose ideals would one day clash with legal restrictions imposed by NIS, Stanford University in 1972 was the perfect breeding ground. Students had a plethora of significant world events to consider, including the infamous Watergate break-in, the near-landslide reelection of President Richard Nixon and Vice President Spiro Agnew (both resigned from office in disgrace), and Henry Kissinger's continued attempts to peacefully end the unpopular Vietnam War at the Paris peace talks.

Against that backdrop, Jonathan Pollard enrolled at the university named after Leland Stanford, deceased son of the noted California industrialist. At the same time, the Zionist noted another example of the persecution of Jews: the abduction and later death of two Israeli Olympic athletes and nine hostages by members of the Black September Group, a wing of the PLO that remained unacknowledged by Yasser Arafat.

For a time it was questionable if young Pollard was destined for college. When Jonathan told his father that he wanted to remain in Israel and become a pilot, Morris said, "Get your education and then move there." After some debate, Jonathan agreed.

College choices included Wisconsin, the University of Chicago, and Notre Dame, which Jonathan could have attended for free. Academic excellence, superior SAT scores, National Honor Society membership, and accolades for his poetry (he was dubbed "Hoosier Poet" in his high school yearbook) permitted him a varied selection. After some debate, Stanford was selected.

During Pollard's freshman year he switched his major from pre-med to political science. Franklin Weinstein, Jonathan's faculty adviser, told the *Washington Post*, "[Pollard] was a very bright, extremely articulate student." He added, "[Pollard] tended to overdo things. If you gave him an assignment to write a paper, it would come in elegantly but much longer than required."

A fellow instructor lauded Pollard's prowess as a student. Between his freshman and sophomore years at Stanford he enrolled in an African history course at Notre Dame. Professor Peter Walshe told the *Washington Post*, "He was one of my best students," one who had a "drive to understand the inner working of politics in all their Machiavellian dimensions." Professor Walshe said Pollard "was especially intrigued with intelligence-gathering. He was interested in the way the CIA operated in this country, he was interested in Israel's capacity to defend itself in that way."

Most revealing was Pollard's apparent fascination at Stanford with impressing friends by portraying himself as a zealot for Israel. Former roommate Steven LaPointe recalled that Pollard talked of the military and espionage operations. "He used to boast that he had dual citizenship and was a colonel in the Israeli Army," LaPointe told journalist Wolf Blitzer.

Pollard was attracted to the glamour of war. He played war games such as "Panzer Blitz," a World War II game where players utilized military strategy to defeat the opponent. He also enjoyed "Diplomacy," a game where each player controlled the destiny of the seven major powers at the start of the twentieth century: Turkey, Russia, Germany, England, Austria-Hungary, France, and Italy.

Fellow students alleged that Pollard swore that he was a member of Mossad, had trained with Israeli forces, and was on the front lines for the 1973 Yom Kippur War. That fabrication wasn't surprising to Stephen Haaser who knew him as a youngster. He told *Washington Post Magazine*, "[Pollard] was an excellent raconteur. Whether what he was telling you was straight truth or embellished, who knew. He had all kinds of great stories."

Student Jonathan Marshall told the *New York Times* that Jonathan was a "committed Zionist" who discussed matters of Middle East policy with an impressive expertise while "describing himself as part of an Israel officers' group that favored more open channels of communications with Egypt." Later Marshall embellished upon those remarks by alleging that Pollard was a spy for Israel when he was in college.

Even more bizarre was a report that during his senior year, Pollard carried a gun as he walked the Stanford campus. At age twenty-two, the impressionable young man had convinced himself and others that he indeed *was* a military officer, to the extent of listing himself in the Stanford yearbook as "Colonel Pollard." He defended himself, saying, "All of it was fun and games, no one took it seriously."

The young student's sense of humor was an important trait that many who knew him appeared reluctant to acknowledge. He was a complex person, but his ability to tell jokes and to laugh endeared him to many who met him. "Jonathan had a 'biting sense of humor,' but warmed to people quickly," Carol Pollard said. His father recalled that in high school, his son had won the National English Teacher's Award by writing a tongue-in-cheek account of how Julius Caesar was a tough taskmaster with his family. That essay was published by Ball State University in March of 1972. It was called, "Discipline in the Home."

Dr. Pollard described his son as being "intellectually brilliant, but a failure when it came to street smarts." He also said, "Jay could quote off the cuff from any book or article, but he was naive when it came to the simpler things in life."

In 1973, Jonathan Pollard had come within an eyelash of departing the United States. The Yom Kippur War was brewing, and he swore to fellow students that he had already been accepted into the Golani Brigade, an Israeli infantry unit of renown. The fact that Pollard knew so much about the inner workings of the Israeli Army was significant to note.

Pollard flew to Los Angeles with others, ready to join the battle in Israel. Fate intervened when El Al flights were delayed, causing several agonizing days of waiting in the airport. Pollard said it was one of the most frustrating experiences in his life, since he believed it was his duty to be fighting for Israel.

By the time transportation arrived, the need for his sojourn to the Middle East had passed. Regardless, Pollard's action had proven one important point: he was prepared to die for Israel.

The importance of the early developments in that war scared the budding Zionist in a manner that affected his concern for Israel's survival. "If the Six-Day War established in my mind that Jews could make good warriors," he said later, "the Yom Kippur War demonstrated just how dangerous a failure of our intelligence services could become. In the space of several hours, Syrian armored units had penetrated the Golan defenses and were within shelling range of Tiberias, a Galilee town with a population of 26,000 Jews, some of whom were related to me."

Pollard swore that during his waiting period in Los Angeles he decided to enter the world of intelligence, believing it would most benefit him when he emigrated to Israel. He was able to test whether that field interested him when he applied for and was awarded a Paris summer internship at the Atlantic Institute, a noted think tank, in 1975.

The college student described the Atlantic Institute as a "CIA operation," alleging that the top two floors of the building were open to only the president of the institute, two American secretaries, three maintenance technicians, and armed guards. He proclaimed that his allegations were confirmed when in 1984, the Atlantic Institute was bombed by Action Directe, a French terrorist organization.

Pollard's duties were to prepare reports on the views expressed by foreign diplomats. He told his parents that if they wanted to understand his mission, they should watch the Robert Redford spy thriller, *Three Days of the Condor*.

* * *

When Pollard entered his senior year at Stanford in 1976, President Richard Nixon had resigned, his Watergate co-conspirators were imprisoned, Gerald Ford became president until defeated by Jimmy Carter, and disgruntled Native Americans had occupied Wounded Knee. Yitzhak Rabin had replaced Golda Meir as head of the Israeli cabinet.

Dr. Pollard urged Jonathan to attend law school at Notre Dame, and his son acquiesced. Carol Pollard, aware of her brother's continuing allegiance to the Jewish homeland, recalled conflicting thoughts she had at the time. She said, "Looking back I think it would have been best if Jay had moved to Israel. Right then."

The Notre Dame experience was short-lived, since Jonathan soon realized that the legal arena wasn't for him. "He just didn't feel he wanted to be a lawyer," Dr. Pollard said. "Jay was never into money."

At Notre Dame, an incident occurred that previewed Pollard's conduct in future years. When a law professor asked the students what they would do if their client informed them he had killed ten people, Jonathan said that he would go straight to the police and tell them. "It would be my duty," Jonathan added, despite the ethics of attorney-client privilege.

After leaving Notre Dame, Pollard entered Indiana University to study political science. Two years at Tufts University in Medford, Massachusetts, where he was admitted to the Fletcher School of Law and Diplomacy, followed. Piquing his interest in world affairs was a summer internship at the Naval War College in Newport, Rhode Island, where he learned about military operations across the globe.

"All through the process of trying to understand Jay's behavior," Dr. Pollard said, "certain incidents flashed back to me. For instance, he was always a caring person. He once told me about a blind Saudi prince at Fletcher who was having trouble with classes. Jay read assignments to him and helped him get through. He said he told the prince, 'You don't know me, I'm Jewish' to which the prince replied, 'Then I know I can trust you.'"

By all accounts, Jonathan Pollard continued to struggle with whether to remain in the United States or emigrate to Israel. Of that struggle he informed Wolf Blitzer, "As time passed, I just continued to sink ever deeper into a spiritual no-man's land. And as with all borders, be they physical or cerebral, it is a sense of conflicting allegiances that causes the most confusion for an individual who feels he might be living under the burden of a double standard."

To placate the "confused" mind, Pollard continued to display bravado regarding his extracurricular activities, telling those who listened that he was now an operative for the CIA spying on Arab students at Fletcher. That bizarre statement was dispelled when he applied to and was rejected by the agency when he sought formal employment.

Fascination with the CIA was a certain by-product of Pollard's knowledge that his father had worked with the agency. While growing up, Dr. Pollard told Jonathan that he had reported to the CIA on his three trips to medical conferences abroad, including one in East Germany. He was there to invite scientists to a conference that dealt with foot and mouth disease, a subject of importance in biological warfare. Dr. Pollard traveled to Holland, East Germany, and France to organize the conference. While there, he provided details to the CIA regarding his experiences. Later, he told his wide-eyed son of his travels and the missions.

Dr. Pollard knew his son was aware of requests by the CIA to report anything pertinent while attending the 1958 International Congress on Microbiology in Stockholm. Russian delegates and others from around the world debated issues involving diseases in the military. "The CIA gave me a list of Russian scientists to check out," Dr. Pollard said. "And told me to 'Read it and burn it.' I asked 'Why me?' and they said, 'Because we have been investigating you for ten years, and have found you to be reliable.' I responded, 'I object, I resent it that you would spy on me,' but I took the letter and read it. Later, I laughed about the whole thing since it seemed so ridiculous. All information I gathered had already been published."

Despite Dr. Pollard's belief that his work was unimportant, Jonathan viewed his father as a CIA operative involved in the clandestine world of espionage. "Certainly my efforts with the CIA could have given Jay a feeling of approval for that type of activity," Dr. Pollard, a very humble man, admitted. "Jay was always a romanticist. Always."

Jonathan Pollard was fascinated by his father's adventures when he was chairman of an advisory committee for the Navy that focused on health issues. For two years, Dr. Pollard traveled extensively, undertaking air purification problems in submarines, refuse disposal in subs, and the probing of immunization procedures for troops stationed abroad. Jonathan was also aware of his father's involvement in the atomic submarine Aquanaut program in San Diego.

Like father, like son, and in 1979, Jonathan's application was submitted to the CIA. Citing polygraph results that uncovered drug use during college, he was dismissed as a potential employee. His father recalled that he was "crushed" by the rejection, but Pollard applied for a position with the Naval Intelligence Service. When he was accepted, it was the proudest moment of his life.

Chapter 8

JEWISH HERITAGE

Entrenched in his new position as a junior intelligence analyst with access to lower level classified documents, Jonathan Pollard's initial priority was tracking Russian air and sea movements in the South Atlantic, the Caribbean, the Baltic Sea, and the North Atlantic.

In retrospect, the Navy was the worst branch of the service that Pollard could have chosen, since anti-Semitism and general ill-will for Israel pervaded. The latter was inflamed by an incident on June 8, 1967, during the famous Six-Day War Israel was fighting against Egypt and other Arab countries. On rough seas along the Mediterranean coast, the USS *Liberty*, a United States intelligence-gathering ship, was patrolling under guise of neutrality. Seconds later, the skies were full of Israeli aircraft that battered the defenseless ship. It sank and thirty-four United States sailors were killed.

Israel pleaded innocent, explaining that their pilots believed the ship to be Egyptian and that—contrary to United States assertions that the Liberty was sailing in international waters—it was stationed in a war zone. Regardless, the Israelis later apologized to the satisfaction of United States government leaders, but members of the military never forgave what they considered to be an act of war.

Since the incident, crude jokes, an insolent manner toward Jews, and a thorough dislike and distrust of Israel had prevailed at Navy operations. Nowhere was this more true than at the Suitland, Maryland, location.

Jonathan Pollard never wore his Jewish heritage on his sleeve during his early months at the naval facility, but he assumed that his colleagues knew he was Jewish. Their conduct reminded him of the anti-Semitism that prevailed during his childhood in South Bend, Indiana.

When the analyst entered the naval facility, he felt like a one-man gang for the preservation of Israel, its silent defender, its paladin against those who cared less if it was scourged from the face of the earth. His feelings intensified when he sensed that not only were Navy personnel, at the direction of those in the Departments of State and Defense, verbally antagonistic toward Jews and Israel, they were doing something about it.

Understanding Pollard's thought process at the time requires analysis of his knowledge of the status of Israel in the mid-1980s. By then his "beloved country" was in the midst of dealing with new policy guidelines in the Middle East implemented by the United States.

In accordance with an agenda promoted by Defense Secretary Caspar Weinberger, a proponent of Arab interests who believed that the destabilization of Israel was necessary, the US had implemented a "balance of power" doctrine in the region. That was based on the Reagan administration's belief that Israel's constant, and more to their way of thinking, reckless, concentration on the buildup of its military had created an imbalance in that part of the world.

For Pollard, the Weinberger doctrine evoked memories of the evolution of Israel, which was intertwined with the emigration of Jews to the United States.

During the first half of the twentieth century, Pollard knew, the United States experienced an incredible influx of immigrants including Irish, Poles, Italians, and Jews. Most came from impoverished backgrounds and many had been orphaned. Others escaped persecution in the hope that the United States would provide the type of freedom they could only dream about. And it did, with one notable exception—considerable bias by those who believed that America was a "land of the free" for Americans, and not for the flock of immigrants descending upon the country.

This bias, as Pollard understood, was most evident regarding the Jews. They experienced social, professional, and institutional restrictions blocking their entry into the mainstream of US culture. Having been expelled from Russia, Germany, Poland, England, and Spain, among others, the Jews must have wondered if they had indeed discovered the promised land where opportunity could blossom into independence, wealth, and peace of mind.

From the moment members of the Jewish community set foot on

American soil, they offended many of those around them. Several became "middlemen" whose bargaining talents caused others to characterize them as "sneaky and onerous."

When some Jews began to achieve success, critics perpetuated the myth that they were only interested in making money and becoming wealthy. The belief that they were inferior prompted accusations that their success came through cheating and the commission of illegal acts. They were branded conspirators who, according to those who distrusted and despised them, scoffed at the Americans who didn't understand the proclamation that they were members of "God's chosen people."

In 1906, the Jews fought back by forming the American Jewish Committee. This group combated anti-Semitism on a wide scale. Nine years later, the Ku Klux Klan was refounded with the express purpose of controlling American Jews and other minorities whom they believed were "harming the American social and moral norms." To confirm those claims, author Madison Grant wrote a book entitled *The Passing of the Great American Race*, which vilified minorities by alleging that the US policy of unrestricted immigration was destroying "America's superior racial stock."

Based on those assertions, Pollard knew from his historical studies that the Quota Act of 1921 was enacted. That act restricted immigration to 3 percent of the "ethnic stock" the US had as of 1910. Three years later, that percentage was reduced to 2 with the qualifying year set back to 1890. The legislation cut immigration of Germans, Russians, Poles, and Rumanians to less than 10,000. That was a far cry from the totals of nearly 160,000 German Jews alone who had entered the country in 1906.

Nevertheless, most Jews who relocated to America were assimilated to the culture, and by the 1930s those of the Jewish faith were perceived as an important part of society. Utilizing a strong work ethic and their parents' determination that education was the key to success, as Pollard's father had preached, Jews contributed to the American way in strong numbers.

Despite these achievements, anti-Semitism was still rampant, and there was even self-hate among those of the Jewish faith. The famed columnist Walter Lippman, son of wealthy clothing manufacturers from

Germany, blamed the Jews for anti-Semitic perceptions they themselves caused. He scalded their behavior, writing that they deserved punishment for being, as he called it, "too conspicuous." Asked to comment on the quotas at Harvard, Lippman wrote, "I do not regard the Jews as innocent victims. [They had] many distressing personal and social habits, which were selected by a bitter history and intensified by a pharisaical theology."

A glimpse into the mind-set of Americans in 1944 provided an understanding of the nonchalance that most citizens had toward Adolf Hitler's attempt to extinguish the race altogether. A poll taken during that year found that nearly 80 percent were opposed to raising quotas to help Jewish refugees. Elmo Roper, the pollster, declared, "Anti-Semitism has spread all over the nation and is particularly virulent in urban centres."

Jonathan Pollard's journey to Germany as a youngster permitted him to witness the brutality. Hitler's anti-Semitism was all-encompassing and nurtured a nation's mentality that lumped Jews together like amoeba. Jews were told that they weren't human, but vermin to be eliminated regardless of whether they were housewives, laborers, or pillars of the financial and legal communities. The Fuhrer's belief that the earth should be cleansed of Jews had repercussions beyond Germany. Wherever Jews traveled, they were considered a dreaded disease to be avoided. By war's end, *six million* of them had disappeared from the face of the earth.

Hitler, his generals, and the anti-Semites around the world perpetuated a fear of Jewish people because they were "different." Pangs of jealousy over their financial success underscored the continued distrust. Terms such as, "They jewed you out of money," flourished as anti-Semitism continued.

Based on those attitudes, it was no wonder that there was no public or political outcry when the United States admitted fewer than 21,000 Jews during the war, 10 percent of the quota allowed. Immigrants, and especially Jews, were the enemy; even the American Legion and Veterans of Foreign Wars applauded efforts to curb foreigners' entry into the country.

American media, Pollard realized, mirrored the insensitivity of the general public. When Jews were gassed in vans near Chelmno, the *Boston Globe* ran the headline, "Mass Murders of Jews in Poland Pass 700,000 Mark." The story appeared on page *twelve*.

American Jewish leaders were slow to respond to the slaughter, agreeing with the government that behind the scenes "negotiation" was preferable to military actions. US President Franklin Delano Roosevelt did nothing to rescue those being exterminated; many believed he possessed anti-Semitic sentiments.

Author Paul Johnson in his book *The History of the Jews* explored the reasons behind the lack of Jewish resistance and provided an analysis of why so many Jews were slow to react to the desperate cause of their brethren if indeed they acted at all. Johnson wrote, "The Jews had been persecuted for a Millennium and a half and had learned from long experience that resistance cost lives rather than saved them. Their history, their theology, their folklore, their social structure, even their vocabulary trained them to negotiate, to pay, to plead, to protest, not to fight." That nonconfrontationalism aids in understanding the passivity of many Jews in the Jonathan Pollard case, since he was one who fought for what he believed in, albeit it illegally, instead of "pleading."

The horror of the Holocaust could not be contained; it is a stain of blood and infamy that spread through time and space. Those who witnessed the Nazi atrocities from afar and those who fled to the United States to describe the massacre now possessed one single frame of mind: "Never again. Never again." Perhaps even more important, Paul Johnson pointed out, was a belief in something so precious that it became the beacon of hope for every Jew. He wrote, "The overwhelming lesson the Jews learned from the Holocaust was the imperative need to secure for themselves a permanent, self-contained and above all sovereign refuge where if necessary the whole of world Jewry could find safety from its enemies. The Second World War made it essential. It persuaded the overwhelming majority of Jews that such a state had to be created and made secure whatever the cost, to themselves or to anyone else."

Johnson's remarks reflected the apparent status of Jonathan Pollard's beliefs as his days at the NIS continued. To him, his beloved Israel was under siege from those who were determined to weaken her defenses, prompting the necessity for him to assist "whatever the cost."

***

From Jonathan Pollard's vast knowledge of history, he knew that the creation of Israel in May 1948 as a safe haven did not occur without obstacles. For supporters, the saving grace was President Harry Truman who, unlike FDR, believed those of the Jewish faith to be underdogs who deserved their own homeland. Truman was encouraged by a close Jewish friend who recognized that the issue was about "Arab oil and access to it, Jewish blood, and the right of the Jews to have a safe haven."

Opponents to establishment of a Jewish homeland could be traced to "anti-Zionists" within the US State Department who believed that Israel should align itself with the Soviet Union. They argued that if that occurred, the Russians could use Israeli military bases to strike its Middle Eastern enemies.

Despite that viewpoint, President Truman provided support, and in November 1947 the United Nations General Assembly voted 33-13 to recognize the State of Israel.

From the beginning, Pollard realized the infant country was besieged with violent attempts to obliterate what the UN had created. Those threats to the existence of Israel did not come from America where the majority of citizens believed that the Jews deserved a sovereign homeland.

During the years after World War II, anti-Semitism had decreased significantly in the United States. New attitudes of tolerance permitted immigrants to continue what some called "the Jewish consciousness," while swearing allegiance to their *new* homeland as well. "Dual loyalty," a term often connected to Pollard, was and is common among immigrants. It ran rampant in a true democracy, and while Washington, DC was the home of the government that ruled them, beloved Jerusalem was the sacred capital of Jewish spiritual existence, much as the Vatican symbolizes the spirit of the Catholic faith.

Spiritual blessing that Jerusalem was precious came, Pollard had learned as a youngster, from the Bible. In *Isaiah 62*, inspiring passages included, "For Zion's sake, I will not keep silent, for Jerusalem's sake I will not remain quiet, till her righteousness shines out like the dawn, her salvation like a blazing torch," and "You who call on the LORD, give yourselves no rest, and give him no rest until he establishes Jerusalem and he makes her the praise of the earth."

Above all, every Jew insisted that preservation of Jerusalem and of Israel was imperative and that there was an absolute duty to defend their existence at any cost. Those people relied on the United States government to honor the Jewish spiritual homeland as it had done when Congress ratified the Balfour Declaration and the British mandate for Palestine. Both ordered that Jews be permitted to return to the land from which they had been driven away by the Romans.

For the United States, in need of establishing a foothold in the Middle East, allying with Israel, the only democracy in that region, was a natural choice. The US also respected Israel's military regimen and its concerns for security.

While United States assistance to Israel increased as the years passed, the key event in establishing relations between the countries was the June 1967 Israeli-Arab war. To its credit, the US became a peacemaker in that region of the world while aligning with the Israelis and their rights to sovereignty. Six years later, after the October 1973 Yom Kippur War, US policy dictated that the Israelis negotiate land concessions to appease its enemies in the war. Although Israel disagreed with that position, they acquiesced, believing it to be in their best interest to placate those who saw the new homeland as a warring nation not to be trusted.

When President Jimmy Carter assumed office, he initiated what was dubbed a "comprehensive approach" to Israeli/Arab relations capped by Egyptian leader Anwar Sadat's historic visit to Jerusalem. The Camp David Accord produced agreements on several issues, providing a road map for future negotiations between all concerned parties. As never before, Jews sensed a stronger bond of unity between Israel and the United States.

President Ronald Reagan's administration changed all that. In the 1980s, through a series of policy decisions initiated by Reagan and his cabinet appointees, Israel found itself questioning the allegiance of its ally. That occurred when US Secretary of Defense Caspar Weinberger and his State Department, aware that Arab oil interests were of paramount importance to the US, had undertaken a mission to deemphasize support for Israel, which they characterized as a "deterrent to peace." While doing so, they intended to support Arab interests so that not only was the balance of power in that region resumed, but the Arabs could be convinced that their finest ally was not the Soviet Union, but the United States.

The result, Pollard recognized, was the "level battlefield doctrine," which earmarked an attitude where the previous "special" relationship with Israel was continued in public while behind the scenes orders were given to treat Israel with caution. In order to satisfy the Israelis that the status quo was still in order, the 1983 US-Israel Exchange of Information Agreement was passed and signed by President Reagan. This subterfuge was promulgated with the knowledge of Weinberger and his supporters that the agreement, to share all relevant intelligence information with the ally, already had been thwarted.

As fate dictated, the United States' altered strategy toward Israel, its Middle East ally, coincided with Jonathan Pollard's accelerating involvement into the world of classified intelligence. The US position toward Israel was on a collision course with a young, idealistic junior analyst who believed that Israel must be provided all intelligence data necessary for its survival. Months into his job, Pollard alleged that vital information regarding Iraqi and Syrian chemical warfare capability, intelligence data concerning potential PLO raids, updates on Soviet weapons shipments to several Arab countries, biological warfare potential, Libyan air defense systems, Pakistan's intention to build an atomic bomb, and Iraq's tentative plans to attack Israel were deliberately withheld from the Israelis by NIS officials. All this in violation of the Exchange of Information Agreement.

Later, the disgruntled analyst discussed his dilemma in a communiqué from prison. "What would you do if you were in a situation where you had information that could save thousands of lives of an ally?" he wrote. "Wouldn't you give it up?"

Unbeknownst to Pollard, Israeli intelligence personnel shared his views. They were disgusted with what they believed to be less than 100 percent cooperation from the Americans regarding transmission of meaningful intelligence information. Objections were noted at every high-level conference between officials of both governments. At one juncture, Israel had suggested that a ground station be constructed near Tel Aviv so that its intelligence department could directly receive transmissions of photographs taken by US spy satellites. That request was denied.

Officials of the Israeli government also chastised the US for its unwillingness to forward classified data regarding its Middle East neighbors Jordan, Egypt, Iran, and Iraq. Unable to sway the Americans into cooperating, the Israelis had been forced to fly their own missions over those countries.

While the Israelis were stewing, so overwhelming was Pollard's frustration that he attempted to quit naval intelligence and join the American Israel Public Affairs Committee, an Israeli lobbying organization. In a brazen act he marched into the committee's headquarters in Washington, DC, and began accusing the NIS of withholding intelligence information from Israel. According to those who were in attendance, he even admitted to being privy to classified documents that proved his theory.

By all accounts, committee members dubbed Pollard a "kook" and disregarded his remarks. One later referred to him as a "raving lunatic." A surface check would have proved otherwise, but the interviewers tore up his job application and forgot he ever existed.

Chapter 9

THE DECISION TO SPY

"Dad, I've been ordered to see a psychiatrist. Can you recommend one?"

Pollard's uttered his request during an incident at NIS that threatened to end his career as an intelligence analyst. Taking advantage of a friendship seeded in graduate school, Pollard had been asked (the Navy said *he* suggested it) to establish what he called "a back channel" to gain intelligence information from Lieutenant General E.W. Van der Westhuizen, South Africa's chief of military intelligence. This was set up through a South African naval officer named DuPlessis, who had returned to his native country.

The concept had merit, since the United States had for all practical purposes cut ties with South Africa over their apartheid practices. That decision prevented the US from securing intelligence information about Soviet ships cruising around the tip of South Africa to and from the Persian Gulf and the Indian Ocean.

The Navy's plan, or Pollard's, met with interest and contact was made. Jonathan later stated that communication between the two countries improved, and that intelligence information, which included South Africa's transmittal of the first photo of a short-range Soviet naval SAM missile, was first-rate. Critics believed the effort was illegal and a dispute between the NIS and the CIA resulted in extinction of the operation.

According to his superiors, Pollard, disappointed at the turn of events, acted in a bizarre manner and fabricated stories about having lived in South Africa. They said he also bragged that his father was an operative for the CIA there. Pollard denied the allegations.

Days later, Pollard filed a report stating that four agents accosted him one evening as he carried out the garbage, drove him to a motel room, handcuffed him to a chair, and interrogated him for hours.

Based on the incident, Pollard threatened to sue the Navy. Superiors claimed he was delusional and ordered an examination by a staff psychiatrist. When the report was filed, the analyst was declared mentally unfit, causing him to lose his top-secret clearance and nearly his job.

Pollard demanded an examination by a private psychiatrist. "Jay said he had to see a psychiatrist," Dr. Pollard recalled. "I called a colleague who recommended Dr. Neil Pauker, based at Johns Hopkins. He saw Jay several times and pronounced him fit."

Dr. Pauker's findings didn't convince the Navy. They required Pollard be examined by a CIA specialist. When that psychiatrist agreed with Dr. Pauker, the analyst was reinstated.

Years later, the Pollard defense subpeoned Pollard's psychiatric file. "It was missing," Dr. Pollard said. "No one ever found it."

* * *

During the next few months at NIS, Pollard's anger festered. When he witnessed the Israelis being shortchanged regarding vital security information, frustration mounted, and he edged closer to his moment of truth.

Pollard's attitude was based on intelligence conferences NIS officials conducted with the Israelis. To his amazement, he discovered that directives authorizing release of intelligence information to Israel were being ignored. In his mind, he believed this was occurring for only one reason: the operatives at NIS were intent on deliberately withholding information from the Jews.

"I was totally unprepared for the level and extent of the anti-Semitism which was tolerated within the organization…" he later told Wolf Blitzer. "In the end, I came to the conclusion that the US Navy…was the last refuge of the patrician bigot."

To a degree equal with the denial of information to Israel was a comment attributed to an NIS analyst. It infuriated Pollard on two levels, his being a Jew and his love for Israel.

"I had just seen a photo of the world's largest poison gas factory being built in northern Iraq," Pollard told his father. "I asked permission to transmit it to Israel and my chief turned to me laughing and said he thought the Jews were overly sensitive about gas due to their experiences during the Second World War. He suggested that they should calm down a bit."

If a single incident triggered Pollard's infidelity, it occurred in 1983. That was the year American President Ronald Reagan labeled the Soviet Union "the evil empire" and Yitzhak Shamir succeeded Menachem Begin as prime minister of Israel.

The event that catapulted Pollard to the brink of spying was the bombing of the US Marine Corps headquarters in Beirut by fundamentalist Shi'ite terrorists. While many mourned the lives of the Americans, the Zionist was seething over the ineffective response of the United States, which countered with an air raid that did little damage and killed more Americans.

Standing in the rear of the National Cathedral during the memorial service, Pollard made the final decision to do the unthinkable—become a spy. Later he told Wolf Blitzer, "I was committed to do something that would guarantee Israel's security, even though it might involve a degree of potential risk and personal sacrifice. I knew what I was contemplating was wrong, but at the same time all I could see was that the ends justified the means."

Months later, government prosecutors alleged that prior to passing classified documents to a foreign power in violation of the loyalty oath Pollard swore to uphold when he became a Navy analyst, he sold out his country merely to impress business friends. By his own admission, one that tarnished his later defense that he became a spy solely to aid Israel, prosecutors were right.

The incident in question had occurred in 1982, when Pollard violated regulations by passing classified information to acquaintances named Laura Caro, Kurt Lohbeck, and Joe Harmon. Pollard later admitted that he provided documents that detailed "economic and political analyses" intended to further the business careers of his associates. Attempting to defend himself, he said, "I got carried away trying to impress friends and my insecurity, in effect, made me show off."

Kurt Lohbeck's version of the incident varied greatly from Pollard's. "He was very secretive," Lohbeck, who alleged Pollard told him arms deals with Argentine and South African insurgents could be lucrative, informed journalist Peter Perl. "Like a wannabe cop who likes to flash badges. He wanted to seem like he was really involved in intelligence, and then I learned he was just a staff analyst."

Lohbeck's comments to the contrary, the "staff analyst" was ready to take action. In order for it to occur, one fortuitous event and one important meeting had to occur.

The event involved a promotion for Pollard, whose outstanding work record had earned three Navy citations for excellence and a medal from the Secretary of the Navy. By June 1984, the year that Shimon Peres became Israeli prime minister, Pollard had been assigned to an elevated position, one in the new Anti-Terrorist Alert Center (ATAC) of the Naval Intelligence Service's Threat Analysis Division. His assignment was to be a watch officer under the command of the new administrator, Commander Jerry Agee. He was a stern, twenty-year veteran with extensive experience in the intelligence community who had just returned from a duty with the Sixth Fleet in the Eastern Mediterranean.

When Pollard's spying scheme was exposed, Commander Agee, whose thinning red hair indicated a quick temper, was blamed. Superiors realized that if he had contacted any of those who knew Pollard, he would have collided with Lieutenant Commander David Muller, Jr., who headed an analytical operation at Suitland. According to Muller, Pollard applied for an opening on Muller's staff. "Initially, I had a lot of respect for him," Muller initially told journalist Seymour Hersh, a constant critic of Pollard's. "He knew a lot about Navy hardware and a lot about the Middle East."

Muller's perception changed during a Monday morning interview with Pollard. "Jay blew in first thing Monday," Muller told Hersh. "He looked as if he hadn't slept or shaved. He proceeded to tell me that on Friday evening his then fiancée, Anne Henderson, had been kidnapped by IRA operatives in Washington, and he'd spent the weekend chasing the kidnappers. Pollard said he'd only been able to rescue Anne moments before the interview."

Recalling the incident for Hersh, Muller said, "I ought to have gone to the security people and said, 'This guy is a wacko.'" Later, Jonathan disavowed Muller's version of the story, saying that he exaggerated the facts.

After Pollard's arrest, Commander Agee blamed his previous supervisor for not revealing the analyst's "personal problems." But Agee had a duty to thoroughly check out the men who were under his new command. If he had done so, including interviewing Muller, he would have noted the South African incident that almost cost Pollard his job. Commander Agee would also have discovered that enough suspicion regarding Pollard's behavior existed to warrant a psychiatric examination.

Commander Agee's defense proved his naiveté. "I didn't even know he was Jewish," the supervisor proclaimed. "…He never came out and said, 'I am Jewish,' but after a period of time I put two and two together, and I assumed he was."

What Commander Agee did know and failed to report or act on was his knowledge that Pollard was, as he later stated, "a bullshitter, a teller of tall tales." Commander Agee admitted that he had heard about Pollard's boasts that he worked for Israeli intelligence, but disregarded the comment and laughed it off as a joke.

How wrong he was. While Commander Agee was dismissing red flags evidencing malcontent, Pollard was already stealing documents, those that he passed on to friends. All while his commander praised his work as "competent."

Working twelve hours at his new post, Jonathan Pollard was now in a position to access higher level intelligence information. During his first days on the job, he monitored messages forwarded to the ATAC involving terrorist activities. To operate, clearances had been obtained for him to have access to Sensitive Compartmented Information (extremely sensitive material relating to technical systems that intercept communication), as well as Top Secret, Secret, and Confidential material. The SCI clearance was essential, permitting access to libraries containing "secure" information, and to computer data for civilian and military agencies ad infinitum. Most important, Pollard was issued his "pass to spy," a "courier card," because it permitted the twenty-eight-year-old zealot for Israel to ferry classified documents between nearby libraries without having to pass through checkpoints.

Pollard's area of concern was the Caribbean/United States corridor, but he had clearance to classified data pertinent to the Middle East as well. With one eye on his assigned area and the other focused on events transpiring in and around Israel, he kept up-to-date on current developments. That permitted him to surmise that Israel was receiving only half a loaf of intelligence information instead of a whole.

The realization had ignited a fierce desire on Jonathan's part to assist his spiritual homeland as soon as possible. To his regret, he had known no one in the Israeli government to contact concerning his decision to become a spy. All had changed when Colonel Aviem Sella became his conduit for espionage, triggering the clandestine mission that had lasted over a year. Then Commander Agee woke up, and Jonathan Jay Pollard was arrested, accused of betraying his country.

BOOK III

Chapter 10

INVESTIGATING POLLARD

On November 21, 1985, a telephone call was placed in Washington, DC to Dr. Morris Pollard's office six hundred miles away at Notre Dame. The caller was Anne Pollard, and when she uttered three simple words, "Jay's in jail," Dr. Pollard's brain nearly hemorrhaged.

"What do you mean?" he uttered as the famed researcher attempted to comprehend the message.

"The FBI arrested him, Morris," Anne said. "He's in the DC jail."

Dr. Pollard recalled that until that disturbing moment, all had seemed well with the Pollard family. Wife Mollie was her usual delightful self and older son Harvey, forty-two, a graduate of Rice University and the University of Chicago, was a noted x-ray crystalographist and head of the laboratory for genetics and cell biology at the National Institutes of Health in Washington, DC. Daughter Carol, thirty-five, a gifted artist and musician, worked in hospital administration in New Haven, Connecticut, while youngest son Jonathan had just completed his sixth year as an analyst with the Naval Intelligence Service in Washington, where he lived with Anne, his wife of several months.

That year, one that included President Ronald Reagan's summit with Mikhail Gorbachev in Geneva, a TWA highjacking by Arab terrorists, and vigilante Bernhard Goetz's shooting of four black muggers on a New York subway, Morris and Mollie had traveled extensively, spending time in Australia, Brazil, and Central America.

Despite their being out of the country, never more than a few days passed without family members talking to one another. The Pollard family was closely knit, love apparent between parents and children.

"What happened?" Dr. Pollard asked.

"They arrested Jay for spying," she replied, her voice raised an octave. "We tried to get help at the Israeli embassy, but they threw us out. And then the FBI was waiting for us."

"The Israeli embassy, spying, what do you mean?" Dr. Pollard bellowed, his mind confused by Anne's words.

For the next thirty minutes, an out-of-breath Anne attempted to explain the circumstances of Jonathan's arrest. When the conversation ended, Dr. Pollard agreed to take the next plane to Washington, hopeful the whole situation was somehow a mistake.

It wasn't. From the moment the security guard received orders to boot Pollard and Anne from the Israeli embassy parking lot, and to use force if necessary, arrest was inevitable. When the gates opened and Pollard drove his Mustang onto Van Ness Avenue, FBI agents swarmed the vehicle, arrested and handcuffed him, and confiscated all of their personal belongings. For the time being, Anne, clutching Dusty, was permitted to remain free.

After Pollard's detention, there had been a hastily conceived plan to assist him. Colonel Sella said he informed Israeli general Ehud Barak, later to be prime minister, that the spy was under suspicion. Officials in Israeli military intelligence were placed on alert, but while they discussed a rescue plan, Pollard entered the embassy compound. Since no one had informed Elyakim Rubinstein of Pollard's importance, the spy was ordered out of the compound.

* * *

Sitting by the telephone in his small, cluttered office that featured a framed photo of Nobel Prize winner John Enders, whom Dr. Pollard admired, the sixty-eight-year-old researcher bowed his head in total disbelief as Anne divulged the details of Jonathan's arrest.

At home, Dr. Pollard notified his beloved wife Mollie, who burst into tears. He notified Carol and Harvey, sparing the shock of learning their brother's fate through news releases.

During the flight to Washington the next day, Dr. Pollard recalled a conversation he'd had with this son a few months before. Jonathan had sounded an alarm only to discover a father unwilling to listen.

Jonathan's message dealt with what he called "trouble brewing" at NIS. Though he listened with interest to the generalities, Dr. Pollard was leery, "I can't hear what you have to say, Jay," he said. "I don't have [security] clearance to do so."

"But yes, you do," Jonathan had replied. "I checked."

Despite the assurance, which Dr. Pollard realized was true based on his former dealings with the CIA, he didn't want to risk a security breach. That despite the fact that he worried about Jonathan and his presence in a world filled with secret data where he might compromise his position and cause him to violate his code of silence.

"I'm sorry, son," he told Jonathan with regret. "I just don't think you should tell me anything."

Those words haunted Dr. Pollard, since he knew that Jonathan in all likelihood was going to confide in him regarding the secret mission resulting in his arrest. "Did I fail my son when he needed me?" he wondered, his heart heavy with guilt.

* * *

With Jonathan Pollard incarcerated, government prosecutors concentrated on preparing a case to convict him. In addition to the stolen documents discovered in his possession, they now knew, or at least believed they knew, that Israel was the recipient of the contraband. When disclosure of Pollard's arrest and the link to one of the United States' closest allies was relayed to government intelligence officials, they were livid.

While prosecutors began working with investigators in order to piece together a case against the spy, Dr. Pollard was permitted to visit him.

"Jay was wearing an orange jumpsuit the first time I saw him," he recalled. "We were separated by a glass partition and I couldn't believe it was him. I wanted to hug him and never let go, but all we could do was talk on the phone. We made small talk and I promised to help, but he had such a strange look on his face, one of sorrow. When I left, I felt awful, like I had truly lost my son. All the while, I kept thinking I'd wake up from a bad dream and the whole thing would go away."

The next day Dr. Pollard witnessed the strong arm of the government. As he and daughter-in-law Anne were walking down the steps of the DC hospital across from the jail (they had eaten in the cafeteria), three stone-faced men in dark suits approached. "What is your name?" one of the gruff agents asked Anne. "Why, Anne Pollard," she replied as the tall agents towered over her. "Then you're under arrest," he informed her. "You will have to come with us." Seconds later, despite the protests of Dr. Pollard, who was threatened with arrest if he intervened, a sobbing Anne was read her rights and then escorted away in handcuffs.

"I walked down the street feeling hollow, frustrated that I was unable to help either Jay or Anne in any way," Dr. Pollard recalled. "The whole thing was a nightmare. Jay had been especially bitter about his treatment from the Israelis, because they had betrayed him. He suggested I deliver a message to their ambassador to the effect that their government lacked *beitzim*, Hebrew for balls."

While the Pollards spent their days and nights behind bars, two important lawyers entered the case. Heading up the government prosecution was forty-year-old United States Attorney Joseph diGenova, a mustachioed law and order zealot with piercing eyes and bushy eyebrows. A Republican known for being outspoken, he was appointed by President Ronald Reagan in 1983, after having been a deputy in the DC office for ten-plus years.

A graduate of Georgetown Law School, diGenova, whose political ambitions were well-known, served as a special assistant and legal adviser to Attorney General Edward Levi regarding matters involving intelligence. His expertise in that area benefited him in positions as a member of the Senate Intelligence Committee and the Senate Judiciary Committee. He was also counsel to the Senate Governmental Committee. "I had extensive experience in federal investigations, prosecutions, the federal legislative process and the oversight of governmental agencies, particularly the Justice Department, CIA, and FBI," diGenova, who served five years as US attorney, explained.

DiGenova's name resurfaced later when he was appointed Independent Counsel for the investigation into allegations that President Bill Clinton's passport file had been altered during the explosive 1992 presidential campaign. A chief suspect was President George Bush's confidant James Baker, who eight years later spearheaded George W. Bush's Florida recount campaign that earned him the presidency.

In December 1995, diGenova, who spent three years investigating the passport incident, released a report that contained 60,000 pages of documents summarized from interviewing more than 140 witnesses. No charges were brought against Baker and his cohorts. Regardless, diGenova characterized Bush administration officials as "stupid, dumb, and partisan." The cost of the investigation: a staggering 2.2 million dollars.

Insight into diGenova's persona was provided by author Bob Woodward in his book, *Shadow: Five Presidents and the Legacy of Watergate*. When diGenova believed he was being stonewalled by Bush administration officials regarding documents to be produced, Woodward described the independent counsel's demeanor by writing, "diGenova, hot by nature, went ballistic." Woodward also quoted diGenova concerning a conversation he had with Baker's attorney, Lloyd Cutler. Addresssing the fact that Baker was concealing information, diGenova bellowed, "…We're going to talk to him again, and this time I want it all. You guys are being dumb, and over-lawyering. I am not a marauding prosecutor, I'm not out to make a name for myself, I already have one."

DiGenova's adversary in the Pollard case was Washington, DC attorney Richard Hibey, a former assistant United States attorney who left to practice criminal law. He had been a senior assistant when diGenova began his tenure in the DC office in 1972.

By the time diGenova became US attorney, Richard Hibey was an experienced criminal defense attorney with many notable clients. Four years after the Pollard case, he defended Clair George, CIA deputy director of operations in the Iran-Contra matter. He was indicted by a grand jury that charged him with ten felonies, among them perjury and obstructing justice. In December 1992, George, whose first trial had ended in a mistrial, was convicted of two counts of lying to Congress.

Richard Hibey was retained by Dr. Morris Pollard. "I didn't know any lawyers in DC, so I contacted the dean of the Notre Dame Law School," he recalled. "He put me in touch with a lawyer in Washington named Gregory, but he only handled commercial cases. He suggested Richard Hibey, and Mollie and I went to see him."

From the outset the Pollards had reservations about Richard Hibey. "We should have known immediately that Hibey was a lightweight and that he was looking for a big case to take," Dr. Pollard explained. "He looked up the sentencing guidelines and played down the charges as not being serious. One thing I'll always remember is that he placed a call to Paris while Mollie and I were there. Afterwards, Mollie wondered if there was anyone really on the line or whether he was just trying to impress us. We didn't feel good about him, but we were just naive. We felt we had no choice. And the choice turned out to be a bad decision. Many times I've wondered if he was in cahoots with the government, for he failed Jay so badly."

The telling point regarding Hibey came later, Dr. Pollard believed, when he raised questions about certain defense strategies. "'You aren't my client, Dr. Pollard,' he told me bluntly. 'So I can't tell you anything.' That despite my being Jonathan's father and being responsible for paying the legal bills."

Midway through the legal proceedings Dr. Pollard sought to replace Hibey. He contacted Nat Lewin, a renowned lawyer in Washington. But he was representing Colonel Sella, thought to be Jay's Israeli "handler." Lewin suggested several lawyers, all Jewish, but when Dr. Pollard called them they claimed to be "too busy."

As the case progressed, Richard Hibey made it clear to Dr. Pollard that defending his son wouldn't be easy. "He said it was a difficult case, a tough one because people equate Zionism with racism," Dr. Pollard said. "That struck me as strange, but I had no one else willing to take Jay's case."

As his frustration mounted, Dr. Pollard confronted Hibey, of Lebanese extraction, about his reckless representation. "Hiring him was the biggest mistake I ever made," Dr. Pollard said. "And I feel I really let down Jay. He never trusted Hibey, and I shouldn't have either. He sold us out. I was just a babe in the woods, stupid, didn't know anything, and I got taken. When we finally argued about what he had done, he said to me, 'Well, look what your people did to my people in Lebanon.' I fired him the next day."

Richard Hibey's response to allegations of impropriety was silence. Since the date of sentencing he was unwilling to discuss the case, oftentimes declining to even return telephone calls regarding the matter. In the mid-1990s the attorney was asked by a New York magazine about his "toughest cases." He included Pollard, but did not elaborate.

If questions about representation for his son lingered, Dr. Pollard was buoyed by the support he received at Notre Dame. "I wondered whether the whole thing was an embarrassment to the university," he lamented, "since my association with Notre Dame was always mentioned in news coverage. I assume it was, but that didn't stop my colleagues from supporting me. Father Hesburgh, who was responsible for my coming to the university, was especially understanding. He came to see me right after the arrest. I wasn't sure how he would react, but he put his arms around me and told me he would pray for me, for my strength. And I will never forget one day when an elderly priest put his arm around me on the way to the post office while saying, 'I am praying for your son.' It made me want to cry. I'm not sure Mollie and I could have made it anywhere else."

* * *

Within hours after Jonathan Pollard's arrest an arraignment hearing was held at Federal District Court in Washington before United States Magistrate Patrick J. Attridge. After the charges against Pollard were read, government lawyers were successful in arguing that bond be denied based on US Attorney Harry Benner's assertion that the alleged spy was a "flight risk" because of "the large amounts of money he received for his offenses." A similar hearing was held subsequent to Anne's arrest, with bond being denied for her as well.

When asked by reporters after the arraignment the essence of the charges against Pollard, Joseph diGenova quipped, "This was not a list of lunchtime attendees at the Press Club. The documents were highly classified."

Despite the magistrate's ruling, Pollard was almost freed a few days later. "While I was standing in the lobby, a jail official announced that Jonathan Pollard was to be released immediately," Dr. Pollard recalled. "I was shocked by the announcement and immediately grew suspicious. I knew that bail had been denied and wondered what was going on. I quizzed the jailer, but he insisted my son was to be released. Fearful that he might be shot if he was on the streets, I informed Gordon Coffee, an assistant to Hibey who happened to be in the jail, of the impending release. 'Block it,' I shouted. 'Block it.'"

Minutes went by while Dr. Pollard waited in agony. "My mind was numb," he recalled. "I was so confused."

Dr. Pollard stood transfixed while Coffee shouted at officials. "When he returned," Dr. Pollard said, "he told me Jay would not be released."

Afterwards, Dr. Pollard had second thoughts regarding his actions. "I wondered if I had made a mistake, not having Jay released. But I'm sure I made the correct decision because so much that was unexplainable was happening that I really did fear for his life."

No explanation was ever forthcoming regarding the mix-up that almost permitted accused spy Jonathan Pollard to be released in violation of a court order. It was just the first of many such instances where the bizarre became commonplace in a case that took on the appearance of an episode of Rod Serling's *Twilight Zone*.

* * *

On 27 November, Magistrate Attridge summoned all parties to US District Court for a full-scale preliminary hearing. Both Anne and Jonathan's request for bail would be considered a second time.

Assistant United States Attorney Charles Leeper, a strong advocate with a voice to match, appeared for the government. Richard Hibey was the attorney for Pollard; Hibey's brother James was Anne's legal counsel.

On that rainy afternoon, Dr. Morris Pollard's eyes glistened as his son, dressed in a pink shirt, paisley tie, and chocolate brown suit, stood before the magistrate. Anne sat as if in a trance at counsel's table wearing a simple purple dress that appeared two sizes too big.

FBI agent Eugene Noltkamper was the government's star witness. He described Pollard's crime by stating that the documents stolen related to "the intelligence-gathering capabilities of foreign countries."

Noltkamper, in answer to Leeper's spit-fire questions, outlined Pollard's modus operandi in stealing the documents. He divulged that more than sixty documents among those stolen marked "Top Secret" related to "weapons capabilities of foreign countries." He added that Pollard had received "twenty-five hundred dollars per month and two trips to Europe" for his spying efforts.

Seconds later Leeper questioned the agent about Anne's part in the spy matter. He noted that she had a suitcase full of classified documents in her possession along with her passport when she and Jonathan entered the Israeli embassy. He also noted that she had "contacts with the

Chinese embassy." Once the agent had completed his testimony, Dr. Pollard was called to testify as to the possibilities of Anne's fleeing if permitted bond. In a tone barely above a whisper, with his now disgraced son sitting just a few feet away, Dr. Pollard told the court of Anne, "I know her. I respect her. I've developed an affection for her."

Dr. Pollard's plaudits aside, Charles Leeper ended the hearing by proclaiming, "Desperate circumstances produce desperate action," in reference to the likelihood that the Pollards might flee the country if permitted bail. Minutes later, Magistrate Attridge agreed and the couple were handcuffed and returned to the DC jail.

* * *

While sorting out the strength of the evidence available to prosecute Pollard, Joseph diGenova and his colleagues must have been pleased with the strong public reaction condemning both the suspected spies and the State of Israel.

Media attention to the arrest of Jonathan Pollard had been swift and strong. And, with few exceptions, misleading.

A November 22, 1985, *New York Times* article by Philip Shenon reported that "Pollard had received less than $100,000 from the Israelis in exchange for 'code information.'" Use of that high figure, which exaggerated what Pollard had accepted and the term, 'code information,' without providing specifics, distorted the truth and left the impression that money was Pollard's ultimate goal.

Shenon also wrote, "In conversations with government agents,...Pollard acknowledged selling classified information to the Israeli government and to an Asian nation." By the 22nd, Pollard, FBI reports confirmed, had confessed to nothing, since questioning was still in the preliminary stages and Pollard was being evasive to protect his handlers and Anne. The addition of the "to an Asian nation" phrase proved to be false; Pollard never discussed such a possibility because none existed.

The quote, "Before the arrest, Pollard talked with Israeli officials, and said that 'the FBI is on to me, I need help,' according to a law enforcement official," was also in error; there was no way at that point for any government official to know of any conversations between Pollard and "Israeli officials" other than those at the embassy.

Shenon's article contained a statement from an unnamed FBI official comparing Pollard's misdeeds with those of John A. Walker Jr., the retired Navy chief warrant officer who had pleaded guilty the same month to charges of passing highly classified documents to the Soviets. "The official said that the information obtained by Pollard was sensitive," Shenon quoted his source, "but added, 'I don't have any reason to believe it's in the Walker category.'" Regardless of the clarification, mention of the Russian spy in the same breath with Pollard connected him with a cowardly act of espionage with an archenemy of the United States.

The article portrayed Pollard as a mercenary by quoting "another bureau official" who stated that, "It appeared Pollard had not been motivated by ideology. It was financial." The text of that statement was pure conjecture based on few available facts.

The charges outlined in the *Times* and other newspapers across the globe following Pollard's arrest made one thing very clear: Israel, the beloved ally of the United States, was an active and knowing participant in the spy mission. From coast to coast members of the American Jewish population, so committed to preserving Israel's freedom, found themselves questioning the conduct of the very country they supported. Their response was to condemn Pollard and chastise Israel for its part in the espionage.

"I tried not to be upset at first over the lack of an outcry by the Jewish community over Jay's arrest, because they were never told all of the facts," Dr. Pollard said, "but it was a revelation to me. I realized that Jews are not monolithic; they are split in many directions. They claim 'Never, never again,' but there can be a Holocaust even when people are not killed."

Initial Jewish condemnation of his son caused Dr. Pollard deep anguish. As he watched in anger, Jewish leaders with few exceptions, preached that Pollard was indeed a traitor not only to his country but to Jews in general.

Leading the charge was Nathan Perlmutter, national director of the Anti-Defamation League (ADL) of B'nai B'rith. Using the op-ed page of the *Washington Post* as his bully pulpit, Perlmutter chastised Pollard, writing, "What began in stupidity quickly sank into irresponsibility." His successor, Abraham Foxman, added to the furor by singling out

Israel in the *Jerusalem Post* for acting in a "cavalier and equivocating manner that borders on contempt for American sensibilities."

Later, Jonathan Pollard shouted back at the Anti-Defamation League's outburst, alleging bias, since Aviem Sella's wife had been a lawyer in the firm of Kenneth Bialkin, the national ADL chairman while his spying escapades were in progress. "They [ADL] always cited dual loyalty as the backbone of their arguments," he lamented. "They simply never understood what I did for Israel never hurt the United States."

Jewish leadership's abandonment of Jonathan caused Dr. Pollard to consider another aspect of the case. "The statement came out that if Jonathan had been black, he would have been treated differently, been released from jail quickly....All because the Jewish community would have risen to his defense. I hate to admit it, but that is true. I can't recall one of their own [a Jew] who has been protected. Can you?"

Regarding specific reaction, Dr. Pollard surmised: "There were Jews who were scared, Jews who were indignant, and Jews who later said they thought Jay got a bad break, but they kept quiet. They were the worst, people like Steven Spielberg or Barbra Streisand, who were asked to get involved. They declined to even talk to us. Silence is the greatest enemy of truth, they know that, but even now, not enough have come around. They simply never wanted to know the other side of the story."

As the case progressed, Dr. Pollard continued to be stumped by Jewish behavior in the case. "One day I was really thinking about all this, and it came to me," he explained. "Fear of the dual loyalty [United States and Israel] is a sign of weakness. You can't judge the patriotism of a man by the size of his flag."

Pollard supporter Beverly Newman believed the Jewish community at large had been misled by the media. "They did not willfully abandon Jonathan," she said. "And when they learned the truth, they supported him through letters, protests, signed petitions, and rallies, all to his benefit."

A "fictional" Jonathan Pollard, Dr. Pollard alleged, was created by government attorneys. "They portrayed him as an evil mercenary whose only motivation was money. They leaked it that Jay was a heavy drug user and had been treated for mental problems for years and was unstable. To embellish these accusations, fictional friends and colleagues were invented as sources. Complete with fictional accounts of what Jay said and did."

Government attorneys disputed Dr. Pollard's claims. DiGenova and his deputies called them "irresponsible" and "not based on the facts."

During the grand jury investigation of his son, Dr. Pollard sought a clear understanding of the potential damage his son had done. Subpoenaed to testify, he said he encountered Deputy United States Attorney Charles Leeper outside the grand jury room.

"I testified about Jay's childhood," Dr. Pollard recalled. "The jurors wanted to know all about him and why he would have done such a thing. I explained that, especially his passion for Israel and belief that it needed protection, but the most intriguing thing was talking to Leeper. Outside the grand jury room, he came up to me and said, 'I know you are unhappy with Jonathan, Dr. Pollard. We have been informed about what you have done for the government [research work], and I want to assure you that he did nothing to damage the United States.' I appreciated his comments and took that as a sign that everything would be all right. It turned out that I couldn't have been more wrong."

As the months passed during 1986, the year when the media broke the story that the United States was unlawfully selling military arms to Iran, Dr. Pollard said he made one thing clear to his son. "I told him, 'Jay, you need to tell them what you did. Make it right so that nobody gets hurt.' I truly believed that if he did that, he would be punished, but not too harshly. Later, I would realize that I was completely wrong. Looking back, I can see that they never intended to release him."

Chapter 11

THE INDICTMENT

When the grand jury returned the indictment against Jonathan Pollard in Case Number 85-0778M-01(cr), it charged him with violation of Title 18, US Code sections 794(a) and 794(c). Section 794(a) alleged that "…Jonathan Jay Pollard did knowingly and willfully conspire, combine, confederate and agree with Rafi Eitan, Aviem 'Avi' Sella, Joseph 'Yossi' Yagur, Irit Erb, coconspirators, not defendants herein…to commit an offense against the United States that is: To knowingly and willfully communicate, deliver, and transmit to a foreign government, that is, Israel, or to representatives, officers, agents, or citizens thereof, directly or indirectly, information and documents relating to the national defense of the United States, having intent and reason to believe that the same would be used to the advantage of Israel." If convicted, the term of imprisonment could be life.

Anne Pollard was charged with two counts: 1) Conspiring to receive embezzled government property in violation of 18 USC PP371, and 2) Accessory after the fact to unauthorized possession of national defense information in violation of 18 USC PP193(e). Both counts carried a maximum sentence of five years.

The specific charges now a matter of public record, prosecutor Joseph diGenova, who visited Israel as part of an eleven-member fact-finding delegation that included his wife, Charles Leeper, Commander Agee, and State Department legal affairs adviser and former federal judge Abraham Sofaer (who advised government officials during the Iran-Contra Affair), continued to assess actual evidence collected against Pollard. He soon became aware that a critical element was missing—the stolen government documents passed by Pollard to his Israeli handlers. Without them, there was no direct link to the Israelis, and a successful prosecution would be difficult.

DiGenova also made plans to demand access to Israeli diplomats suspected of being in the conspiracy with Pollard. By interviewing them he hoped to weave together the events that led to the spying.

DiGenova's efforts were aided by high level talks between American and Israeli officials. Attempting to avoid responsibility, the latter projected a smoke screen campaign that portrayed Jonathan Pollard as a rogue spy who had conducted illegal dealings through an unofficial and radical clandestine intelligence unit that top Israeli government officials knew nothing about.

To confirm their position, they issued a statement from the Foreign Ministry, which read in part: "Israel's political leadership received with shock and consternation the reports from Washington, according to which an employee of the US Navy was accused of espionage for Israel. Actions of that kind in the United States stand in total contradiction to the policy of the Israeli government."

Responsibility for communicating with the Israelis was assumed by Secretary of State George Schultz, a former Marine and veteran of cabinet posts in the Nixon administration. He had been on the receiving end of a "Why are they [Israel] doing it?" question from an exasperated President Ronald Reagan. Intent on taking an offensive stance, Schultz telephoned Prime Minister Shimon Peres in Jerusalem. At first both Peres and Shamir denied accountability, but after checking with other Israeli officials, including Yitzhak Rabin, under whose department of defense Jonathan's activities took place, they altered their stance.

Media reports detailed the continuing negotiations. On December 2, 1985, Philip Shenon wrote a revealing article in the *New York Times* titled, "Shultz Welcomes Apology By Israel." The first paragraph read, "Secretary of State George P. Shultz said today that the United States welcomed Israel's apology for the purported espionage activities of Jonathan Jay Pollard, a Navy counterintelligence analyst accused of spying for Israel." Shenon also reported that the statement by the Israelis had come after "a lengthy telephone conversation between Shultz and Prime Minister Shimon Peres" which followed a State Department communiqué the previous Friday to the effect that the United States "was 'dismayed' by Israel's lack of cooperation in the Pollard investigation."

Shenon quoted Peres as saying, "He was sorry for whatever Israeli spying on the United States took place, and said if the espionage allegations were confirmed, the unit involved would be dismantled."

To the eyes of the world, Israel had disavowed any allegiance to Pollard, but it had admitted guilt in betraying its allegience to the United States, its most coveted ally. In doing so Israel had infuriated government officials, including Secretary of Defense Caspar Williard Weinberger, long suspicious of Israel's intentions.

Left unclear was whether FBI agents would be able to interview diplomats Ilan Ravid, the deputy science attaché at the Israeli embassy in Washington, and Yosef Yagur, the science attaché in the Israeli consulate in New York. Unidentified United States district attorneys were quoted as saying that while they expected to interview both men, they looked upon the Israeli apology as an "invitation to participate in the investigation."

To Pollard supporters the message was loud and clear: Jonathan was on his own—Israel was not going to back him up.

Years later, in 1989, Dr. Morris Pollard traveled to Israel on a fact-finding mission to discover the motives behind the government's abandonment of his son. He attempted to meet with Yitzhak Rabin and Yitzhak Shamir, but both men refused his requests. Only Shimon Peres assented. "We met at a military installation," Dr. Pollard said. "I entered one end of the building and he entered the other since they did not want anyone to see us together. I asked him, 'Why did you disavow Jonathan?' He looked at me and said, 'We were scared.'"

The admission didn't surprise Dr. Pollard. "Politicians never make a decision based on principle. The Israelis simply called Jay a rogue and that was that. [Later] they were instrumental in having him locked up so he wouldn't tell the truth. In effect, he was to become a political prisoner."

As for Shimon Peres, Dr. Pollard said, "I told others after meeting with him that I wouldn't trust that guy with my car keys."

For Jonathan Pollard, who believed he had given his heart and soul to his beloved Israel while placing himself in great legal jeopardy, Israeli top government officials' denials that they knew of his spying efforts was a crushing blow. In a memorandum filed with the US District Court in August 1986, Pollard provided his reasoning regarding the matter:

...First of all, the number and type of Israelis who were associated with this affair suggest a high degree of government awareness if not intimate supervision of their behavior. Given both the comparatively small size of the Israeli intelligence community as well as its notorious infra-service volubility, the plausibility that seven members could carry out a "renegade" operation unbeknownst to security and fiscal management personnel is beyond reason. Even with the availability of a bureaucratically unaccountable "slush" fund, the expenses of this operation could not have passed unnoticed by the Inner Cabinet's intelligence auditor, who has an extremely broad mandate for regulating these sensitive financial outlays. Furthermore if one takes into account both the quality and highly specialized professional expertise of the personnel who were involved in this affair, it seems unlikely that their collaboration could have been the product of random selection: a near famous advisor to the Prime Minister, a highly decorated member of the Air Force, two senior science attachés, and a leading international arms broker do not simply coalesce out of thin air.

Secondly, the type of collection guidance I received suggested a highly coordinated effort between the Navy, Army and Air Force intelligence services. At the end of each month, I was given an extremely detailed list of material which was needed by the various organizations that included an explanation of why the information officially transferred did not satisfy their requirements. Although the acquisition lists appeared to have been submitted by each service separately, since dissimilar plans and formats were used by the three organizations, there was always one prioritized list which had evidently been agreed upon by the respective military chiefs of intelligence and bore their combined seal. While it is possible that the Mossad considered this affair to have been "unauthorized" because they were evidently never a party to it, the same cannot be said of the General Staff, which was intimately involved with identifying which type of scientific and technical intelligence was to be the object of my activity. From what I could see, Rafi Eitan only served as the individual responsible for managing the covert side of this uniformed service operation.

Thirdly, I was routinely provided with finished technical assessments of the material which had been passed to the Israelis. The turnaround time for these assessments was very quick and when I inquired how this was accomplished was told that a special team of analysts had been established back in Israel just for the purpose of evaluating the operational applicability of all the new information collected. Given the unique nature of this material, such as satellite photography and SIGINT-derived studies (CENSORED) this team was not only fully aware of when the information was being acquired, but was also cognizant that it was not being transferred through official channels. Although I was never told how large this group was, it had to have been rather well staffed with extremely competent scientists in light of the volume and diversity of the material I collected.

Fourthly, there were three occasions on which I was told that the higher levels of the Israeli government had purportedly extended their collective thanks for the assistance I had provided the state. After I had supplied Yosef Yagur with a very detailed study of Pakistan's facility, he informed me that a special studies committee, directly subordinated to the Prime Minister's office, had presented its conclusions to the Cabinet on the growing dangers of the Pakistani weapons effort and had emphasized, in writing, that the intelligence material obtained from a "special source" had been critical to its evaluation. I was also congratulated by Yagur after an Israeli drone, or unmanned reconnaissance aircraft, had been able to successfully negotiate its way through the entire Syrian air defense system in 1985. According to the Israeli Air Force, this remarkable achievement was only possible due to the material I provided.

...Fifthly, since Eitan was physically located in the Prime Minister's office and was evidently involved in some type of intense bureaucratic competition with the Mossad, it is very likely that he provided both my name and position to the select group of Israeli politicians and General Staff representatives who would have been briefed on the agent responsible for such intelligence coups as the photos of Pakistan, the aerial romp over Syria and the raid against the PLO's North African headquarters. The inner Cabinet would have wanted to know who provided this information and Eitan could never have resisted the opportunity to score points against the Mossad in front of the government. Yagur mentioned several times that specific documents had been used by Eitan to embarrass the Chief of Mossad at Cabinet meetings and, as stated earlier, the material was so unique that anyone present at the carefully orchestrated confrontations would have known about the existence of an agent working in the American intelligence establishment....

* * *

Following Pollard's arrest a flurry of activity in Israel aimed at damage control was centered on making the best of a bad situation. Once the leadership was convinced that action was required, an ad hoc committee was formed under the code name "Siren." Three members from Labor and Likud, the ruling parties, were appointed. Results of their internal investigation were immediate: Yes, Pollard was a spy for Israel. Yes, he had done so under handlers associated with LAKAM, an intelligence unit within the Israeli Defense Ministry. And, yes, Jonathan Pollard had been a most expedient and resourceful spy who provided essential material for the defense of his spiritual homeland.

Despite these admissions, several members of the committee were unwilling to aid the United States with their investigation. After a vociferous debate, a deadlock resulted when three members of Labor backed Peres's inclination to cooperate while three Likud representatives dissented. Among the dissenters were members of the Israel intelligence community, which believed that capitulating to the Americans would be a mistake and that doing so meant further betrayal of Pollard, who had been left to fend for himself. They asserted that if any documents were to be turned over, a tit-for-tat deal should be struck so that both Anne and Jonathan Pollard would be exchanged.

The course of action decided upon by Shimon Peres was predictable. Forced to choose between loyalty to a spy, no matter how helpful he had been, or the United States, he chose the latter.

Peres's decision to sell out Pollard was delivered with the intention that the US would accept the shaky explanation that the spy was part of a "rogue operation" and had done little harm to American security. Further discussions between Peres and Schultz produced a promise by Peres to produce documents Pollard had stolen. In return, Schultz accepted the "rogue" excuse, and the apology, and promised not to indict any Israeli conspirators.

By doing so, Peres disconnected Pollard from Israel and set a dark precedence in the intelligence community. For the first time in history, a country assisted in convicting one of its own spies. Not only had Israel denied Pollard asylum at its embassy, it now had become a critical member of the prosecution team.

Dr. Aaron Lerner, director of the IMRA (Independent Media Review and Analysis) analyzed Peres's actions and those of the members of the committee that voted to authorize passage of the stolen documents to the US government. Dr. Lerner, a Middle East news analyst and commentator, stated in a June 2000 Israeli radio broadcast that Israeli leaders produced the documents, but "conditioned cooperation on the consent of the Americans to the fact that the documents returned would not be used to convict Pollard." Citing his possession of a copy of the May 26, 1987, Eban Committee Report, prepared by a subcommittee of the Foreign Affairs and Defense Committee of the Knesset, Dr. Lerner said, "I was astounded to find the…passage under the heading, 'The Decision To Cooperate with the FBI.'"

Prosecutor Joseph diGenova called the Knesset report "absolutely false." He stated, "We were [in Israel] to gather evidence. We even interviewed the Israeli embassy officials who fled the country [US] in contravention of their promise to the US government that they would not. The Israelis gave us a few documents, saying the rest of them had been destroyed, which of course, we knew was a ludicrous claim. There were no restrictions on the use of those documents. And they were used in the investigation. Those documents were United States government documents.…We weren't about to have restrictions put on them."

DiGenova also spoke to the usefulness of the documents and of Israeli cooperation. He stated, "The documents were of little if any value. They were used in the questioning of Mr. Pollard and other people, but we got other information about those documents which was far more compelling and helpful than anything we got from the Israeli government. We didn't expect the Israelis to be forthcoming. We expected them to do exactly what they did which was to claim that all of the documents that they had gotten from Mr. Pollard had been destroyed and therefore they couldn't be returned."

When diGenova was asked to comment on the Israelis' reluctance to admit that higher-ups in their government were aware of Pollard's spying, he said, "My God, yes, the Israelis were denying it categorically. In fact, during our first trip there, they did everything they could to hide from us the most important secret, which of course we didn't know until months later. That the real reason they were trying to give us false information and put us on a sidetrack was because they were trying to protect the identity of Pollard's original handler, Colonel Aviem Sella.…Once we discovered that when we were back in the United States, we made another trip back under different circumstances armed with new information."

In a court document filed in June 1987, government attorney John Fisher admitted that the "new information" assisted in the prosecution of Pollard. The pertinent paragraph read, "Cooperation was not forthcoming in this case until several months after defendant's arrest. Indeed, defendant agreed to enter a guilty plea and cooperate only after government attorneys and investigators returned from Israel with additional evidence of defendant's guilt."

Despite Joseph diGenova's allegations, several members of the Eban Committee, convened after the spy was sentenced, still insisted that the documents turned over were key to Pollard's demise. Dr. Lerner, quoting the same section of the Eban report, wrote, "...three members of the Eban Committee condemned Israel's return of the documents and concluded...these documents constituted the basis for the conviction and life sentence that Pollard received, in spite of...an American commitment not to use the documents against Pollard."

While there remained confusion regarding the documents and what promises were made about their use, it is apparent that the Israelis assisted in the prosecution of their own spy. They had not only abandoned Pollard, but assumed an active role in locking the door to his prison cell.

Chapter 12

THE PLEA AGREEMENT

During the first month of incarceration, Anne Pollard, in excruciating pain from her worsening stomach condition, diagnosed as biliary dyskinesia, lost over fifty pounds. She was twenty-five years old, but observers noticed that her personal turmoil and stress over the fate of Jonathan caused her to age considerably. Later, Anne described the horror of being in prison to new attorney Leon Charney, a Pollard supporter who characterized Jonathan's contribution to Israel as "invaluable to their security."

The letter was published by her father Bernard Henderson in his book, *Pollard, The Spy's Story*. Anne had written, "Prison life has been particularly brutal to us. At first, prosecutors concocted wild stories that I was a Chinese and Israeli spy in order to secure my wrongful detention for nearly 100 days. I was locked in a tiny, windowless, roach and rat infested cell for 23 1/2 to 24 hours a day. I was deliberately denied essential medical treatment and prescriptions for my numerous health problems, and almost died as a result of this. My hair even turned gray."

With Anne's health in question, and a mountain of evidence facing both her and Jonathan, the time was ripe in the spring of 1986 for a plea bargain to bring closure to the case. Prosecutors did not want to endure a trial for fear of compromising national security. They had been startled to hear Jonathan proclaim, "There are much bigger fish to fry here." That statement caused them to wonder who Jonathan's lawyers might call as witnesses at a trial that could prove embarrassing to the government.

For all concerned, a plea agreement had merit. Richard Hibey feared life imprisonment for his client, and his brother James had similar concerns regarding a lengthy sentence for Anne if the Pollards were convicted at trial.

Negotiations between the parties in March and April 1986 produced the plea agreement. Cooperation by Pollard began before the arrangement was reduced to writing in a May 26, 1986, eight-page letter from diGenova to Richard Hibey. In return for Pollard's plea of guilty to 18 USC Section 794(c)—Conspiracy to Deliver National Defense Information to a Foreign Country, the government agreed to request a "substantial sentence." They also promised to show leniency for Anne, who faced consecutive (served one after the other) five-year penalties.

The plea agreements signed by Anne and Jonathan were "wired," a common tactic utilized by prosecutors. Each was a mirror image of the other containing obligations to cooperate with government investigators. If either violated the provisions, the other suffered.

Later, Jonathan Pollard charged that he had no choice other than to plead guilty. He alleged he was shown Polaroid photographs of Anne that portrayed her deteriorating condition. Time and time again, he said, he was informed that if he wanted to help her, the only way to do so was to plead guilty. When he was shown a photo, according to him, of Anne lying on a cot in excruciating pain, he relented and agreed to the demands.

Anne's condition had become exacerbated after her incarceration. In a memorandum to the court her attorney alleged that, "Mrs. Pollard's medical problems, for which she had undergone a surgical procedure the day before her arrest, were far from over. Rather, her condition worsened dramatically in jail. Initially, she was deprived of the medication on which she depended to regulate her condition….She endured long periods of constant pain and frequently was unable to eat. Her frequent requests for medical treatment went largely ignored."

Despite the Pollards' accusations, Joseph diGenova labeled Jonathan's assertions regarding the photos and his being forced to plead guilty "absurd." "We demanded a dual guilty plea in the case," he explained, "because that is what the government does in cases where there are co-conspirators. And Henderson-Pollard [Anne] had assisted Mr. Pollard in violating espionage laws….There was absolutely no relationship to her health whatsoever in anything having to do with the guilty plea. [Pollard] saying he plead guilty because Anne wouldn't get medical treatment if he didn't is false."

Dr. Morris Pollard disagreed with diGenova's statements about the plea agreement. "DiGenova was just a political animal hoping for higher office and he came up with an idea, one diabolical in nature but perfectly legal. Basically, it came down to putting the squeeze on Anne, depriving her of proper medical attention while submitting her to vile prison conditions. In effect, he broke her spirit and caused her much suffering while making it clear to Jonathan that the key to her cell lay in his hands."

Anne's views regarding her participation in the spying scheme were quite revealing. In a letter to Attorney Charney published in the Bernard Henderson book, *Pollard: The Spy's Story*, she said:

> As Diaspora Jews, our families instilled in us the vital importance of preserving human life through the deterrence of war. Their convictions stemmed largely from their recent memory of World War II, in which 6,000,000 Jews were systematically massacred during the Holocaust. As a result of our upbringing, our perceived moral and racial obligations dictate that we should do everything in our power to prevent another systematic slaughter of mankind (especially Jews) from ever occurring again whether it is directed against a nation or a person. Human life is too precious to sacrifice. It is because of this rationale that Jay and I felt compelled to take certain actions which have ultimately resulted in our own personal Holocaust.

Regardless of those strong feelings, Anne insisted she was opposed to pleading guilty. She agreed to do so under pressure from her attorney James Hibey, and her father Bernard Henderson. He said Anne was told, "If you refuse, Jonathan will risk being given the maximum sentence. And Anne simply could not take a chance on that occurring."

Significant to the plea bargain were paragraphs detailing Jonathan's continuing cooperation. One read, in part:

> Several interviews of Mr. Pollard followed, conducted in your presence by Government attorneys and agents of the Federal Bureau of Investigation. During those interviews, Mr. Pollard revealed the details of his espionage activities on behalf of the government of Israel, including the specific classified documents and information requested by his co-conspirators, the means by which he acquired classified

documents and information for his co-conspirators; the nature and extent of classified information compromised; and the nature and amount of the compensation which Mr. Pollard received for his espionage activities. It should also be noted that the veracity of the foregoing information was confirmed through independent investigation and several polygraph examinations of Mr. Pollard which you authorized agents of the Federal Bureau of Investigation to perform.

Paragraph 4(a) of the plea bargain referred to anticipated plaudits for Pollard at sentencing. It read:

When he appears before the Court for sentencing for the offense to which he has agreed to plead guilty, the Government will bring to the Court's attention the nature, extent and value of his cooperation and testimony. Because of the classified nature of the information Mr. Pollard has provided to the Government, it is understood that particular representations concerning his cooperation may have to be made to the Court "in camera." In general, however, the Government has agreed to represent that the information Mr. Pollard has provided is of considerable value to the Government's damage assessment analysis, its investigation of this criminal case, and the enforcement of the espionage laws.

So that Pollard understood the government could strike back if he wasn't cooperative, Paragraph 4(b) was inserted. It stated:

Notwithstanding Mr. Pollard's cooperation, at the time of sentencing the Government will recommend that the Court impose a sentence of a substantial period of incarceration and a monetary fine. The Government retains full right of allocution at all times concerning the facts and circumstances of the offenses committed by Mr. Pollard, and will be free to correct any misstatements of fact at the time of sentencing, including representations of the defendant and his counsel in regard to the nature and extent of Mr. Pollard's cooperation. Moreover, Mr. Pollard understands that while the Court may take his cooperation into account in determining whether or not to impose a sentence of life imprisonment, this agreement cannot and does not limit the Court's discretion to impose the maximum sentence.

While many Pollard supporters alleged that the plea agreement was unfair, prosecutor Joseph diGenova defended it. When asked whether the agreement was too open-ended, the former United States attorney said, "Open ended? The [plea agreement] was negotiated by one of the best criminal lawyers in this town [Washington, DC], Richard Hibey. It was a classic agreement, basically boilerplate. It required cooperation and it is the judgment of the government as to whether or not there has been full and complete cooperation. That is the language in every plea agreement that the United States enters into. There was nothing vague about the agreement....It required Mr. Pollard to be completely forthcoming, to be completely cooperative, to assist the government, not to divert the government."

In addition to the principal provisions of the plea agreement covering cooperation and penalty, it contained requirements for permission if Pollard elected to be interviewed by the media or write a book. The pertinent text was:

> Mr. Pollard understands and acknowledges his legal obligation to refrain from the unauthorized disclosure, either orally or in any writing, of classified information derived during his employment by the United States Navy and/or in the course of the activities which resulted in his arrest in the above-captioned case. Should Mr. Pollard at any time author any book or other writing, or otherwise provide information for purposes of publication or dissemination, he hereby agrees to first submit said book, writing or information to the director of Naval Intelligence for pre-publication review and deletion of information which, in the sole discretion of the director of Naval Intelligence [is or should be classified]....

In essence, Jonathan Pollard was agreeing that the secretary of the Navy had to approve any media interviews and the specifics of their content before they occurred. Little did he realize that it was this provision that would haunt him several months later.

BOOK IV

Chapter 13

GUILTY

Assigned to the Jonathan Pollard case was Federal Court Judge Aubrey Eugene E. Robinson III, a sixty-three-year-old light-complected African-American. On June 4, 1986, Jonathan first glimpsed the man who would decide his fate.

Having shed considerable weight during his six-month incarceration, a lean Pollard appeared before the judge. Attired in a cloudy gray business suit, he appeared to be a young Wall Street stockbroker upset with the market. His dour, chastened mood was evidenced by a worrisome scowl, especially when he glanced at Anne. Hunched over in apparent pain, she sat nearby wearing a black dress that fit the occasion.

On this monumental day Pollard, a thirty-two-year-old man who evolved from a young boy dreaming of saving his beloved Israel into a defendant about to admit his guilt in a criminal case, stepped to the lectern. Jonathan was about to waive his constitutional rights to trial by jury, or even trial by court, by entering a plea of guilty to charges that he had betrayed the United States of America.

According to Middle East analyst Emanual Winston, Judge Robinson, born March 30, 1922, "had an interesting reputation for being rotated into certain cases in which the Justice Department and intelligence agencies had a deep interest." A rigid, no-nonsense man who ruled his courtroom with an iron hand, he was a native of Madison, New Jersey, population 900, who earned first a bachelor's degree and then a doctor of jurisprudence from Cornell University in 1947. His father had gained a degree in veterinary medicine from that same university.

One of four children, Judge Robinson, proficient in the violin and clarinet as a youngster, had been interested in becoming a doctor. "I had contemplated for some time the possibility of studying medicine," the judge said in an interview with the Historical Society of the District of Columbia Circuit in 1992, "but I determined that I didn't think I wanted to go through the drudgery because I didn't have that gut feeling that medicine was what I was really inclined toward."

Judge Robinson's law school years were interupted by the army during World War II. In 1945 his army unit was scheduled to set sail for the fighting front in the Pacific. Days before their scheduled departure, the atomic bomb was dropped and the orders were canceled.

During his days at Cornell, Judge Robinson witnessed racial bias. "…I was incensed that I could not belong to the legal fraternity in the law school," he said in 1992. "Though neither could the Jewish students, and we protested rather strenuously."

Judge Robinson discovered upon graduation that being a black attorney restricted job placement. Several months elapsed before he joined Belford Lawson, who maintained a law practice on Eleventh Street in Washington, DC with his wife Marjorie Mackenzie, and George Windsor.

During his tenure as a private attorney, Judge Robinson successfully handled a memorable 1949 case, *Henderson v. The Southern Railway.* "I had a friend and client who was Legislative Assistant to Congressman Dawson," the judge recalled in 1992. "His duties required him to travel and he was headed on Southern Railway through the South and they wouldn't feed him in the dining car. He was incensed. And he came back and we undertook that litigation and it went to the Supreme Court."

After maintaining the private practice for eighteen years (1945–1963), Judge Robinson became an associate District of Columbia juvenile court judge in 1965. A year later he leaped from the juvenile bench to the DC Federal District Court through an appointment from President Lyndon Johnson.

Only 42 at the time, Judge Robinson initially believed that the envoy who informed him of the pending appointment was joking. "I damn near flipped backwards in my chair," the judge said when he learned the envoy was serious.

Judge Robinson, known for his distinctive penmanship, was an associate judge on the district court until being named chief judge in 1982. When asked in the 1992 interview by the Historical Society to name his "cases that had the most memorable impact on society," the

Pollard case was not mentioned.

Judge Robinson died in March 2000, at the age of seventy-seven, best known for the Pollard case and his decision, later reversed on appeal, that awarded punitive damages to victims' families killed in the 1983 Korean Air flight 007 shot down over Soviet airspace.

Other cases of note that the judge oversaw included the 1980 theft of government documents by Church of Scientology officials Jane Kember and Morris Budlong. Each was sentenced to six years in prison. A year later Robinson ruled that a US Air Force order barring Rabbi Captain Simcha Goldman from wearing a yarmulke while in uniform was illegal.

Of the three-hundred-plus decisions Judge Robinson delivered, more than eighty-five were reversed. Most interesting was a 1975 case involving the Anti-Defamation League which sought to enjoin the National Mexican-American Anti-Defamation Committee from using "Anti-Defamation" as part of its name. Robinson dismissed the league's claim, only to be reversed by the Court of Appeals.

Prosecutor Joseph diGenova called Judge Robinson "an African-American of distinction," adding, "he was one of the finest Federal judges I ever appeared in front of."

* * *

During the guilty plea hearing, Judge Robinson queried a nervous Jonathan Pollard, whose hands were shaking. The judge asked, "Do you know of any reason why I shouldn't accept your plea?" A beat or two later Pollard uttered a weak, "No sir, I don't." To remind Pollard that he wasn't bound by any agreement between him and the prosecution, the judge said, "You realize I could still impose life imprisonment." With a lump in his throat, Pollard nodded, then said "Yes."

Seconds later Anne Pollard pled guilty to one count of "conspiring to receive and possessing stolen documents," which carried the five-year maximum sentence. She and Pollard were now convicted felons, each at the mercy of Judge Robinson.

Later, lawyer David Kirshenbaum, who practiced in Israel, alleged that Jonathan Pollard's guilty plea was faulty since he was not asked the proper questions. "[Federal Court] Rule 11," the attorney said, "provides that a court 'shall not accept a plea of guilty without first…determining that the plea is voluntary and not the result of force or of threats or of promises apart from the plea agreement." Based on that provision, Kirshenbaum stated, "Judge Robinson's failure to inquire of Pollard directly whether his plea was voluntary…is not merely a technical defect."

Regardless, as required after the guilty plea hearing, Pollard cooperated with government investigators while submitting, according to him, to more than 130 lie detector tests to check the veracity of his story. Pollard swore the tests verified his version, but the results, in another abnormal twist to the bizarre case, mysteriously disappeared days before his sentencing. They were never found. Efforts to locate agents who conducted the test proved unsuccessful.

Despite Pollard's assertion that his statements regarding all aspects of the case were truthful, Joseph diGenova was convinced he was lying. At one point, Pollard alleged, the US attorney placed a list of twenty-five prominent American Jews in front of him and demanded that he place an "X" in front of those involved in what he dubbed the "espionage conspiracy." One man listed, Pollard said, was Jewish journalist Douglas M. Bloomfield, who later called the spy, "a loose cannon with a messiah complex."

Pollard's "reward," he swore, was that Anne would receive her proper medication. Despite his concern for Anne, Pollard didn't acquiesce. That caused an outrage by diGenova, who accused Jonathan of being uncooperative. DiGenova, in later interviews, denied that a list of Jews was ever brought to Pollard's attention.

Noted attorney Alan Dershowitz and other Pollard supporters questioned whether diGenova was anti-Semitic. They pointed out that the prosecutor believed that a Jew who spied for an ally like Israel should be punished more severely than a non-Jew spying for an enemy such as the Soviet Union. DiGenova dismissed such accusations as "being ridiculous."

* * *

In late 1986, a year marked by such diverse events as President Reagan's admission of secret arms deals with Iran in breach of the US arms embargo ("Iran-Contra"), the taking of the Fifth Amendment by

Colonel Oliver North at Congressional hearings, and boxer Mike Tyson's emergence as the heavyweight champion of the world, correspondent Wolf Blitzer, the Washington-based reporter for the *Jerusalem Post*, requested an interview with Jonathan Pollard.

Blitzer, whose beard had not yet turned gray, did so after being contacted by Bernard Henderson, Anne Pollard's father. According to the journalist, he was told of a furious debate that occurred between Jonathan and his wife regarding the importance of speaking to the media prior to the sentencing date. Based on the government's attitude, Anne and Jonathan felt that prosecutors did not intend to honor the plea agreement, but instead would request maximum or near-maximum sentences for both. Each agreed, Anne more than Jonathan, that if that occurred they would be incarcerated and silenced without the opportunity to tell their side of the story.

The Pollards' queasy frame of mind was caused by a sudden awareness of the "Weinberger memorandum," a thundering attack of disparaging remarks by the secretary of defense that had been delivered to Judge Robinson. Anne had told her father, "There is something wrong here. If I get back to jail (she had been released for 'medical reasons' after ninety-five days in isolated detention), I'll be cut off and nobody will know [what really happened]."

Jonathan was also concerned with his treatment, both by the government and the media. "I am being done in by a campaign that is a combination of Dreyfus and McCarthy; I can't win a war in the shadows," he wrote in a communiqué to his father.

A different side of Anne emerged to Blitzer, who quoted Bernard Henderson in the journalist's book *Territory of Lies* as saying, "Jay wanted this done quietly, discreetly, from day one. He was most reluctant of all to open it. Anne had to scream at him a lot of times to do things." This time the screaming resulted in disastrous consequences.

At Henderson's suggestion, Blitzer called and then wrote the warden at the Petersburg, Virginia, prison where Jonathan Pollard was being held. Within days, Blitzer, after filling out the proper forms and mailing them back, gained acceptance. He realized he was staging an unbelievable coup: he would be the first journalist to interview the spy who had become famous around the world.

On November 20, 1986, the same month that Ronald Reagan was informed by Attorney General Edward Meese that ten to thirty million dollars in profits from the arms sales to Iran had been passed on to the Nicaraguan rebel Contras, Blitzer met with Pollard. His hair was thinning, a bald spot was pronounced, and he sported an unruly mustache which Pollard told his sister Carol was the result of being denied scissors to trim it.

The anxious journalist spent more than two hours with Pollard, camera in tow. Asked his reaction to prison, the spy stated, "The right way to describe where I am is a pit. It's totally frustrating and scary." Concerning his motives for his actions, Pollard quipped, "I'll be the first to admit that I broke the law. But give the kid a little empathy. I thought I was helping Israel and the United States."

Pollard told Blitzer he couldn't sleep due to the sound of other prisoners, "sharpening their spoons against the concrete floor." Blitzer also reported, "[Pollard] told me he was under death threat. 'We're going to get you, Jew boy,' he said." The threats, Pollard alleged, were from "both the Aryan Brotherhood and Black Muslim prisoners."

While Pollard's comments were revealing, they were less important than the fact that the interview occurred. A true professional, Blitzer had gone through what he believed were proper channels. The interview was conducted in broad daylight with no sense of secrecy since guards were everywhere. If there was objection by government officials, permission could have been withdrawn while the interview was in progress, for Pollard was a high-profile inmate known to all administrators at the prison.

Pleased with the interview, but thirsting for more, Blitzer again petitioned to visit Pollard. A few days later permission was granted, and on 29 January the journalist traveled to Petersburg for a second session with the spy. No objection was made to the interview, which proceeded in a similar fashion as the first.

In the days that followed, as Blitzer wrote his article, no government official contacted him to protest that Pollard had violated any agreement regarding contact with the media. That despite the full knowledge of prison administrators who were in constant contact with government prosecutors and members of the Department of Justice.

The text of the interview, entitled "Befuddled Pollard: Why did Israel Abandon Me?" was published simultaneously in the *Jerusalem Times* and the Sunday, February 15, 1987, *Outlook* section of the *Washington Post*. Eighty-seven days had expired since the first interview with Pollard; seventeen since the second.

The article targeted Blitzer as a much-coveted expert on Pollard and he became a frequent guest on national radio and television programs as well as BBC broadcasts. Little did he know that the government would later argue that the interviews were a direct violation of Pollard's plea agreement with the government, based on their belief that the spy had not commanded the proper approvals.

Caspar Weinberger also mentioned his distaste for the spy's actions in meeting with Blitzer in the memorandum he filed with the court. He alleged, "Pollard's loyalty to Israel transcends his loyalty to the United States."

When Blitzer learned that prosecutors were criticizing Pollard's conduct, he questioned whether he had been used by the government to trigger a technical violation of the plea agreement regarding media access. To discover what had occurred, Blitzer later confronted Joseph diGenova and asked him whether the interview had been a setup to trap Pollard into defying the terms of the agreement. In *Territory of Lies*, Blitzer wrote, "I told diGenova that the government's pre-sentence memorandums, in my opinion, should have pointed out that I had received permission from the Justice Department to interview Pollard. DiGenova said, '...You were just doing your job....' But he insisted that according to Pollard's plea-bargaining agreement, it was up to Pollard to first clear any newspaper interviews with the director of Naval Intelligence. It wasn't up to the warden to make that kind of decision, diGenova stressed. 'It was Pollard's responsibility.'"

DiGenova embellished upon those remarks in October 2000. He stated, "Actually Mr. Pollard decided he was not going to get permission of the Navy to do that interview with Mr. Blitzer...Remember this is prior to sentencing, and it was Mr. Pollard who chose not to notify the Navy. [And] you know who wasn't there? Mr. Pollard's lawyers. He didn't even notify his own lawyers. Now, why did he do that? [Because] Mr. Pollard had decided along with one or two persons that they were going to go over the head of the judge to the American people and make it a political attempt to affect his sentencing." DiGenova then added, "The question here is not for Mr. Pollard, not me, or the judge or anyone else as to why he decided [that]. His conduct was an example,…to show that he could not be trusted not to compromise classified information in the future."

Regardless, the more Blitzer pondered the question of whether he was used by the government, the more the journalist became convinced that he had. "I suspected that they [the government] wanted Pollard to commit some technical violation of his plea-bargain agreement," he stated in the book. "That would enable the Judge to impose a stiffer sentence. And in fact the Judge, in announcing…the sentence, cited, among other things, Pollard's interviews with me as having shown that he had no remorse for his crime and that he was still incapable of protecting classified information."

During a July 1987 visit to Israel, Blitzer tested his theory. "Several senior Israeli military and intelligence officials said for a fact that I had been used by the prosecution," he wrote, exasperated by the turn of events.

The Blitzer article, viewed by many as sympathetic to Pollard, did not contain the entire text of the two conversations at Petersburg. Blitzer divulged more in his book, writing that, "During the second session, Pollard was much more depressed than at our first meeting. He was more nervous and edgy. He told me he was now convinced he was going to get a life sentence even though the prosecution had promised as part of the plea bargaining agreement, not to ask for life. He felt he had been set up. And he placed most of the blame on Defense Secretary Caspar Weinberger.…"

After Blitzer's article was published, Pollard said he learned of the government's displeasure with his deed. He alleged that on the Jewish holiday of Hanukkah, a guard stormed into his cell in Petersburg and told him "You are going home to Israel." Pollard said he then proceeded to chain his arms, legs, and neck, and then spread-eagle him to both sides of an unheated van. Pollard alleged he was transported at speeds of more than one hundred miles an hour to the federal prison at Lewisburg, Pennsylvania. There he was dumped in a dank cell without blankets or a mattress. The government denied his charges, calling them "completely unfounded."

Even though diGenova was confident that he possessed evidence that Pollard had violated the plea agreement, he continued to build the case against the spy. Colleagues informed him that Pollard, while cooperating, continued to conceal critical information, showed little remorse for his actions, and was in fact gloating to others regarding his spying efforts. Based on these factors, diGenova primed himself for a day of reckoning with the spy whose case had catapulted the prosecutor into the media spotlight.

Chapter 14

MR. WEINBERGER

At 2:00 P.M. on March 4, 1987, a sunny, pleasant day to everyone but the defendants, a weary Jonathan and Anne Pollard returned to the same pristine Washington, DC federal courtroom where they had pled guilty nine months earlier. That evening President Ronald Reagan spoke from the Oval Office to the nation. He told his fellow citizens, "A few months ago, I told the American people I did not trade arms for hostages. My heart and my best intentions still tell me that's true, but the facts and the evidence tell me it is not."

The day before, the government announced that a federal grand jury had indicted Aviem Sella, dubbed by the *Washington Post* as "Pollard's Spying 'Handler.'" The article, to the chagrin of prosecutors who believed Colonel Sella should be returned to the United States, acknowledged that the colonel had been promoted to command the Tel Nof Air Base outside Tel Aviv (the promotion was later rescinded). Regarding the question as to whether Colonel Sella would ever see the inside of an American courtroom, the article quoted unnamed sources as saying, "No, since the US-Israeli extradition treaty does not cover espionage offenses."

The article mentioned conflicting stories apparent between Israeli government leaders and the convicted spy. It reported that while Pollard indicated "last week he was told that the highest levels of the Israeli government knew of his espionage efforts," Israeli officials "repeatedly have said that the Pollard ring was a 'renegade operation' not authorized by the government."

The day after the sentencing, United States Representative Dick Cheney, later Vice President under George W. Bush, supported Pollard's statements. Cheney told Charles Babcock of the *Washington Post*, "I don't think the Pollard case was a rogue operation. I think this was a major, very successful penetration of the US government and our intelligence agencies by the Israeli government…behavior that doesn't behoove an ally."

Embroiled at the time as a member of the House Select Committee investigating the Iran-Contra Affair, Cheney added, "On the one hand, Israel pleads a special relationship with the United States. On the other hand, they run a major intelligence operation against us. There isn't much they couldn't get if they asked for it. But they chose not to do it that way. And I think the Israeli government ought to know that some of us are deeply concerned about that kind of conduct."

Representative Henry Hyde, the Republican from Illinois who later gained fame as a fervent opponent of President Bill Clinton during his impeachment trial, said, "Israel shouldn't be considered our 51st state. I think Pollard is what he is: a spy in the pay of the Israeli government, and that's really outrageous from one of our closest allies."

Those concerns about the Israeli government may or may not have been of interest to Judge Aubrey Robinson as he anticipated the sentencing of the Pollards. His brain, according to Pollard supporters, was infiltrated by troubling information provided him regarding the connections of Pollard to the government of South Africa.

Recreating the scenario at a later date was Harvard lawyer Alan Dershowitz, a media seeker and admitted supporter of Pollard's right to review of his case. He said he had read a September 12, 1989, letter from retired Supreme Court Justice Arthur Goldberg to the *Jerusalem Post* outlining Goldberg's views about the Pollard case. He urged members of the Jewish community to ignore the spy's efforts to be released due to the "terrible offenses" committed.

Shortly thereafter, Dershowitz said he contacted Goldberg, the last of eleven children born of Ukrainian Jewish immigrants, to discuss Pollard's lengthy sentence. That discussion precipitated a March 27, 1990, affidavit that Dershowitz filed with the United States District Court for the District of Columbia.

In the affidavit the outspoken Jewish lawyer, famous for defending among others Claus Von Bulow and Mike Tyson, swore, "During the 1963–64 Supreme Court term, I was a law clerk to Mr. Justice Arthur Goldberg. Between that time and his death, I remained a close friend and associate of Mr. Justice Goldberg. We worked together on many projects, spoke and met frequently, and jointly authored articles and proposals."

Regarding the Pollard case, Dershowitz then told the court, "Following the publication of a letter to the *Jerusalem Post*, on September 12, 1989, I spoke to Justice Goldberg [after he had retired] on the telephone about the sentence imposed on Jonathan Pollard....Subsequent to that conversation, Justice Goldberg called me to tell me that he had personally met with Judge Aubrey Robinson and discussed the Pollard sentence with him. Justice Goldberg told me that Judge Robinson had told him that he [Judge Robinson] had been provided by the government evidence that Jonathan Pollard had given Israel American satellite photographs proving that Israel had tested Jericho missiles in South Africa and had provided South Africa with missile and nuclear technology. Justice Goldberg told me further that Judge Robinson was particularly outraged by the Israel–South Africa connection and Pollard's role in providing Israel with evidence that the United States had satellite evidence of it. Justice Goldberg told me that he understood why Judge Robinson, a Black man, would be particularly sensitive to this evidence."

Dershowitz then added, "Justice Goldberg told me that Judge Robinson told him that the Pollard–South African connection had weighed heavily in his [Judge Robinson's] decision...."

To check the validity of the charges, Dershowitz first contacted Richard Hibey, the spy's original attorney. Dershowitz said Hibey, who had been privy to the Weinberger memorandum, told the Harvard professor that there was no mention of South Africa in that memo. He also stated that as far as he knew the government had no evidence against Pollard for aiding South Africa.

Dershowitz related the Goldberg story to Hamilton Fox, Pollard's appellate lawyer. Fox discussed the matter with Pollard and reported to Dershowitz that Pollard denied the allegations made against him. Based on the information related to him by Hibey and Fox, Dershowitz then swore in the affidavit, "After being assured...that there was no truth to the [charges], I wrote Justice Goldberg the attached letter [dated January 10, 1990]." It read, "I have now completed my checks, and I am confident that Jonathan Pollard never provided information to Israel regarding American satellite [or other] surveillance of Israeli supplied missiles or weapons in South Africa. Indeed, Pollard was never even accused—formally or informally—of providing any such information to South Africa." After reviewing Goldberg's conversation regarding Judge Robinson's assertions concerning sentencing of Pollard, Dershowitz wrote, "If I am correct that Pollard provided no such information, then it is possible that the prosecution was pandering to Judge Robinson's hatred of South Africa. As an Afro-American, Judge Robinson could be expected to react strongly to any suggestion that Pollard was part of the Israeli–South African connection. If the government did pander in this racially sensitive manner, it behaved outrageously, especially if the information it provided to Judge Robinson was not true. I would be very interested in your reaction to this matter."

In the sworn affidavit, Dershowitz then asserted, "On January 15, 1990, I spoke with Justice Goldberg on the phone. He was quite upset at the content of my letter and promised to get to the bottom of it. He told me that he would phone Attorney General Thornburgh for a meeting to discuss this issue and the sentence. He told me that if the facts were correct, then the Justice Department had improperly 'pandered' [that was his precise word] to Judge Robinson's racial sensitivities as a Black judge by providing him with false, inflammatory, ex parte information."

Before the intended meeting between Justice Goldberg and the attorney general could occur, Dershowitz stated, "On Friday morning, January 19, 1990, I learned from Robert Goldberg that his father, Justice Arthur Goldberg, had died in his sleep during the night."

In the memorandum demanding that Pollard be permitted to withdraw his guilty plea filed simultaneously with the affidavit, Dershowitz argued that a defendant had a constitutional right not to be sentenced on the basis of false information. Dershowitz alleged that since the false accusations were forwarded to Judge Robinson by the government, they violated the terms of the plea agreement and it should be declared invalid.

Goldberg's death robbed Dershowitz of further investigation and the potential to call him as a witness at a court proceeding. Without that testimony the memorandum fell on deaf ears, with Judge Robinson declaring the information "hearsay" while stating, "The court's recollection of events is in stark contradiction…to the declarations in the Dershowitz affidavit."

Pollard supporters noted that Judge Robinson never denied that conversations took place between him and Justice Goldberg, and that the judge failed to respond to charges that he was influenced by the information regarding the Pollard/South African connection. A follow-up request by Pollard attorneys to examine the Weinberger memorandum was denied.

Responding to Dershowitz's allegations of impropriety regarding Judge Robinson was former assistant United States District Attorney Charles Leeper. He declined to discuss the Pollard case in detail during a brief September 5, 2000, telephone interview ("I don't talk about the case because so much time has gone by it is difficult to separate what is classified information about the case and what isn't"); but said defiantly, "[Dershowitz's] comments are patronizing toward such a fine man as Judge Robinson."

If Charles Leeper was reticent about debating Dershowitz's allegations, his former boss Joseph diGenova was not. He stated, "We forwarded no such information to the judge [about the South African connection] or anyone else. The allegations that Professor Dershowitz makes are preposterous. [He] never made public any of this information until Arthur Goldberg was dead [so] Professor Dershowitz is quoting a dead man who cannot speak for himself."

Asked if he had discussed the Goldberg matter with Professor Dershowitz, diGenova said, "I do not speak with the professor anymore. I do not talk to him, I don't appear with him on television. I simply have lost all confidence in his ability to be professional." DiGenova then added, "Dershowitz is walking legal graffiti."

DiGenova had high praise for Judge Robinson. "He was a respected judge. All of Pollard's supporters who want to continue to tarnish his reputation have no basis for doing so. All they do is make allegations, but none of it is substantiated, particularly the ludicrous assertion by Alan Dershowitz of quoting a dead man who cannot possibly be cross-examined about these alleged conversations."

Whether Judge Robinson was provided information regarding Pollard's connections to South Africa is subject to speculation. Since the judge was sensitive to racial matters based on his experiences in law school at Cornell and during his years of practicing law, Pollard's ties to an apartheid government in South Africa could have poisoned him against the spy. Goldberg's death, and Dershowitz and diGenova's bias toward Pollard make it impossible to discern the truth about the matter.

* * *

Preparing for the sentencing of Jonathan Pollard, Joseph diGenova and his colleagues concentrated on providing the court with their updated assessment of the spy's impact on the ultimate victim of the crime: the United States of America. Acting under the auspices of the Federal Rules of Criminal Procedure, they provided the court with a document entitled Victim Impact Statement (VIS). In part, it read:

> The specific instances of damage to the national security caused by Mr. Pollard's offense will be described in a classified damage session affidavit to be submitted to the Court *in camera*. Generally, it can be said that the breadth and scope of the classified information compromised by Mr. Pollard is among the greatest of any espionage operation uncovered by Federal authorities. Thousands of pages of Top Secret and Sensitive Compartment Information were sold to the Israelis by Mr. Pollard. As explained in detail in the government's *in camera* affidavit, Mr. Pollard's unauthorized disclosures have threatened the US relations with numerous Middle East Arab allies, many of whom question the extent to which Mr. Pollard's disclosures of classified information have skewed the balance of power in the Middle East. Moreover, because Mr. Pollard provided the Israelis virtually any classified document requested by Mr. Pollard's co-conspirators, the US has been deprived of the *quid pro quo* routinely received during authorized and official intelligence exchanges with Israel, and Israel has received information classified at a level far in excess of that ever contemplated by the National Security Council. The obvious result of Mr. Pollard's largesse is that US bargaining leverage with the Israeli government in any such further intelligence exchanges has been undermined. In short, Mr. Pollard's activities have adversely affected US relations with both its Middle East Arab allies and the government of Israel.

The VIS marked a turning point in the case against Pollard. While the government promised that "specific instances of damage" would be presented in secret through an "in camera" proceeding as agreed to in the plea bargain, they alerted Judge Robinson that the documents the spy passed to the Israelis were of significant substance. By doing so, they alleged that Pollard had already affected US/Arab relations, and that the betrayal had altered what they believed to be the bargaining power that the US posessed in dealing with Israel concerning intelligence matters. Whether the claims were inflated was subject to debate, but the strong allegations earmarked Pollard as among the worst of the worst spies in the history of the United States.

The VIS having been forwarded to the court, the government decided to further attack Pollard. To deliver the knockout punch, Joseph diGenova engaged the perfect sleuth, Secretary of Defense Caspar Weinberger. Already incensed by the betrayal of Israel, he was pleased to prepare for delivery to the court not one, but two directives which he believed would ensure incarceration of Jonathan Pollard for the rest of his life.

The first directive came in a forty-six page memorandum. The exact details of the government's version of Pollard's notorious behavior were outlined. The day prior to sentencing, a follow-up letter from the secretary of defense was delivered by courier to the judge's chambers. Both the memorandum and the letter were admitted into the record and sealed from public view. Later, the memorandum, with relevant material crossed out for "national security reasons," was released. The contents of the letter, however, were not released, though reports suggested that Weinberger, among other things, criticized the recent promotion of Colonel Sella to general and commander of the Tel Nof Air Base in Israel. He also wrote that "the Pollards had succumbed to the same virus of treason which had infected the Rosenbergs."

To all those concerned, it appeared that Weinberger's memo and letter had been submitted *by him* to assist diGenova's pleas for a life sentence. That assumption was clouded by the startling revelation in 1999 that the former secretary of defense had submitted the memo and letter *at* the invitation of Judge Aubrey Robinson.

Weinberger, who according to journalist Wolf Blitzer later told the Israeli ambassador to the United States that Pollard "should have been shot," wrote, "It is difficult for me, even in the so-called year of the spy to conceive of a greater harm to national security than that caused by the defendant in view of the breadth, the critical importance to the United States and the high sensitivity of the information he sold to Israel...I respectfully submit that any US citizen, and in particular a trusted governmental official, who sells US secrets to *any* foreign nation should not be punished merely as a common criminal. Rather the punishment imposed should reflect the perfidy of the individual actions, the magnitude of the treason committed, and the needs of national security."

Emphasis on the word "any" in Weinberger's letter appeared significant since that underlined the secretary of defense's belief that Pollard's misdeeds should not be diminished because the secrets he passed were to a US ally—Israel. By noting that fact, in addition to misusing the word "treason"—defined in the Constitution as levying war against the United States or aiding US enemies—Weinberger upgraded the severity of Pollard's actions.

Weinberger's memo alleged that Pollard had passed along capability assessments of Libyan air defense, diagrams of the PLO headquarters which Israel bombed in 1985, Syrian and Iraqi chemical warfare production capacity, and details of Soviet arms shipments to Syria. Pollard denied those charges.

Most startling was Weinberger's accusation that Pollard had compromised United States intelligence—gathering "sources and methods." That meant the Israelis had knowledge of United States electronic eavesdropping potential, code-breaking procedures, and the topper, identities of agents and spies in foreign countries.

To those who knew Weinberger, the scathing tone of his memo was not surprising. Secretary of State George Schultz, who had no sympathy for Pollard, later characterized Weinberger's memo as "a nasty piece of work."

* * *

Caspar Weinberger's rise to power began after the San Francisco native graduated from Harvard Law School and earned a Bronze Star as an Army captain. A conservative Republican, the articulate attorney served six terms in the California legislature before becoming chairman of an economic committee and state director of finance under Governor Ronald Reagan.

Jonathan Pollard's future tormentor arrived in the big leagues of Washington as chairman of the Federal Trade Commission. As director of the Office of Management and Budget under President Nixon, he became known for his penny-pinching, earning the nickname "Cap the Knife." A stint as general counsel to the Bechtel Corporation (future Secretary of State George Schultz was president—Pollard supporters dubbed them the "Bechtel Babies") followed. That company had pro-Arab ties to the extent that it constructed a chemical plant in Iraq for Saddam Hussein. Weinberger's position with Bechtel, dubbed by *The Secret War Against The Jews* authors John Loftus and Mark Aarons, "One of the most anti-Semitic companies in the United States," preceded his appointment to President Reagan's cabinet as Secretary of Defense after the California cowboy/actor became president.

Former Assistant Secretary of Defense Lawrence Korb wrote to Dr. Pollard, "I know that Weinberger had an almost visceral dislike of Israel and the special place it occupies in our foreign policy." Several critics alleged that Weinberger never forgave his grandfather for his Jewish name.

History proved that in the midst of condemning Pollard's conduct, the secretary of defense was illegally participating in a scheme to sell arms to Iran and divert the profits to rebels fighting a civil war in Nicaragua. That campaign had begun in 1985 when the US covertly authorized the government of Israel to sell arms to Iran. In return the US would replenish those arms while Iran agreed to assist US efforts to win release of the American hostages.

While Weinberger crucified Pollard for breaking the law, he was doing so as well. That was the opinion of Independent Counsel Lawrence Walsh and a grand jury that indicted Weinberger on June 16, 1992. He was charged with five counts, including obstruction of justice and perjury. When those charges were dismissed on technicalities, Weinberger was re-indicted on the Friday before the presidental election between George Bush and Bill Clinton.

During the course of the Iran-Contra investigation, four other individuals were charged with criminal violations designated "operational crimes," those dealing with the illegal use of funds generated while the scheme was operational, and "cover-up crimes," which concerned false statements and obstruction of justice. Among those indicted were: National Security Advisers Robert McFarlane, who pleaded guilty to four counts of withholding information from Congress, and John Poindexter, convicted of conspiracy, making false statements, destruction and removal of records, and obstruction of Congress. Oliver North was convicted of altering and destroying documents, aiding and abetting in the obstruction of Congress. His conviction was later reversed.

Richard Secord pled guilty to making false statements to Congress, and Elliott Abrams was charged with four counts of providing false statements. He was pardoned by President Bush before trial. Secretary of State George Shultz, who condemned Pollard's actions and those of Israel, was investigated as to whether he misled or withheld information from Congress. Independent Counsel Walsh refrained from prosecution though he was suspicious of Shultz's actions. Abrams, McFarlane, and Richard Secord, who was indicted on six counts but pleaded guilty to one of providing false statements to Congress, were all given probationary (suspended) sentences by District Judge Aubrey Robinson.

Four of the five specific charges against Weinberger portrayed him as a clever liar. According to the independent counsel's executive summary, the secretary of defense, "From on or about March 11, 1987, up to and including August 3, 1987,…acting unlawfully, willfully and knowingly did corruptly influence, obstruct and impede…the due and proper exercise of the power of inquiry of the Select Committee [on Intelligence] (Obstruction of Congress)." Weinberger was also charged with "false statement," regarding a deposition where he "unlawfully, knowingly and willfully made a material false, fictitious and fraudulent statement to a department or agency of the United States Government." A third charge, this involving perjury, stated that Weinberger, "having duly taken an oath before competent tribunals, to wit, the Select Committees…that he would testify truthfully in [the said] proceedings, did willfully and contrary to said oath make a material statement that he did not believe to be true." Finally, fourth, Weinberger was charged with a further count of "false statement," with the grand jury alleging that "[certain] statements made to a Special Agent of the FBI, in the presence of the independent counsel's staff, were false, fictitious and fraudulent."

The crux of the case against Weinberger concerned his refusal to acknowledge possession of 7,000-plus pages of notes (1,700 dealing with Iran-Contra) he wrote during the Iran-Contra (IC) Affair. Lawrence Walsh, in his book *Firewall: The Iran-Contra Conspiracy and Cover-up*, alleged that Weinberger's refusal to cooperate impeded the investigation. "Our fascination with the disclosure [discovery of the notes Weinberger said didn't exist]," Walsh wrote, "was matched by a deepening realization that Weinberger, hero or not, had deliberately lied to the Tower Commission, to Congress, and to us."

Walsh, whose motives were questioned in the probe just as Ken Starr's were in the Bill Clinton/Monica Lewinsky case, pointed out that Weinberger sought to influence others involved in the IC probe as well, writing "Weinberger had disparaged Schultz for having suggested, 'telling all.'" Summarizing, Walsh added, "Weinberger had opposed Schultz's efforts to tell the public the truth."

While deciding whether to request an indictment of the former secretary of defense, who left his post in 1987, Walsh recalled in his book Weinberger's mind-set. He observed, "…when a witness lied to us as arrogantly as Weinberger had done, we had to react.…In my judgment, we had been exceptionally courteous to Bill Rogers [Weinberger's lawyer] and had given Weinberger a chance to come in and tell us the truth. If he had done so, we would have had a difficult decision to make. But Weinberger had chosen to continue lying. I did not see how we could look the other way."

Robert Bennett, another of Weinberger's DC lawyers (he defended President Bill Clinton during the Monica Lewinsky scandal) attempted to exonerate Weinberger's memory failure regarding the notes. He explained to Walsh that the former secretary's denials were "innocent mistakes," since "his note-taking was so habitual" it was "like brushing his teeth, it left no impression on his memory." Walsh and his associates enjoyed a good belly laugh after Bennett left their offices.

Walsh believed that Weinberger was lying for one single, paramount reason. "We considered our case strong because Weinberger had had such a powerful motive," Walsh wrote in the book. "He had lied to protect the President, who, Weinberger believed, had committed an unlawful act. Once having lied, he had been forced to conceal the existence of the notes that would have exposed him as a liar."

Weinberger's response to the charges against him, Walsh alleged, was to lie again. At a news conference, Weinberger blasted the independent counsel, telling reporters that the only reason he had been "charged with multiple felonies" was due to his refusal to "give them statements which were not true about myself and others." He also alleged that in effect a plea bargain had been offered, to which Walsh responded, "Weinberger's insinuation that we had conditioned a plea bargain on false accusation is a brazen lie."

Several journalists chastised Walsh for being biased against the Republican administration and Weinberger, but syndicated columnist Mary McGrory weighed in with astute observations concerning Weinberger's conduct after being accused. "When he was indicted," she wrote, "Weinberger gave a little glimpse of the knife he has always carried with him during his long career—and not just to cut welfare budgets. He has always been a street fighter, and he showed it again with his savage strike at Walsh...It was breathtaking and poisonous, but not totally out of character. Weinberger's way with those who oppose him is viperish...."

One man disagreeing that Weinberger had broken the law was President George Bush. Although Anthony Lewis of the *New York Times* labeled the President a "candidate without shame" and alleged that "Lies, hate, vulgarity, nothing has been too shameful for George Bush" during the election he lost to Bill Clinton, Bush decided to save his stricken friend just before leaving office. Describing the indicted Weinberger, about to face trial for his alleged offenses, as a "true patriot" who had "rendered long and extraordinary service," Bush stated on Christmas Eve, 1992, "I am pardoning him not just out of compassion or to spare a seventy-five-year-old patriot the torment of a lengthy and costly legal proceeding, but to make it possible for him to receive the honor he deserved....Some may argue that this will prevent full disclosure of some new key facts to the American people. That is not true. The matter has been investigated exhaustively."

Predictably, Walsh, who had gained "guilty" verdicts against Weinberger during three mock trials he conducted, was upset at the president's actions, telling reporters, "A lie to Congress is not a matter of political controversy, it is a crime." Ever defiant, Weinberger held a news conference thanking the president and condemning Walsh. AP captured a photograph depicting the former secretary of defense laughing as he stood between lawyers Bennett and Carl Rauh. Later, Bush blamed his election loss on the Walsh investigation. Pollard supporters said Weinberger belonged in prison.

If Weinberger's illegal conduct had been known at the time that Anne and Jonathan Pollard were being discredited in the secretary of defense's memorandum and letter, a far different reaction would have occurred to his harsh allegations. Like those he accused, Weinberger had seen himself as being above the law, acting on his own and in concert with other individuals who believed they could disregard the United States Congress.

Critical of Weinberger was Lieutenant Colonel Oliver North, who charged in his book *Under Fire* that the secretary of defense "Seemed to go out of his way to blame the Israelis for every problem in the Middle East." North added, "Weinberger's hatred for Israel adds to his disdain for his Jewish ancestry."

An addendum to the evaluation of the Weinberger memo appeared in a February 2000 article in *The Nation* written by Milton Viorst, the author of *In the Shadow of the Prophet: The Struggle For the Soul of Islam.* The article, titled "Pollard and Haddam: Prisoners of Secret Evidence," provided comparisons between the Pollard case and that of Anwar Haddam, an Algerian identified with Islamic fundamentalism imprisoned by Immigration and Naturalization Service (INS) officials.

While Viorst believed that both men had been incarcerated based on evidence kept from public view and thus assessment, he was critical of the Weinberger memorandum. "The intelligence community—the FBI, the CIA, the Pentagon agencies live by leaks," he wrote. "What the FBI and CIA say to the press is incredible, and in publishing it the press is willing to be used. An assistant of Weinberger who helped draw up the memo told me it was shocking what his boss would say. He said the memo, pure speculation at best, would never pass a polygraph test. The agencies still have their thermostats high over Pollard. Most people in my business think they want to scare any sympathizers that Israel may still have in the agencies."

Through the years Weinberger defended his actions, telling the American Jewish Committee, "I am a strong supporter of Israel, and an admiring witness to the democracy they have built and preserved under the most trying conditions."

In a letter written to Robert Cohn of the *St. Louis Jewish Light*, Jonathan Pollard discussed Weinberger's paranoia. "A friend of mine who happens to be a clinical psychologist has recently observed that the Secretary of Defense evidently suffers from what might be called a 'Kreisky Complex,' in which because of his Jewish ancestry, he has a strong unconscious need to distance himself from Jews and Israel....I would suggest that Caspar Weinberger's problem would more accurately be diagnosed as an 'Amalek Complex,' since he seems to despise Jews *more* than is absolutely necessary."

Pollard believed that Weinberger detested him for another reason. "One final matter which absolutely infuriated Mr. Weinberger," Pollard told journalist Elliot Goldenberg, "not to mention the CIA, was that I had forewarned the Israelis of several impending terrorist operations against Israel's security forces in southern Lebanon. By doing this, Weinberger charged, I had violated a long-standing CIA policy of withholding that type of information from the Israelis."

* * *

Weinberger's onslaught regarding Pollard may have been rooted in the spy's inadvertent exposure of the Iran-Contra Affair. In the summer of 1984, the junior analyst monitored ships passing from Greece to Yemen, known to be a PLO outpost. Positive that the Israelis required knowledge of the activity, he informed his espionage partners of his suspicions. They alerted the Greeks, who then apprehended a ship loaded with arms for the PLO. Those arms, according to Pollard supporters, were destined for Lebanon to be exchanged for American hostages.

As Weinberger's secret dealings with Iraq unfolded, it became clear that Pollard had been first to warn the Israelis of Saddam's intended use of germ warfare. His muddling into those affairs was disruptive to the secretary of defense, so intent did he appear to be on lessening Israeli security. When Weinberger discovered, through Pollard's admissions, what the spy had accomplished, he must have been enraged. Though he has never divulged the exact motives that compelled his venom-like memorandum and letter to the court, it appeared that he despised Pollard for having intervened in his grand scheme.

Pollard's appellate attorneys later alleged that neither Pollard nor his initial lawyers were able to inspect government documents, including the Weinberger communqués, prior to the sentencing. Joseph diGenova disputed that claim, stating "Pollard's counsel had access to all classified documents and the classified sentencing memorandum.... [They] had access to everything the government had access to. His [later lawyers] play a game, 6, 7, 8, 9, 10 years later, they say they did not have access, but the later lawyers had no right to the documents."

To be certain, Richard Hibey was permitted to scan the Weinberger memo and make notes before returning the document to the court for sealing. In haste, he filed a brief in opposition to Weinberger's severe allegations of impropriety on Pollard's part.

The paperwork completed, the stage was set for Judge Robinson's pronouncement of sentence on Anne and Jonathan Pollard. No one realized that he intended to do so in a voice loud enough it could be heard all the way to Israel.

Chapter 15

MOMENT OF DESTINY

When Dr. Morris Pollard entered the Washington, DC federal court room on the fateful Thursday afternoon of March 5, 1987, he and daughter Carol sat in the back row (no seats had been reserved for them) alongside Bernard Henderson. Mollie, his companion, his strength, his wife of nearly fifty years, had remained at lawyer Richard Hibey's office stricken with fear.

An eerie electricity pervaded the courtroom full of spectators, journalists, sketch artists, and twenty of Pollard's former colleagues at NIS including Commander Jerry Agee. At 2:12 P.M. the court clerk announced, "Criminal Case Numbers 86-207 and 86-208, *United States of America vs. Jonathan Jay Pollard and Anne Henderson Pollard.*"

Perched on the bench, Judge Robinson, known for his disdain of those who betrayed the public trust, called the proceedings to order. Initially he informed the participants that he was restricting the time for argument. Later, realizing that was poor public relations, he recanted.

Early on, Jonathan Pollard had risen from the dark oak counsel table, his legs rubbery, his voice trembling, as he tried to explain the "whys" of his actions. Dr. Pollard sighed as his son attempted to show remorse, to provide the court with the reasoning behind his having broken the law.

Richard Hibey, resplendent in the colors of the American flag, had preceded his client, but his argument, though delivered with passion, rang hollow. "The damage from the spy ring is minimal, Your Honor," he argued, "since the information was given to Israel, an ally and partner in democracy, not to the Soviet Union or China....The damage to US security is nothing like that caused by that of John Walker or Ronald William Pelton." In closing, he remarked, "There is room, your Honor, for leniency while at the same time justice will be served."

Once Hibey's legalistic soliloquy had ended, Pollard dressed in a dark suit, had delivered his own impressions of his illegal deeds. "My actions were never intended to hurt the United States, just to help Israel," he uttered in a hushed tone. "But it does not matter that my activities may benefit this country in the long run. I realize I broke faith and took the law into my own hands."

"I realize," Pollard continued on, "that my actions were tantamount to intellectual laziness, that I should have gone through the proper channels to correct weaknesses in the intelligence information being provided to the Israelis. Instead I betrayed my country, and for that I am truly sorry."

"Sorry for betraying your country, or sorry that you were caught?" Judge Robinson interrupted in a strong voice that pierced the quiet of the courtroom. "I suggest it is the latter."

Pollard's shoulders slumped at the harsh words, and it appeared he might collapse. Several times during the hearing, Anne moaned so loudly at the counsel table, her head hung over her lap, court observers thought she might faint. Two recesses were taken and nurses called to comfort her.

"No, no, I am truly sorry," Pollard lamented, his voice now an octave lower. "I realize I should have recognized the infectious nature of an ideology, Zionism."

"But do you realize that you made decisions on national security reserved for the President, the cabinet, and the national security agencies?" Judge Robinson queried.

Pollard's head bowed before he answered. His voice quivering, he said, "If everybody followed my course of action, your Honor, it would be nothing short of a Lebanon."

When the judge didn't respond, it appeared that Pollard was finished. Then he began to speak of Anne, who had pleaded guilty to being an accessory to his crime. "I feel I broke a second violation of trust," he explained as he glanced at his mate. "My wife's trust in me. That, Your Honor, is an unmitigated tragedy."

Moments later, Jonathan continued. "I recognize that I broke the law. And that I hurt a woman who was relying on my good judgment."

In a rambling discourse to the court, Anne Pollard told Judge Robinson, "I pray to God every single day of my life that I will be reunited with my husband." Her voice less and less audible, Anne stated. "I never thought God would bless me with anyone as good and wonderful as my husband," she said smiling at Pollard. "I want to raise a family with him, grow old with him, spend the rest of my life with him. I need him so much right now. He is my soul, my best friend, and my intellectual conversationalist, my greatest love."

"Anything else you wish to say to the court," Robinson barked in an unyielding tone of voice.

"Yes," Anne had replied, her voice a whisper. "Yes, Your Honor. I'm very sorry, very sorry for this incident to have gotten so blown out of proportion. I pray for leniency and mercy."

"Does the government wish to be heard on this matter?" Judge Robinson asked.

"Yes, Your Honor," Assistant US Attorney Charles Leeper, a brazen man with persuasive powers, answered. "Yes, we do."

Standing before the lectern, Leeper glanced at a legal pad before beginning. "Your honor, it was the defendant Pollard's arrogance and deception that drove him to commit criminal acts: He believed everyone else was wrong and he was right when it came to Israel."

As Leeper extolled the evil being he thought Jonathan to be, Dr. Pollard was tempted to rise and speak his mind. He wanted to alert the court to the conversation he had with Leeper after his grand jury appearance where he characterized Jonathan's damage to the country as "minimal."

Before he could do so, Leeper said, "Pollard believes that if he keeps repeating 'this case does not involve the Soviet Union' that there was no harm to national security. This defendant has admitted that he sold to Israel a quantity of classified documents 10 feet by 6 feet by 6 feet, ones that included disclosures about the location of US ships and the timing and location of US training exercises."

After a glance at the legal pad, Leeper continued his attack. "It is plain and simple, Your Honor," he argued, "Jonathan Pollard made a judgment up front of 'Israel right or wrong.'"

While Leeper spoke, Jonathan stared straight ahead as if comatose. He knew that the sentence imposed by Judge Robinson could be severe, anywhere from a few months in prison to life. Most observers felt, based on previous spy cases, that he'd be sentenced to ten years, perhaps twenty at the most.

His voice rising and falling with dramatic emphasis, Leeper continued. "And in the Weinberger memorandum," he exclaimed, "we find these words most revealing. 'It is difficult for me, even in the so-called "year of the spy," to conceive of a greater harm to national security than that caused by the defendant in view of the breadth, the critical importance to the US and the high sensitivity of the information he sold to Israel.'"

At the mention of the memorandum, Dr. Pollard's face portrayed a quizzical look. What is the Weinberger memorandum, he wanted to know? And why is the secretary of defense involved?

Before Dr. Pollard could sort out his thoughts, Judge Robinson, over the objection of lawyer Richard Hibey, permitted discussion of the letter received by the court. Hibey asked to read the document, then approached the judge's bench. He and the US attorneys huddled as if they were calling a play during the last seconds of a football game.

Five minutes later, Hibey returned to his seat. The ashen look on his face portrayed a crestfallen man.

"Once I saw Hibey return from the judge's bench after examining Weinberger's letter, I knew Jonathan was in deep trouble," Dr. Pollard recalled. "What I couldn't understand and never have is why he didn't ask for a continuance, for more time to sort the new evidence through."

To Jonathan Pollard, the state of affairs was evident. "My attorneys simply sat back and permitted me to commit judicial suicide," he alleged after the sentencing.

As a confident Joseph diGenova, clad in a slate gray double-breasted suit, watched from counsel table, Leeper's baritone voice once again rang throughout the courtroom. He condemned Pollard for his "high lifestyle," a reference to his monthly stipend and the Swiss bank accounts promised in the future. Leeper then accused Pollard of "conducting a public relations campaign glorifying his actions," calling him a "recidivist" and "vengeful," and proclaiming him "contemptuous of this court's authority."

The reference was to Pollard's Wolf Blitzer interview. Earlier, Judge Robinson had asked Richard Hibey if he was aware of it before the interview occurred. Hibey admitted that he was not, causing the judge to comment, "I didn't think so."

Summing up, Leeper's words were direct and clear. "When it comes to protecting against any further disclosure of US secrets," he shouted, "Jonathan Jay Pollard is not a man of his word. And in combination with the breadth of this man's knowledge, the depth of his memory, and the complete lack of honor that he has demonstrated in these proceedings, I suggest to you, Your Honor, that he is a very dangerous man."

Stepping away from the lectern, Leeper sat down, a look of satisfaction on his face. He had thrown everything at Pollard, building a case that he was the grandest spy of the modern era.

Assistant US Attorney David Geneson, a Jew who believed that the Pollards were a disgrace to their heritage, was next to argue. During a twenty-minute diatribe he chastised Anne for her actions in aiding Jonathan and for the lack of remorse she had displayed during a *Sixty Minutes* interview that aired the Sunday before the sentencing.

During that interview, a wide-eyed Mike Wallace said, "Listening to you Anne, I get the impression that you feel that everyone else is wrong, and you and your husband are right." Anne had responded, "I feel my husband and I did what we were expected to do, what our moral obligation was as Jews, what our moral obligation was as human beings, and I have no regrets about that."

Geneson's comments about Anne's defiant words were strong. He said, "She characterizes her conduct in terms of a political crime. This is not a political crime, Your Honor. It is a criminal act. The government would suggest, Your Honor, and the government requests, that the Court impose a sentence of incarceration reflective of her lack of remorse and contrition and commensurate with the severity of the acts in which she was engaged."

Lawyer James Hibey's rebuttal defended his client regarding the *Sixty Minutes* interview, telling the Court, "You have to understand as I am sure virtually everyone in the courtroom does, that the format of that program is such that things are taken in and out of context."

Anne and her supporters swore that CBS broke a promise not to broadcast the segment until after the sentencing. It was later aired in Israel, causing a firestorm of protest from supporters there.

Concerning Anne's interview with *Sixty Minutes*, prosecutor diGenova disagreed with their position. In an October 2000 interview, he said, "[It] was taped some time before the sentencing and scheduled to broadcast after the sentencing. But then prior to the sentencing, Mr. Pollard and his cohorts asked *Sixty Minutes* to run it before." Asked if he had verification of that, diGenova said, "From *Sixty Minutes*, from Mr. Wallace."

DiGenova believed the interviews provided by the Pollards had a definite purpose. "[Her interview] was part of a plan," he stated. "Coupled with the Blitzer interview, to go over the head of the judge to the American people and make the sentencing political and thus force the judge's hand. The [interviews] were calculations which misfired on the part of Pollard and his cohorts. They were arrogant and unremorseful attacks on the judicial process and they were correctly and rightfully taken note of by the Court."

* * *

Once James Hibey concluded his remarks, a nervous silence pervaded the courtroom. Reporters readied their pencils and sketch artists honed on creating a lasting image of the unfolding courtroom drama.

"Will the defendants please rise?" Judge Robinson, his blank face staring at Anne and Jonathan, ordered.

As if in slow motion, Dr. Pollard watched Jonathan grasp Anne's hand and attempt to comfort her. He placed his arm around her shoulder and together they stood steadfast, poised for their moment of judgment.

Later, Dr. Pollard recalled three never-to-be-forgotten words that Judge Robinson uttered. First, the word "life" convulsed his body like an electric shock. Simultaneously, Anne collapsed and fell to the floor in anguish as she screamed "God!" and "No! No!"

Jonathan attempted to steady her, but Anne was still moaning as the final two awful words, "five years," her sentence, rolled out of the judge's mouth. Dr. Pollard heard cries of protest from the crowd, including someone who blurted out, "Is this justice?" Irritated, Judge Robinson pounded his gavel and issued stout warnings to those who might consider disrupting the proceedings.

Dr. Pollard's mind was reeling, but before he could react he heard the panicked voice of Bernard Henderson, Anne's father. He was protesting the denial of bond for his daughter despite her lawyer's plea that she remain free until adequate facilities could be found to treat her digestive disorder. Judge Robinson, his face filled with anger at the disruptions, was in no mood to be lenient, and with the final sound of his gavel banging away, he swiveled his chair 180 degrees and retreated to the sanctity of his chambers as the minute hand on the wall clock ticked to 5:03 P.M.

Stunned at the nightmare, Dr. Pollard stood beside Carol and watched as his son led a whimpering Anne, her face as red as her closely cut hair, toward a holding cell at the front of the courtroom. As the door closed, Dr. Pollard heard Anne's piercing screams. Minutes later, Joseph diGenova encountered the media on the courthouse steps and continued the venom-filled tirade against Pollard. "The sentence imposed reflects the severity of the damage," the steely-eyed prosecutor triumphantly announced for the benefit of television cameras. "It is likely Pollard will never again see the light of day."

diGenova later defended the actions of his deputy prosecutors in court against those who believed that their words were too harsh and violated the spirit of the plea agreement to avoid requesting a life sentence for Pollard. He stated, "Mr. Leeper and Mr. Geneson were career prosecutors....They did not argue for a life sentence without explicitly doing so. In fact, they argued and used the precise words in the plea agreement, which provided for a substantial period of incarceration...it was tough arguing, this was a very serious espionage case, one of the four worst espionage cases in the twentieth century."

Commenting on the sentence imposed on Pollard, diGenova said, "During the plea, Judge Robinson made it very clear to Mr. Pollard, and this is a matter of public record, [that] he was not bound by any recommendation of the government, [so] the sentence could have been less and it could have been more."

* * *

When Dr. Morris Pollard informed Mollie that her son had been sentenced to prison for life, she could barely breathe. A frown covered her entire face as she fought to hold back tears.

Later, Mollie told her husband she had a premonition of what was to occur. "While sitting in Hibey's office prior to the sentencing, I overheard an argument between him and his secretary. She said, 'You aren't doing things right.' He shouted back 'I can't listen to you because I just fired you.'"

Dr. Pollard said Mollie also informed him of a conversation she had with Hibey that had left her speechless. "He told me that he had run into Judge Robinson at a cocktail party in Williamsburg, Virginia, and that while the two were drinking, the Judge had told him, 'I don't care what evidence is presented, he [Pollard] will get life.'" Hibey, when contacted to refute Mollie's allegation, did not return telephone calls. Skeptics questioned whether he would have uttered such words to his client's mother.

Pollard's supporters denounced the life term, but there were those who believed the sentence was too lenient. Retired Rear Admiral Sumner Shapiro, the first and only Jewish director of Naval Intelligence., told the *Washington Post Magazine*, "[Pollard] had a Walter Mitty complex. He saw himself as kind of a James Bond....He tries to sell himself as a hero, a savior of Israel and the Jewish people, and, in point of fact, that emerged after he was in jail and tried to reinvent himself."

Continuing, Shapiro said, "Whether it was Pollard's initiations or the Israelis', the idea that an American Jew would spy for anyone bothers the hell out of me. It bothers me because it puts all Jews in a position like that under a certain cloud....We work so hard to establish ourselves and to get to where we are, and to have somebody screw it up...and to have Jewish organizations line up behind this guy and try to make him out a hero of the Jewish people, it bothers the hell out of me."

On 6 March, the day after the sentencing, Glenn Frankel's article in the *Washington Post* offered Israeli views of Pollard's sentence. He quoted Israeli foreign minister Shimon Peres as saying, "A man was sentenced, not a nation. Even before the trial, Israel saw the whole affair as a mistake and I hope it won't happen again....It was not done on purpose and now we have to make every effort to overcome this. There is no point in throwing oil on the fire."

Official government response came from Foreign Ministry spokesman Ehud Gol, who stated, "We said in the past and we repeat that the activities involved were wrong, the government of Israel apologized, the unit involved in the activity was dismantled and necessary organizational steps were taken to ensure that such activities were not repeated." He added, "Our relations with the United States are based on solid foundations of deep friendship, close affinity, and mutual trust. Spying on the United States stands in total contradiction to our policy."

In effect, Jonathan Pollard had become what was known as a "cigarette," a term used to describe a low-level, expendable source to be exploited and then discarded.

Chapter 16

PUNISHING THE "GHOST OF THE SEALED ROOMS"

When the prison doors clanged shut behind Jonathan Pollard following his sentencing, it must have reminded him of that fateful day when the gates at the Israeli embassy irrevocably closed. Instead of being permitted to emigrate to Israel by that government in November 1985 prior to his arrest, Pollard had now been ordered to serve the lonely life of a convicted spy for his remaining days on earth.

Headlines around the world heralded Pollard's sentence. A page one article in the *Washington Post* announced, "Pollard Gets Life Term For Spying." The same day President Reagan delivered a speech refusing to acknowledge that several of his advisers, including Secretary of Defense Caspar Weinberger, had secretly and illegally covered-up the Iran-Contra Affair.

That mattered little to Pollard, whisked from the courthouse by federal marshals. To them he was now a "lifer," and their orders were to transport the spy briefly to the Washington, DC jail, then back to Petersburg, and then to the airport. In anticipation of Judge Aubrey Robinson's pronouncement of sentence, a government plane awaited the felon. Destination: the United States Medical Center for Federal Prisoners in Springfield, Missouri.

Anne Pollard, in turn, was flown to the federal prison in Lexington, Kentucky, where officials, her father reported, prevented her from taking Tylenol to block the pain from her constant stomach disorder. Later, Anne informed reporter Leslie Katz that she was transferred "eight times from one prison to another," including a maximum security facility in Rochester, Minnesota, where she was the only female prisoner. Anne told Katz that in one prison she was called a "dirty Jew Israeli spy bitch," and held in isolation "where my closest friends were rats and cockroaches."

In the early 1990s, Anne informed syndicated columnist and television talk show host Arlene Peck that when she entered the Rochester facility, the warden said, "We're going to fix your ass, Pollard." "I was constantly watched," she added, "and notes were made of my every move. They stared at me twenty-four hours a day."

According to a communiqué from Michael Quinlin, director of the Bureau of Prisons, the order to transport Jonathan Pollard to Springfield was directed by "Attorney General Ed Meese, the Justice Department, and the Office of Navy Investigations." If Judge Robinson had done his part to make an example of Pollard by sentencing him to the maximum time allowed, the new attorney general decided to do likewise when it came to punishment.

From March 6, 1987, until June 10, 1988, Pollard was held for all practical purposes incommunicado in the hospital wing of the center set aside for the criminally insane, even though there was no evidence that Pollard possessed any mental deficiencies. Information was disseminated by government officials alleging that Pollard's incarceration was the "norm" for his "type" of prisoner, but supporters believed he was singled out and punished to set yet another example as to how an Israeli spy would be treated.

Those sympathetic to Pollard fought to gain his release from the mental ward, where they believed he was being treated like a lunatic. On behalf of the spy, attorney Hamilton Fox, III wrote a February 1990 letter to Senator Dennis DeConcini. After chastising the government for their double-talk in rationalizing the continued incarceration of his client in the mental hospital, he wrote, "I realize there is little public sympathy for incarcerated prisoners, and that Jonathan Pollard probably receives less sympathy than most prisoners. But there is something terribly wrong when a non-violent prisoner is treated in a fashion, unless recent events have changed things, that exemplifies the way the KGB treats its prisoners."

Government resistance persisted until respected Indiana Congressman Lee Hamilton intervened. He complained about the deplorable conditions and Pollard was transferred from the mental ward.

Responding to allegations that Pollard was submitted to torture through the isolation, the government argued that "Springfield is divided into several main areas: diagnostic and observation, surgical, mental health treatment, forensics, work cadre, and medical. Pollard was initially assigned to the diagnostic and observations area....He was housed in a single room in this area, separated from other inmates....Mr. Pollard was not in contact with psychiatric patients, nor was he given psychiatric treatment while housed in the diagnostic and observation area. In January 1988...Mr. Pollard was reassigned to the surgical area, where again he was housed in a single room separated from other inmates."

That watershed description differed from the image Jonathan projected in a letter to his father:

> The inhuman screams of the patients around me sounded like something straight out of Dante's *Inferno*. Can you imagine what it is like to live in a nine foot by six foot cell under such appalling conditions? Apart from my lack of sleep, washing tends to be rather difficult. The single shower available to all the inmates on the ward generally has the appearance of a latrine by the time I am given permission to use it. So although I really don't enjoy smelling like an animal, it seems preferable to stepping into AIDS-infected fecal matter. Perhaps the most difficult thing for me to deal with, however, is the fact that my commode backs up on a regular basis, inundating my cell with organic matter I can't even begin to describe....And then there is the attempted suicides. Witnessing a man cut his own throat from ear to ear is something I can do without. In fact, I see this happen so many times that I actually have developed the ability to distinguish between the ones who are serious about killing themselves and those who are merely bent on a little self-mutilation.

During one visit, Dr. Pollard said, "An assistant warden told me he was ashamed that his facility used KGB-type tactics."

Unable to incarcerate Pollard at Springfield due to Lee Hamilton's efforts, the government transported the spy to a real hellhole, the Level 6 prison at Marion, Illinois. Its reputation for being escape-proof provided comparisons of the maximum security facility to Alcatraz. "Guests" at Marion included Colombian cocaine kingpin Carlos Lehder and Mafia boss John Gotti.

At Marion, Pollard was housed in the penitentiary's most secure section, K-Unit, which could have been dubbed "house of spies." Alongside Pollard were the infamous John Walker Jr., who sold classified documents to the Russians for seventeen years, and Edwin Wilson, the CIA agent convicted of supplying weapons to Libya's Muammar Khadafy.

Dubbed by prominent psychologist David Ward, a noted expert on the US prison system, a prison "that shows what the US Government can do if it really gets angry," K-Unit featured regulations like no other facility. Inmates such as Pollard were housed in cells where they nearly expired experiencing 107 degree temperatures in the summer and froze when the thermometer dipped below freezing from lack of heat in the winter.

Prisoners were required to spend twenty-three of every twenty-four hours in their cells. To keep the convicts disoriented they were relocated every seven to ten days without notice, prompting them to keep all of their belongings in plastic bags. When visits to the dentist or doctor were permitted, a "black box" was attached to the prisoner's wrists. Any movement of the hands caused the box to tighten, causing excruciating pain.

While Anne was imprisoned at Lexington, Jonathan began to serve the first of *five years* spent in solitary confinement. Dr. Pollard's initial visit to see his son was one he never forgot. "We passed through seven gates and two steel doors and walked down two flights of stairs," he recalled. "Jay had been in solitary for a long time, and he told me he couldn't even remember what grass looked like. My heart was broken. I could barely drive the car when we left. Later, he told me he considered Marion to be the 'Bates Motel' of the federal prison system."

Dr. Pollard knew that his son alleged harassment on the part of prison guards due to his Jewish heritage. "During one incident, Jonathan said, 'A guard grabbed me by the testicles.'" Prison officials denied any such incident.

Pollard's sister Carol wasn't mystified by the treatment. She alleged, "The government couldn't kill him, so it put him in a living tomb." Supporter attorney Larry Newman, agreed, stating, "They put Pollard in there to drive him crazy. They were worried about what he knew since he was a walking encyclopedia."

Despite the incarceration, one bit of news was positive. Carol told Jonathan that to many Israeli citizens, he was a hero.

The alleged heroics occurred when Iraqi dictator Saddam Hussein, after having directed his Republican Guard toward Kuwait, focused on destroying Israel by use of poison gas. In anticipation of the attack, Israeli soldiers and civilians alike were required to prepare for any on-slaught that might occur.

Prior to the launch of the "El-Abed" missile that Saddam had tar-geted toward Israel, the Israeli government had issued a dictum that every house, apartment, and building have a totally encased "sealed room," one enclosed with plastic that could withstand a poison gas at-tack. When more than forty Scud missiles fell from the sky in 1990, hundreds of thousands of civilians hid in the sealed rooms.

None of the missiles carried poison gas warheads, but the Israelis had been prepared. That due, Carol Pollard told Jonathan, to the infor-mation he provided in 1985 regarding Iraqi gas, chemical, and biologi-cal capabilitities. It had been utilized by Israeli intelligence, and they had spearheaded a campaign to prepare the country for Saddam's at-tack.

Carol told her brother that in Israel he was known as the "Ghost of the Sealed Rooms," and that the gas masks utilized were dubbed "Pollies." For the first time in months, a smile washed across the imprisoned spy's face.

In 1989, a year prior to the Iraqi attacks, Pollard explained the mo-tives for passing intelligence information about Saddam's poison gas potential in a letter to Rabbi Morris Werb. Poignant paragraphs in-cluded:

In retrospect, Rabbi, I know that there may have been other ways in which I could have exposed Weinberger's treachery. At the time, though, I was so scared of what might happen if the embargoed intel-ligence did not reach Israel that I threw caution to the wind. But tell me, Rabbi, what would you have done in my situation? Go to the press and run the risk of having sensitive information inadvertently leaked? Turn your eyes away from what was going on and try to live with the potential consequences? Convince yourself that the security of 4 million hard-pressed Jews was worth less than your loyalty to a man who was pledged to destroy them? The decision I made may have been illegal but I honestly thought that I was doing something morally right. Should I have just sat there and done nothing while Israel was being stabbed in the back? What kind of self-respecting Jew could do that? Oh, I know that there are many within the American community who are absolutely furious over what I did. No matter what, they wail, I should never have endangered our position here by exhibiting such loyalty to Israel. So what was I supposed to do? Let Israel fend for herself? If you think that this is what I should have done, then how can we condemn all those smug, self-righteous "American" Jews during the Second World War who consciously participated in the abandonment of European Jewry? Seriously, Rabbi, what would be the difference between what they did and a decision on my part to have kept silent about the Iraqi poison gas threat to Israel? After all, the same gas which the Nazis used 40-odd years ago to murder our European brethren could just as easily be used today by the Arabs to exterminate the Jewish population of Israel. Was I really expected to just let history repeat itself without doing anything to protect our people from such a calamity? Could you have stood by and let this happen? Granted, I broke the law. But, to tell you the truth, I'd rather be rotting in prison than sitting Shiva for the hundreds of thousands of Israelis who could have died because of my cowardice. I ask you, sir, have the fires of the concentration camps grown so cold that people have forgotten that 6 million Jews were butchered while the whole world looked on in silence? Have the screams of Neve Shalom grown so faint that people have forgotten that we are still considered fair game for slaughter? Have the burial ceremonies on Mount Herzl grown so commonplace that people have forgotten the grim price of independence? Well, I didn't forget these gruesome images. I kept them in the forefront of my mind to serve as constant reminder of just how precarious our existence really is. So you see, I just couldn't walk away from the problem of intelligence embargo and pretend it didn't exist. I had to act.

Chapter 17

JEWS JUDGING JEWS

W orld reaction varied considerably when Jonathan Pollard's life sentence was announced. Some viewed the penalty as light, believing he should have been shot. Others condemned the actions of Judge Aubrey Robinson and questioned whether justice had been served.

A *Washington Post* editorial on Friday, March 6, 1987, entitled "And What About Israel?" was indicative of the mood. It centered on criticism of the Israelis for failing to cooperate with the investigation and refusing to punish Colonel Aviem Sella and others involved with the case. The editorial chastised Pollard by stating: "Jonathan Pollard got life imprisonment for spying for Israel. He deserved severe punishment. He took money for stealing massive quantities of major secrets over a period of eighteen months. To go easy because he shoveled information to a country that is a friend would condone his compromising of specific secrets, of intelligence sources and methods, and of American freedom of action."

Despite scathing condemnations of Pollard, supporters protested the life sentence. Over the next decade and a half, during the height of the crusade to free the spy, 123 Jewish organizations totaling more than three million members rallied behind Pollard, causing *Washingtonian* magazine to dub him "The Spy with a Fan Club."

Pollard's crusade attracted several Hollywood supporters. Among those who signed a letter to President Clinton demanding review of the spy's case were actors Jon Voight, Jack Lemmon, Whoopi Goldberg, Gregory Peck, and Barbara Hershey. Others who later supported Pollard were New York mayor Rudolph Giuliani, who said, "The sentence is disproportionate, and should be commuted," former Senator Carol Mosely Braun, who opined, "I think Mr. Pollard's sentence should be commuted to time already served," and Pennsylvania Senator Arlen Specter, who said, "I continue to favor clemency for Mr. Pollard because I think the sentence is excessive considering all of the facts."

Pollard's never-ending paladin was his sister Carol, who resigned her position as a hospital administrator after the sentencing and formed "Citizens For Justice," a nonprofit entity with one goal in mind—"Free Jonathan Pollard." Not a day passed when Carol failed to attempt to help her brother just as she had when he was growing up.

Carol Pollard's ability to organize supporters proved successful. At the peak of the "Save Jonathan Pollard" movement, a million-and-a-half concerned individuals signed petitions and more than four hundred volunteers worked countless hours in his behalf. Forty-plus members of Congress added their support, as did the majority of the Israeli Knesset.

Support for Pollard crescendoed at a rally held in New York City at Manhattan's Kehilath Jeshurun Synagogue. A combination of Jews and Christians (Carol Pollard announced, "This is not a Jewish issue, it's a fairness and human rights issue") met there to denounce governmental conduct in Pollard's case. Speaking were a wide array of supporters including evangelist Pat Robertson, founder of the Christian Broadcasting Network, who proclaimed, "We are here today in support of justice, and we're also here to let the powers-that-be in our nation hear a cry of rage from our lips at the injustice that is being done to Jonathan Pollard." Pulitzer Prize winner Elie Wiesel told the crowd that several years earlier he had made the pledge to "never leave a Jew to feel alone." He asked, "Why did it take six-and-a-half years for such a gathering to take place? Why hasn't the Jewish community responded earlier? Why has Jonathan Pollard been abandoned so long?"

Dr. Pollard, an educator with limited funds, added more than thirty thousand dollars of his own money to the crusade. He, Mollie, and Carol traveled the country speaking at rallies, civic gatherings, and religious meetings to spread their belief that Jonathan had been denied equal justice. Signed by thousands of supporters, petitions were forwarded first to President George Bush and then to Bill Clinton.

Hindering those efforts was Pollard's erratic behavior toward those trying to save him. As the years passed, he became less and less willing to cooperate. Such believers as Senator Patrick Moynihan, Orthodox Rabbi Aaron Soloveichik, Rabbi Avi Weiss, and Israeli businessman

Annon Dror all experienced Jonathan's wrath. He initially supported their efforts. Later he disavowed them.

David Luchins, one of Senator Patrick Monyihan's senior officials, told the *Washington Post Magazine,* "There is a pattern that when people try to help him [Pollard], he grows paranoid, distrustful and delusional. Any suggestion of fault or frailty on his part by supporters leads to his denouncing them as his enemies and reaching out to a new, more compliant group of supporters, whom he will embrace until they grow weary or commit some sin against his ever-changing perception of martyrdom."

Dr. Pollard understood his son's erratic behavior. "Who would you believe anymore after all of those you trusted deceived you?" he asked. "Jay simply doesn't know what to do and many times, he has received terrible advice from those who say they love him." When retired former Federal Judge George Leighton attempted to assist him with an appeal, Jay rejected it. Judge Leighton opined that Pollard suffered from "Stockholm syndrome," a common disorder affecting prisoners who have been incarcerated too long. "They simply don't trust anyone any more," the judge said.

Supporter Beverly Newman agreed, stating, "Such erratic behavior is predictable for any human being subjected to subhuman conditions for a prolonged period of time. Extreme temperature shifts, being moved around from cell to cell, isolation, being constantly threatened; that would make anyone distrustful."

Pollard's life support system shifted dramatically during the 1990s. After serving forty months in prison, wife Anne was released on March 31, 1990. She was placed on probation until November 1991.

In late 1990, Jonathan Pollard divorced Anne. She was served legal documents while recovering from a flare-up of her stomach disorder. "With tubes and IVs hooked up to my body," Anne told Arlene Peck, "a man dressed as a hospital orderly entered my room. To my total disbelief, he dropped divorce papers on my lap."

Conflicting accounts of the break-up were provided. One version related Jonathan's belief that he had become reconciled to the fact that he was never going to be released, and that Anne should move on with her life. Another attributed the divorce to a difference of opinion as to how to proceed with legal remedies. Regardless, since the fateful day in court when both were sentenced by Judge Robinson, Anne and Jonathan were never reunited.

Anne told journalist Leslie Katz in 1999 that "bad influences" had convinced her husband that he stood a greater chance of freedom without her. Anne indicated that she still believed Jonathan's sentence should be commuted, "as a matter of principle."

Following her release, Anne emigrated to Tel Aviv. On the day before Yom Kippur in September 1991, she was granted Israeli citizenship. In the Jewish publication *Amici Curiae*, a smiling Anne was shown in a photograph standing under a sign that read State of Israel Ministry of Immigrant Adoption. The caption under the photo read, "Truly a victim, held hostage by the government."

After residing in Israel, Anne moved to Los Angeles. In 1999, she said she was considering changing her name, telling journalist Katz, "I want a new life and to be separated from this matter."

Replacing Anne as Pollard's love interest was a devoted woman named Esther Zeitz, a Canadian Orthodox Jew whose admiration and support for Jonathan after he and Anne divorced catapulted her into his inner circle. So much so that she became Jonathan's wife under the name Esther Zeitz-Pollard. This was in line with their mutual beliefs, in full accord with Halachah (Jewish law and tradition comprising the law of the Bible).

Esther told the *Canadian Jewish News* that she became intrigued with the Pollard case in 1990, while working in the Ministry of Justice and teaching English at Hebrew University in Israel. She wrote to Jonathan and received a packet of information and a personal letter. "I expected the person who wrote it to be angry and bitter," she explained. "Instead, his letter was full of love for the land and people of Israel. It was such an overwhelming human, patriotic, compassionate tone, that I was very touched. Thus began the beginning of our communications."

Many of Jonathan's supporters questioned Zeitz-Pollard's motives, believing that she thwarted bona fide support group attempts to free Jonathan. Carol Pollard swore that at one point "we were within ten days of gaining Jay's freedom. Then Esther blocked our attempt." Jewish journalist Douglas M. Bloomfield believed Esther was a deterrent to gaining Pollard's freedom. In a 2001 letter published in the *New Jersey*

Jewish News, he labeled Esther a "megalomaniac." Responding to the allegation, Esther chastised Bloomfield for his irreverence. She reminded him that while in prison Jonathan could have won his freedom if he had singled out certain Jewish leaders as coconspirators. One of them on a list provided to him, she said, was Douglas Bloomfield.

Esther was vocal in her demands, both in the United States and Israel, where she frequently traveled. In 1996 , she read a statement into the official record of the Israeli Knesset which scalded most everyone associated with the case. "Jonathan Pollard," Esther extolled, "has been the scapegoat exploited by anti-Semite elements within the American administration, to call into question Israel's reliability as an ally....Mr. Prime Minister, it is time for the Jewish leader of the Jewish state to act in a manner befitting a Jewish leader, and through strong actions to let the Americans know that Jewish blood is not cheap." Later, when Prime Minister Netanyahu stood ready to demand the immediate release of Pollard, Zeitz-Pollard called him and other Israeli officials "stupid" and "afraid" to challenge the "liar" Americans.

To her credit, Esther organized the www.jonathanpollard.org internet website, which featured a loving photograph of her and Jonathan. From her home in Canada she updated the site and provided the latest news in his case. Thousands of articles articulating his cause are listed. In early 2001, Dr. Pollard acknowledged her support of his son, realizing that she has been a strong beacon of light in an attempt to free him.

Shortly after their long-distance love affair began, Esther explained the motivation behind her efforts. "This is the kind of issue I feel very strongly concerns every Jew and every decent, law-abiding citizen," she said. "The issues are much bigger than Jonathan and myself....Like it or not, we are writing a page of Jewish history."

In recent years, Jonathan rejected family and friends. Morris, Mollie and Carol Pollard had their names removed from Jonathan's approved prison visitor list.

"We had words when Jay wanted to become an Israeli citizen in 1995 [Pollard became one a year later when the Israel Supreme Court ruled he 'had done a service for Israel']," Dr. Pollard said. "I didn't approve, believing it would hurt his chances of being released. He saw my actions as being wrong, and looking back, I probably should have kept my mouth shut."

Expanding the wedge separating Esther and Jonathan and the Pollards was the remark, attributed to an upset Carol, that Jonathan's marriage was a "sham." He was so incensed at his sister that he forbade her from acting in his behalf. Later, in 1996, he filed a lawsuit against Carol condemning her actions and requesting an accounting of all moneys collected and spent by her. Carol was crushed after having spent so much of her life seeking her brother's release.

In the summer of 2000, Dr. Pollard attempted to visit his son by forwarding a letter requesting permission. The message, "It wouldn't be convenient" was delivered by one of Esther's associates. Despite the rejection, the eighty-four-year-old scholar and researchist traveled to Purdue University and delivered an inspiring speech to interested supporters and students. In the fall, his worry over Jonathan, and the continued worsening of wife Mollie's health, perpetuated his undergoing successful open heart surgery.

University of Baltimore professor Kenneth Lasson, a diehard Pollard supporter who penned numerous articles about the case dealing with constitutional issues, was the one man who spoke with Jonathan on a consistent basis. "He calls me nearly every other day when I am in the country," Lasson said in late August 2000. "He's like the captain of a ship seeking safe harbor. We commiserate about his case and he tells me how forsaken he feels."

Professor Lasson reported that any conversation about Pollard's family was forbidden. "Somehow he has erroneously gotten the idea that his parents and his sister Carol have sabotaged efforts to win release," Lasson said. "He won't even discuss the subject."

Regarding Pollard's plight, Professor Lasson said he believed the case involved "a matter of fairness." He also stated, "For ten years I never believed that anti-Semitism had anything to do with the sentence Pollard received, but now I see it as the only logical reason for what happened to him."

Another who attempted to intervene on Pollard's behalf was Notre Dame's Father Theodore Hesburgh, a 2000 recipient of the Congressional Medal of Honor. During the presidency of George Bush he visited the White House and proposed clemency for Pollard based on the condition that he renounce his American citizenship and be banished to Israel. According to Father Hesburgh, he ran into a "stone wall twenty-five feet thick" and the plan was ignored.

Though he attempted to assist Jonathan's release, Father Hesburgh's allegiances were to Morris and Mollie Pollard, not to their son. He told the *Washington Post Magazine*, "It is a terrible drag on this man [Dr. Pollard]. He's a great scholar and a good father, and he and Mollie, they have really suffered, and they don't deserve it."

Concerning Jonathan's behavior, Father Hesburgh had little sympathy. "The boy was a real nerd to do what he did. I think with all his intelligence, he was a hopeless romantic and he used to fantasize, and I think he got caught up and it became a passion with him. He got sucked in, and they hooked him with money, and he assumed he was important."

Regarding his efforts on behalf of Pollard, Father Hesburgh questioned the prosecutor's manner of handling the case. "You make a deal, you keep the deal, even if you are not a great admirer of Pollard, and I am not, but I can't say I am proud of our judicial system."

All the while, Jewish groups and individuals continued to debate Pollard's case. Attorney Alan Dershowitz, who had spoken on behalf of Pollard throughout the country, surmised, "Almost as soon as the sentence was announced, the Jewish community broke down into warring factions. One faction consisted of those who saw the sentence as outrageously excessive and an illegal breach of a plea bargain....Another was comprised of Jews who privately believed that the Pollard sentence was unjust, but who were afraid to speak out publicly, out of fear that Jewish support for a Jewish spy would foment anti-Semitism. Yet another camp—tiny in comparison to the first two—regarded Pollard as a hero to be praised, and sought to justify his actions as legitimate civil disobedience. The final camp—also small—consisted of apologetic Jews who tried to prove their super-patriotism by leaning over backwards to condemn Pollard even more loudly than they would have condemned an American who spied for an enemy nation."

Dershowitz then added, "Where one stood in the Pollard case became a kind of barometer for measuring one's comfort level as a true American entitled to criticize one's own government when it engaged in an injustice. Far too many American Jews became frightened of losing their status as first-class Americans, and in order to protect that hard-earned status, they acted—ironically—like second-class citizens who were not entitled to demand equal justice for one of their own."

Dr. Pollard and fellow supporters of his son were incensed by individuals such as former New York City mayor Ed Koch, who denounced the spy. "I can't understand intelligent Jews taking the word of an indicted felon and avowed enemy of Israel like Weinberger," Dr. Pollard professed. "It is the worst kind of ignorance. Don't they really want to know the truth? What Jonathan did was wrong, but he still has rights to due process. That's what the case is all about."

Pollard supporters targeted David Luchins, the aide to Senator Patrick Moynihan, who like Koch was Jewish. They alleged he caused harm to Pollard's case by announcing that he had seen secret documents confirming that Pollard's spying had resulted in the loss of lives of US intelligence agents. He later recanted his remarks by writing to Pollard lawyer Ted Olson that "I have never suggested that I am in possession of any information concerning the scope and character of Jonathan Pollard's crimes." Regardless, the Pollard supporters alleged, the damage was done.

Aid to Pollard's case by members of the Jewish community was promoted in November 1993, through what was known as "1000 Rabbis' Letter to President Clinton." Prominent Rabbis from across the country wrote, "We wish to voice our plea for Justice for Jonathan Pollard....The lifetime sentence imposed on [him] is unduly harsh and grossly inconsistent with punishment given other Americans convicted of similar and even worse crimes." Duplicated as a full-page ad in the *New York Times*, the letter concluded by requesting that Clinton commute the sentence of Pollard. Later, 700 members of the Rabbinical Alliance of America joined in the call. Neither plea was successful, but the Jewish leaders had shown their support for Pollard's release.

* * *

Grassroots campaigns continued attempting to free Pollard while various legal actions assaulting all aspects associated with his case were instigated.

Initially, Pollard had quelled his attorney's argument to appeal his case. Concerned that his plea bargain was still, in effect, "wired" to Anne's and that any development in his case would affect hers, he prohibited legal action. Jonathan later said he was certain that if he appealed his case, Anne would be deprived of critical medical attention in prison to treat her digestive disorder.

Pollard's decision to delay any appeal until after his wife was released would come back to haunt him. Later, he professed that his lawyers never told him of the deadlines for filing.

Once Anne's sentence was served, Pollard's attorneys acted. An exhaustive motion to withdraw his guilty plea and stand trial and/or to have his sentence reconsidered was filed, but on September 11, 1990, Judge Robinson, to no one's surprise, denied those requests.

In June 1991, Pollard's lawyers appealed Judge Robinson's decision. Supporters filed an amicus brief in Jonathan's behalf in anticipation of an appellate hearing to be held in September. Among those adding their names to the "friend of the court" brief were Father Hesburgh, by then president emeritus of Notre Dame, Elie Wiesel, Nobel Prize-winning author and Holocaust survivor, Seymour Reich, past president of B'nai B'rith International, noted Notre Dame law professor Charles Rice, and Philip Klutznick, former president of the World Jewish Congress.

In conjunction with the appeal, Jonathan wrote a hand-written letter to his parents dated June 6, 1991. Forwarded from his Marion Prison cell, it read in part:

Dear Mom and Dad,

I have always accepted the fact that I am not above the law, and deserve to be punished for my actions, however well motivated I may have believed them to be. At the time, I was faced with a cruel dilemma in which I thought I had to choose between the law and my conscience. That danger that I perceived to Israel's existence was so acute that I instinctively chose action over reflection. I now know that that was wrong. I should have made the effort to discover a legal solution to the predicament I faced. For this error in judgment I am profoundly sorry.

Also, I regret the adverse effect which my actions had on the United States, and the Jewish community. I am now and have always been very proud to be a citizen of this country. However, the loyalty of American Jews to their nation and its law have been unwavering and intense. In fact, American Jews have been particular champions of our legal system in good part because they know that American law is the major bulwark against bigotry toward minority groups. In taking the actions I did, I failed to understand the critical nature of this stance, and the ammunition my actions provided to anyone who might want to accuse American Jews of having dual loyalties.

During my six years in prison, I have also reflected on how and why, despite my idealism about the world and Israel's place in it, I was capable of taking the actions I did. The answer has come to me I think through the maturity gained since the day of my arrest. My problem stemmed not from dual loyalty, but from my anxiety that the past would repeat itself unless I intervened. Unfortunately, I failed to appreciate the fact that such concerns did not justify my indifference to the law. In my mind, though, assisting an ally did not involve or require betraying the United States. I never thought that enhancing Israel's security would in any way jeopardize America's strategic interests. But that judgment was not mine to make.

I say all of this not as a defense for what I did, but as an explanation to my friends and family, so that they understand why I made mistakes that have caused the people I love and admire to suffer so grievously from my actions…nothing will alter the remorse I feel as a result of my actions.

When Pollard's attorneys stood before the United States Court of Appeals, a three-member tribunal consisting of future Supreme Court Justice Ruth Bader Ginsburg, Laurence Silberman, and Stephen F. Williams, their hopes of gaining a new "trial" for Pollard were high.

Prior to the oral argument held in the case, *Wall Street Journal* reporter L. Gordon Crovitz wrote an article entitled, "Even Pollard Deserves Better Than Government Sandbagging." His final paragraph read, "The Pollard case raises broad questions about how to treat spies for our allies, but also presents a more constantly pressing domestic issue. This is that no crime entitles prosecutors to induce plea bargains with broken promises or bullying tactics. Nothing Pollard passed to the Israelis would harm American interests as much as a declaration by judges that there are no limits on prosecutors."

When the court was convened, attorney Theodore B. Olson, Ronald

Reagan's personal attorney during the sixth year of the Iran-Contra investigation and Soliciter General under President George W. Bush, rose to defend Pollard. He was a surprise entry into the Pollard case based on his conservative background.

Olson, a handsome, principled man who permitted a shock of blonde hair to drape over his forehead, had escaped prosecution by the government in 1983. That year he was investigated by Independent Counsel Alexia Morrison, a gruff former assistant US attorney, regarding accusations that he had provided false and misleading testimony regarding Congress's rights to inspect EPA documents. Twenty-nine months later, Olson was cleared, although Morrison described his actions regarding the EPA documents as "less than forthcoming."

Before that report was issued, Olson's attorneys challenged the constitutionality of the Independent Counsel Act and a federal appeals court agreed with them. The judge who wrote the opinion favoring Olson's position was Judge Silberman, the staunch conservative who was now hearing the plea for Jonathan Pollard.

Olson's arguments centered on three main points: 1) The government, to avoid a public trial that might prove embarrassing, secured Pollard's cooperation by "purchasing" his guilty plea in exchange for a promise of leniency of sentence for him and Anne. At the sentencing, Olson argued, the government reneged on its part of the bargain, in effect requesting a life sentence for Pollard and maximum punishment for Anne; 2) In accordance with the plea agreement the government promised to inform the court of Pollard's cooperation with the investigation, but instead ridiculed him for lack of cooperation even though he provided valuable information for them; and 3) By use of the Weinberger memorandum and letter at sentencing, which charged that Pollard had committed treason, the government inflamed the judge, causing him to impose the maximum sentence on Pollard.

The latter, Ted Olson assailed, constituted "an outrageous abuse of power." Assessing the prosecutor's conduct, he exploded, "Although [they] didn't use the words 'life imprisonment,' it certainly moved in for the kill at sentencing time."

During one spirited exchange with Judge Silberman, who had chastised the government for the "winks and nods" conduct utilized during the sentencing of Pollard, the question was asked by Silberman of the government attorney, John Fisher, "How in God's name can you justify Weinberger's use of the word 'treason' in his memorandum to the sentencing judge?" Fisher hesitated with the answer, and before labeling Weinberger's actions "regrettable." He apologized for them, but the judge was on the attack, pointing out, "The message the prosecutors seemed to convey in the Pollard case was that you'd better be damned careful when you deal with the United States government." When Fisher responded that Weinberger's choice of words did not violate the plea agreement, Judge Silberman retorted, "As long as they didn't use the words 'life sentence,' it was okay?"

Attorney Olson argued that the alleged plea agreement violations concerning the interview of Pollard by journalist Wolf Blitzer were bogus. "All of Pollard's visits, including Blitzer's were 'approved, permitted, and facilitated' by the government," he explained. Olson's performance impressed Carol Pollard, who told *Washington Jewish Week*, "Ted was the Pablo Casals of the legal world in court."

Journalist Gary Brookins believed the Pollard case deserved review. He wrote, "Though free-lance espionage operations, even those on behalf of allies, cannot be condoned, it is clear that Pollard has been wronged. This can be rectified by the Court of Appeals, which should grant the petition, vacate the plea, free Jonathan Pollard, or at least grant him a new trial."

In the end, a door that appeared to be inching open was slammed shut when Silberman, a former member of the Republican National Committee who later voted with the majority to overturn the conviction of Iran-Contra figure Oliver North, and Ginsburg refused to grant a new trial to their Jewish brethren. They characterized the prosecutor's behavior as "hard-nosed," but did not see it as "excessive." They based the decision on the fact that the appeal was not filed in a timely fashion by Pollard. That required him to prove not just that he was unfairly sentenced, but that he was a victim of a complete miscarriage of justice.

The adverse decision prompted an outcry of disbelief from Ted Olson. Dr. Pollard said the attorney told him, "Beware of Jews judging Jews," a reference to the fact that both Judge Ginsburg and Judge Silberman were Jewish. The decision brought to mind the revealing comment by Harvard professor of Judaic Studies Ruth Weiss, who said, "When Jews become prominent in government, they will sacrifice other Jews."

Judge Stephen Williams's dissent presented a far different view of the case. "I agree with the majority that the 'plea wiring' was not an unlawful coercion of Pollard's guilty plea and that Chief Judge Robinson did not abuse his discretion in refusing to recuse himself or to conduct a hearing into the claim of ex parte contacts. But because the government's breach of the plea agreement was a fundamental miscarriage of justice requiring relief under [federal law], I dissent."

After asserting that the government made three promises to Pollard (bringing to the attention of the court his cooperation, not asking for a life sentence, and limiting its reserved right of allocution to facts and circumstances of the case), Williams wrote, "The government complied in spirit with none of its promises; with the third, it complied in neither letter nor spirit." Of the promise not to argue for a life sentence, the judge stated, "The repeated use of superlatives implied an appeal for the maximum. Weinberger's reference to treason took the point further. Whereas treason carries the death penalty, and involves aiding the nation's enemies, Pollard was charged with espionage, carrying a maximum of life imprisonment."

Regarding the government's promise to confine its summation to the court specifically to the facts and circumstances of the case, Justice Williams wrote, "The government told the district judge that Pollard's expressions of remorse were 'both belated and hollow' and 'grounded in the fact that he was caught;' that Pollard was a 'recidivist' who was 'contemptuous of this Court's authority' and 'unworthy of trust;' that Pollard felt 'blind contempt' for the US military, and had a 'warped' and 'skewed' perspective; that Pollard was 'traitorous, arrogant [and] deceitful, without remorse,' and 'literally addicted to the high lifestyle funded by his espionage activities.'"

Summing up, Justice Williams wrote, "Though I do not wish to be too critical of the government, and though the analogy is inexact on some points, the case does remind me of Macbeth's curse against the witches, whose promises, and their sophistical interpretations of them— led them to doom: *And be these juggling fiends nor more believ'd, That palter with us in a double sense; That keep the word of promise to our ear. And breat it to our hope.*"

The adverse ruling, which jolted those who believed Pollard deserved resentencing, was duly appealed to the United States Supreme Court. In mid-October the case was not selected to be heard by the court. The *New York Times,* which had botched the initial reporting of the Pollard case, did so again. In a November 29, 1992, "Correction" column, it admitted "A brief article on October 18 about the Supreme Court's declining to review the life sentence of the former Navy analyst Jonathan J. Pollard described his crime incorrectly. Mr. Pollard pled guilty to spying for Israel, not treason...."

Chapter 18

POLLARD'S PAROLE

Attempts to consider a plea for parole for Jonathan Pollard in 1995, the earliest possible year, were considered, then abandoned. According to the Pollard website, legal opinion by several prominent attorneys familiar with federal guidelines warned of dire consequences. One of those, Benson Weintraub, wrote to Pollard advocate Nancy Luque of his concern that if Pollard applied for parole, the request would be denied. That opinion was based on knowledge that the Parole Commission considered only "file information," all of which was negative, about the subject and did not permit new evidence to be submitted.

Worse, Weintraub said, if Pollard were denied parole, he'd be subject to "the 15 year set-off" rule, and he could not be considered for parole for that many years. "Against this background," Weintraub wrote, "I reaffirm my previous recommendation that pending further [political] developments, Mr. Pollard should decline to apply for parole at this time." Based on Weintraub's advice, no parole application for Pollard was filed.

Joseph diGenova, Pollard's prosecutor, possessed a different viewpoint regarding parole. He chastised those who claimed Pollard had been sentenced to life without parole. "If you have the sentencing transcript," he stated, "the Judge said, 'I sentence you to life.' At the time that sentence was imposed, there was not even a sentence of life without parole in the Federal Code. This is classic Pollard deception carried on by his representatives....He has been eligible for parole since 1995 and as a legal strategy he has purposely refused to ask for it so he can use executive clemency as his only real appeal vehicle."

* * *

Arguments by Pollard's supporters that Judge Aubrey Robinson committed legal judicial misconduct were buoyed by a 1999 interview provided by Caspar Weinberger to *Middle East Quarterly*. Prefacing his remarks regarding events surrounding the memorandum and letter he submitted to the court was a litany of caustic remarks about the spy:

MEQ: You have been quoted saying that Jonathan Pollard "should have been shot." Is this accurate?

Weinberger: Any traitor who did what he did should be shot.

MEQ: You describe him as a traitor.

Weinberger: I thought Pollard did a very great deal of damage to the United States....My views have nothing to do with his religion or his beliefs or anything of that kind.

MEQ: You are saying that calling Pollard a "traitor" is in the general sense, not in a lawyerly sense?

Weinberger: It's the smallest kind of footnote. The fact is he did tremendous damage and how you want to define it doesn't really make any difference.

The exchange made apparent Weinberger's distaste for the "traitor," but more important to Pollard supporters was a startling revelation concerning Judge Robinson. Midway through the questioning, Weinberger, in discussing the nature of the memorandum he filed with the court, admitted, "I said everything I knew about Pollard at the request of the United States District Court....I gave them an affidavit that was classified because it went into great detail about the extent of the damage that was done and the number of lives of our people that were endangered." Later, when asked about the motive behind the affidavit, Weinberger answered, "That was the exact subject matter of the information that the judge wanted in the case, and he made a formal, official request to me for it."

Weinberger's admission was startling since for twelve years the concensus had been that either the United States District Attorney's office requested the memo and letter or that Weinberger had provided them of his own accord. If the former secretary was now telling the truth, then Judge Robinson had been less than candid with the defense and should have permitted full access to the documents and proper time within which to respond to the accusations therein. Instead, the atmosphere created by the judge, Pollard supporters alleged, blindsided the defense and left them powerless to act.

If that was the case, former Federal Judge George Leighton said Judge Robinson's conduct "undermined the integrity of the judicial system." Notre Dame law professor Charles Rice suggested, "The trial judge's apparent request to Weinberger that he submit that classified memo and his withholding of that information from the defendant's attorneys, to whom he gave only limited access to that memo, raises a legitimate issue of bias. At the very least, his case cries out for discovery to learn what actually happened."

A side issue to the flap over the Weinberger memo and letter involved assessing the conduct of Joseph diGenova. If Weinberger was telling the truth, and did not voluntarily submit the memo and letter, or do so at the behest of diGenova, then the prosecutor misled defense attorneys who believed that was the means by which the communiqués had reached the court.

Based on the revelation of potential misconduct on the part of all parties, lawyer Alan Dershowitz spearheaded attempts to gain entry in court to hear the charges of impropriety. He was unsuccessful.

Joseph diGenova called Weinberger a liar. "The judge did not communicate with Caspar Weinberger. He was requested to submit his sentencing memo at the request of the government. At my request. Because in espionage cases, there is always a damage assessment provided by either the Secretary of Defense, the CIA, or the Secretary of State. In this case, because Pollard was working for the Navy, the damage assessment was provided under the auspices of the Secretary of Defense. Weinberger was actively involved in the assessment and asked to participate in it."

* * *

On September 20, 2000, lawyers for Jonathan Pollard filed a motion for resentencing in Washington, DC District Court. Represented by attorneys Eliot Lauer and Jacques Semmelman, the motion was accompanied by a sworn declaration by Pollard as well as a memorandum in support of the motion.

The argument that Pollard be resentenced centered around allegations of impropriety by Jonathan's previous lawyer Richard Hibey. In his declaration, Pollard stated, "My petition is based upon the complete and utter failure of my attorney, Richard Hibey, to protect my fundamental rights in the district court." The spy added, "I now understand that my sentence of life in prison was imposed as a result of Mr. Hibey's inadequate and unprofessional handling of my sentencing. His failure to represent me properly deprived me of my constitutional rights to effective rights of counsel."

Among the poignant arguments that Pollard made was the allegation that Hibey "failed to tell the sentencing judge that I had sought and obtained approval for the [Wolf Blitzer] interviews, and he erroneously conceded that the interviews were unauthorized." Jonathan also stated that "Hibey breached the attorney-client privilege by telling the sentencing judge that I had given the interviews against his advice, thus further inflaming the judge against me."

In his declaration, Pollard alleged that "I later learned that most of his [Hibey's] fees were paid by the Government of Israel." The spy also stated that while his main contention was Hibey's failure to tell him he had to file a notice of appeal of his sentence within ten days of the judge's ruling, he also was upset with the lawyer's handling of Caspar Weinberger's letter to the court. Of that Pollard alleged, "I was scheduled to be sentenced March 4, 1987. That day, I was brought to a holding cell adjacent to the courtroom. Mr. Hibey came in, waving a document. He said that Secretary of Defense Caspar Weinberger…had just submitted a second declaration to the Court. Mr. Hibey handed it to me. I read it. It was devastating. But it was not true. It accused me of 'treason.' I had never even been charged with treason, let alone found guilty of it."

Continuing, Pollard argued, "At no time did Mr. Hibey tell me that I had a right to adjournment, the right to offer evidence that could rebut the damaging allegations, the right to ask the Court to make findings of fact on the allegations, or the right to an evidentiary hearing at which the government would bear the burden of proving its allegations.

To the contrary, Mr. Hibey told me that the sentencing could not be adjourned and that nothing could be done."

Addressing the question of his having violated the spirit of his plea agreement by permitting the interview by journalist Wolf Blitzer, Pollard stated, "I was aware that under the terms of my Plea Agreement, any interview had to be approved by the director of Naval Intelligence [not Justice Department]. Because no one—let alone a journalist—can walk into FCI Petersburg and interview, photograph, and tape record an inmate without government authorization, and because the high profile nature of my case left me without any doubt that a request for an interview would be reviewed at the highest levels of government, I believed and understood that, by filing the form provided to me by the government, the approval process would proceed up the chain of government authority, and that the director of Naval Intelligence or his delegate would either approve or disapprove the interview." Pollard also noted with irony that on the day of the first interview, "Using Blitzer's camera, a Bureau of Prisons official took a photograph of me with Blitzer. The photograph later appeared in a book Blitzer wrote about the case."

Besides arguing that the government knew about Blitzer's first interview and indeed the second one, Pollard raised new questions about Hibey's competence. He alleged that Hibey chastised him for submitting to an interview with the press. Pollard stated that "[Hibey] erroneously confirmed the government's accusations, and even volunteered, inappropriately, that he had advised me not to submit to the interviews. Citing my 'Judgmental Deterioration,' Mr. Hibey wrote that I had 'lapsed' and 'against better judgment and advice, has spoken to the press.'" Summing up, Pollard declared, "Mr. Hibey allowed the government to portray me, inaccurately, as a person utterly contemptuous of governmental authority who brazenly violated his own Plea Agreement and Protective Order and who gave unauthorized interviews to a journalist."

Alleging that Hibey never informed him of the requirement to file a notice of appeal, Pollard recalled his final meeting with his lawyer before being transported to the plane departing for Springfield, Missouri. "Immediately after the Court imposed sentence on March 4, 1987, I was taken to a holding cell next to the courtroom," Pollard swore. He then added, "Mr. Hibey told me I would be in jail for thirty years. His parting words were, 'You can handle it.' I never saw him or spoke to him again."

In his Declaration, Pollard was critical of lawyer Hamilton Fox, III, whom the spy alleged had been retained by the Israeli government in 1988 or 1989. At no time, Pollard stated, "did Fox ever inform me of any alleged unprofessional conduct on the part of Richard Hibey." Instead, Jonathan explained that Edward Jason Robinson, a fellow inmate at Butner, North Carolina, expressed surprise that no one had ever appealed his case.

Pollard swore that he learned of his rights from attorney Larry Dub, a civil lawyer who practiced in Israel. That led to a meeting with his current attorneys who convinced the spy to file a habeas corpus petition demanding review of the sentencing procedures utilized in his case.

The declaration, signed by Pollard on August 28, 2000, closed with a simple plea. He stated, "My sole request is that my sentence be vacated and that I be resentenced at a fair proceeding."

Pollard's lawyers promoted his request with an emotional argument of their own. Citing the fact that neither Hamilton Fox nor any other lawyer in Washington chose to criticize Hibey's woeful performance, they stated, "Pollard's life sentence was based on false factual allegations that Hibey did not challenge. It would be a fundamental miscarriage of justice to say that, because of Hibey's shortcomings and Fox's reluctance to criticize a colleague, no appellate court can ever conduct a direct review of Pollard's life sentence. Pollard should not have to spend the rest of his life in jail based upon false accusations simply because one member of the DC bar could not bring himself to criticize another."

In early October 2000, District Court Judge Norma Holloway Johnson ordered the government to respond to the allegations promoted by Pollard's attorneys. To Pollard supporters, that was a sign that the court believed the spy's allegations were legitimate.

The government disagreed. In their reply brief filed on November 28, 2000, they avoided the merits of Pollard's arguments instead arguing that the petition for relief had been filed beyond the statute of limitations under the provisions for appeal listed in the Antiterrorism and Effective Death Penalty Act of 1996 which limited prisoners' rights. Pollard lawyers counterattacked in their reply brief, stating that no statute could toll until the moment that Pollard was aware of what they dubbed irregularities with "prevailing professional norms," the standard of conduct that lawyers were held to. That date, they said, was March of 2000, when the appeals lawyers notified Pollard of lawyer Hibey's failure to provide competent representation.

A setback for the Pollard appellate attorneys occurred on January 12, 2001. Judge Johnson denied a motion for Lauer, who had Top Secret level security clearance, to inspect the classified portion of the Pollard court docket. The Court dismissed his claim that there was a pressing need to view the documents so as to refute the false charges contained therein. The judge expressed concerns regarding security matters, stating, "The Court has viewed the classified materials and finds that the exceptionally grave concern over national security is warranted. These documents contain information that if disclosed, even accidently, would pose a grave risk to national security."

A *Justice4JonathanPollard* press release condemned the decision, stating, "it reveals that the American Government continues its policy of deliberately misleading the Court in its on-going persecution of Jonathan Pollard."

Bolstering the Pollard lawyer's claims was an amicus brief filed by the American Civil Liberties Union on December 5, 2000. It supported lawyer Lauer's request that he be given access to the classified documents filed at the time of sentencing.

Weighing in on the matter were a group of staunch Pollard supporters led by professor Kenneth Lasson. On December 28, 2000, their amicus brief in support of Pollard's petition for relief was filed with the headnote that the "Amica are law professors and individuals from around the country with an interest in the fair administration of justice, principled interpretation of law, and protection of rights guaranteed by the Constitution." Listed along with Lasson were fifteen others, including Anthony Amsterdam, professor of law at New York University, Robert Drinan, professor of law at Georgetown, US Congressman Anthony D. Weiner, Reverend Theodore Hesburgh, George Leighton, and Charles Rice.

Whether a court hearing would occur remained unclear as of June 2001. Better yet, Pollard supporters hoped, the government would agree to a new "plea bargain," one that would reduce Jonathan's sentence to time served, permitting his release.

Vigorously opposing early release for Pollard was Joseph diGenova. In October 2000, he spoke about both the latest court attempt by Pollard's lawyers and whether Pollard had indeed served enough time in prison.

DiGenova said, "I have seen all of the pleadings and they are a joke. They are pathetic. [There is] no substantiation for them." Regarding Richard Hibey, he stated, "[He] is, was, and remains one of the most respected private defense attorneys in the United States....He is one of the finest litigators in the country....He did a very good job. He was paid, I'm sure, handsomely, by Mr. Pollard's supporters. We've always wondered where the money came from for all these lawyers, but so be it. I think he did what any good lawyer would do, he did the best he could to negotiate the best deal he could."

Concerning whether Pollard should be released after fifteen-plus years in prison, diGenova said, "Absolutely not. Pollard has not paid his debt [to society]. The damage he did is irrevocable....I don't believe in releasing people who commit espionage until their sentences are completed." Asked whether Pollard should serve the full life sentence term, diGenova added, "He should apply for parole and he has never done so. Pollard actually may be the one who is keeping himself in prison...."

Chapter 19

POLITICS AND POLLARD

Blinding the legal issues presented in the Jonathan Pollard case was the determination by government officials to treat the spy as a political football. Whether in Israel or the United States, politicians either supported the spy or opposed him based on personal agendas. Nowhere was that more true than with the president of the United States.

In late October 1998, Pollard believed his release was imminent. "I was packing; I thought this was it," he told the *Jewish Week*. "Everybody was coming around my room asking for books, clothes, deodorant, food. Everybody was claiming things. That's what happens in prisons."

Pollard's hope for freedom was based on an alleged promise made by President Bill Clinton to Israeli leaders during the Wye River Peace Conference. According to Dani Naveh, head of an Israeli task force intent on securing the release of Pollard, "At the summit, Clinton promised Netanyahu that Pollard would be released, but then a crisis erupted over the issue. At the emergency meeting of the ministers that Netanyahu convened at the time, there were conflicting opinions. Ariel Sharon insisted that Clinton keep his word. Yitzhak Mordecai thought there was no point in insisting on Pollard's release and blowing the Wye Accords. Netanyahu dug in his heels. He felt deceived by Clinton. [Secretary of State] Albright and [Security Adviser] Berger tried to convince the Israeli ministers not to ruin the Wye Accords by insisting on Pollard....In the end, in spite of the insistence of Netanyahu, the Israelis gave up on Pollard."

At two subsequent peace conferences, Pollard was again a topic of conversation. According to journalist Uri Dan of the *New York Post*, Prime Minister Ehud Barak was offered a deal. If he signed an accord with the Palestinians, Clinton promised "as a bonus" to: grant Israel $750 million to compensate for the retreat from Lebanon and additional money to defend against long-range missiles from Iran, a US upgrade of the strategic relationship with Israel, and freedom for Pollard. Later, Dan wrote, "Barak's enthusiasm for peace led to two summits, both in vain. And none of the three bonuses have come about."

* * *

In January 1999, Clinton considered clemency for Pollard. Based upon his "promise" to the disappointed Israelis at the Wye River Peace Accord to review the matter, White House counsel Charles Ruff, a former US attorney who had been the fifth and final Watergate prosecutor in the 1970s, solicited views from US Intelligence and security agencies, all of whom favored Pollard's continued incarceration.

Opposed to clemency were Secretary of State Madeleine Albright, United States Senator Richard Shelby, the Alabama Republican and head of the Senate Intelligence Committee who asserted that "releasing Pollard would set a dangerous and unwise precedent that crimes against the United States are not serious and would undermine our country's ability to act as an honest broker throughout the world." CIA director George Tenet joined the others, dubbed by Pollard supporters as "the lynch mob," by, according to media reports, threatening resignation if Clinton set Pollard free.

Adding his opinion to denial of clemency was prosecutor Joseph diGenova. He asserted, "If Clinton releases him [Pollard], it will be one of the most disgraceful acts by an American president."

Supporting the opposition were four retired admirals who had served as directors of naval intelligence, sixty senators including fourteen Democrats, Secretary of Defense William Cohen, and Attorney General Janet Reno. A few months earlier, Senate Majority Leader Trent Lott had espoused that "Jonathan Pollard is a traitor" in a much publicized letter that included text stating that "According to former Secretary of Defense Caspar Weinberger, Pollard gave away so much information that the US Intelligence community's bargaining power in official exchanges with Israel was severely reduced."

Lott's directive echoed those expressed whenever it appeared Pollard's sentence might be commuted. In December 1993, a *USA Today* editorial entitled, "Pardon Convicted Traitor? Not This One, Not Now," espoused the belief that "Pollard is a traitor, plain and simple." In January 1999 the same newspaper ran an editorial titled, "Magnitude of

Pollard's Betrayal Justifies Rejection of Clemency," which included the words "Traitor deserves to remain in prison despite Israel's pleas."

Opposing any consideration of clemency in the 1999 letter to President Clinton was Senator Joseph Lieberman. Joining him were colleagues Diane Feinstein, James Jeffords, John McCain, and Herb Kohl. They and the other senators urged the president "to deny clemency in the interest of justice and in the interest of national security."

Lieberman's actions had infuriated Pollard supporters and others who questioned the Connecticut politician's actions. Controversial New York Rabbi Mordechai Friedman was quite vocal, telling a television audience that "Lieberman is evil" while suggesting that assassination might be in order.

An Orthodox Jew who impressed purists with his disdain for working on the Sabbath in accordance with his religious beliefs, Lieberman had leaped into moral prominence when he chastised and ridiculed Clinton on the Senate floor for his immoral conduct during the Monica Lewinsky scandal. Even his Democratic colleagues cheered his speech, calling him a true patriot with the best interests of the county at heart. But when the stakes were elevated, he voted not guilty against the same man he had so criticized weeks earlier.

Senator Lieberman, a former Connecticut attorney general, was a perplexing figure who appeared unsure of his true beliefs. That was evident when it came to examination of his collaboration in joining former Secretary of Education Bill Bennett in condemning Hollywood-influenced violence in films, music, television programs, and videos. They began awarding "Silver Sewer Awards" to those who condoned the violence, believing it to have impacted several youth who committed sensational acts of violence. That seemed worthy until it was disclosed that Lieberman owned stock in Twentieth Century Fox and CBS, two media companies that had won Silver Sewer Awards.

When Vice President Gore chose Senator Lieberman as his running mate, the praise was instant, with Rabbi Bary Fruended of Kesher Israel proclaiming, "His [Lieberman's] integrity and commitment to good values are the most impressive things about him. He's not afraid to put life's most important things in front of politics." Those words about a man who amazingly enough told *Time* magazine, "I grew up in a multiethnic, multiracial, multireligious community, and I was lucky. I cannot remember a single instance of anti-Semitism in my youth…"

Lieberman, whose wife Hadassah's mother had survived the death camps at Auschwitz and Dachau, handled questions about his position regarding the Pollard case by repeatedly expressing the belief that there should be no interference with the judicial process. In an April 2000 letter to New York Assemblyman Sam Coleman, the senator wrote, "I believe that Mr. Pollard's betrayal of his country, his violation of his oath to his employer, and his dishonesty were serious breaches of law and morality….Notwithstanding those conclusions about the Pollard case, as a general personal policy, I believe the courts, which have access to the full breadth of evidence and testimony in criminal cases, are in the best position to decide matters of guilt, innocence, and sentencing. They should do so without influence from elected legislators, or our courts will not be truly free and independent."

Lieberman's position in the year 2000 that he urged non-intervention in the Pollard case conflicted with his stance in early 1999, when he had been one of the senators who approved the letter urging President Clinton to deny Pollard clemency. By his very participation in affixing his signature to such a letter he was in fact intervening in the process, something he condemned.

Spokesperson Leslie Phillips defended Senator Lieberman's actions by saying, "The Senator has been in several highly classified briefings on Pollard's actions and the repercussions of those actions and he feels pretty strongly that Pollard is guilty of serious crimes against the people of the United States."

While the media overlooked Liberman's inconsistencies, ridicule for the senator was evident in a *Justice4JonathanPollard* media release dated August 8, 2000. "If the Pollard case can be considered an example of what voters can expect of Joseph Lieberman as Vice President of the United States, then there is much to be concerned about. Where will such a man stand on matters related to Israel and the Jewish community? Will he continue to do what he has done in the Pollard case? Will he continue to advocate to the detriment of his own kind, to prove that he is a loyal and true American? How can anyone—Jew or gentile— trust a man who has placed himself outside of his own community, refused to advocate for equal justice for one of his own, and ignored the rulings of his own religious leadership?"

Based on the letter and other feedback President Clinton received from Senator Lieberman and those within government agencies, Clinton failed to act in the Pollard case. Supporters had hoped that the issue of Pollard's fate would surface at the July 2000 meeting in Washington between Clinton, Yasser Arafat, and Israeli Prime Minister Ehud Barak, but nothing occurred of substance. Of the Camp David meeting, attorney David Kirshenbaum wrote in the *Jerusalem Post*, "It is a sorry truth that the American government's conduct in the Pollard case and its posture toward Israel as a consequence thereof is distinguished by broken promises, double standards, and bad faith…"

* * *

Political affairs in Israel had caused the government to at long last acknowledge its responsibility in the Pollard case. The revelation had come in May 1998, during a prison visit to Pollard in North Carolina by Israeli cabinet secretary Dani Naveh. He was there at the request of Israeli prime minister Benjamin Netanyahu.

With Pollard's new wife Esther present as well as an officer from NIS who monitored all conversations, the Israeli messenger acknowledged that "Jonathan Pollard was an Israeli agent, handled by high-ranking Israeli officials…and in light of this fact the State of Israel acknowledges its obligation to Mr. Pollard and is ready to assume full responsibility accordingly."

Dr. Morris Pollard's face tightened when he first heard of the declaration. "It means nothing really," he said. "Where have they been all these years?"

While the Israelis were admitting their responsibilities, albeit a bit late, First Lady Hillary Clinton, a candidate for the Senate from New York, chose a neutral position regarding the Pollard matter. In December 1999, she told reporters, "It would be wrong for me, not having read the classified data, to jump in and take a position for political reasons." As the election neared, Mrs. Clinton continued to ponder her position regarding the case. On 24 August, New York Assemblyman Dov Hikind pressed the issue of release with Mrs. Clinton at a meeting in Manhattan. "I was very strong in bringing some of the [Jewish] community's concerns to her," Hikind reported.

Just nine weeks before the national election, Mrs. Clinton, according to the *New York Post*, "went to bat for [Jonathan] Pollard last week after Jewish leaders told her prison officials planned to move him from the relatively safe unit called Clemson [one that primarily houses sex offenders]…to a new unit [Virginia] said to house violent inmates, including white supremacists." Mrs. Clinton's intervention, along with others who contacted the Bureau of Prisons, were actions described by her spokesman, Howard Wolfson, who said, "The issue was brought to Hillary Clinton's attention, and she was concerned on humanitarian grounds."

Esther Zeitz-Pollard welcomed the First Lady's intervention, writing her that, "If a silver lining is to be found [from this matter] perhaps it is that I am aware for the first time of your humanitarian interest in my husband's welfare."

Congressman Rick Lazio, Hillary Clinton's opponent in the New York Senate race, chastised her for the intervention and called upon her husband to announce his intentions regarding Pollard. "The President owes it to America to announce [if he is going to provide clemency] or not," Lazio stated. He also accused President Clinton of dragging his feet on the Pollard matter, saying Clinton's promise to review the case was "600 days late." White House spokesman Jake Siewert responded, "This decision will be made on the merits, without regard to politics."

Answering Lazio's argument, Hillary Clinton spoke of Pollard during their Senate debate in September. In answer to a question from moderator Tim Russert, the First Lady said she had "concerns about the due process issues concerning the way Pollard was sentenced." She also stated that "fair-minded people should ask similar questions."

Mrs. Clinton's observations appeared during a time when her husband was questioning the behavior of the Justice Department, particularly his own loyal Attorney General Janet Reno, concerning the case of Wen Ho Lee, the Chinese-American nuclear scientist. President Clinton issued a statement declaring that he was "quite troubled" over the treatment of Lee, who was branded a spy by federal authorities, incarcerated without bond in solitary confinement, and then permitted to plead guilty to a lesser offense providing no prison sentence. Pollard supporters hoped the Lee case would propel the president to reconsider Jonathan's plight.

The Lazio-Hillary Clinton debate produced a demand by Pollard attorneys that moderator Russert apologize. During the question and answer, he asked the candidates their position on the case while stating, "Mr. Pollard had been sentenced to life for espionage and treason." In their letter to Russert, Pollard attorneys charged him with "sloppy journalism" while alleging that his comments "unfortunately reinforced a popular misconception about Mr. Pollard."

To his credit, Russert apologized on *Meet The Press*, but added that the "chief prosecutor" in the case had called him and said that "agents in the field were identified by Pollard." Pollard's attorneys sprung into action again and demanded to know who the "chief prosecutor" was. Russert notified them that it was Joseph diGenova. He informed the attorneys that it was his "professional opinion" that Pollard had disclosed agents. Since no hard evidence had been produced, the attorneys once again demanded an apology from Russert, but he declined to do so.

In his response to Pollard's attorneys, diGenova supported declassification of the secret documents sealed in the case. He echoed those thoughts when he said, "Should the documents be declassified? I would love to see the pleadings in the case be declassified. I would love to see the damage assessment declassified. I think if they were, they would frighten people to no end as to what he [Pollard] did."

As to whether the documents would indeed be declassified, diGenova stated, "Now that is wishful thinking because the government does not declassify damage assessment. It has never done that in any espionage case in history."

In mid-October, Mrs. Clinton stiffened her resolve regarding the Pollard case. The *New York Post* reported that Hillary revealed she had spoken to the president and quoting her as saying, "I have made my views known, yes." The *Post* stated that Mrs. Clinton said that certain "secret evidence used to prosecute the case should be released so that the public can determine whether Pollard received a fair sentence."

Joseph diGenova possessed strong feelings regarding Mrs. Clinton's statements about the Pollard case. "I think Hillary Clinton's involvement in the Pollard case is pathetic, and it is part and parcel of the way the Clintons view government. It's a little toy to be used by them. Her mouthings on this case are so ill-informed that they ought to be embarrassing to the people of New York....She's playing a game here, a dangerous nasty game, and her participation in it demeans her position both as a candidate for the Senate and as the First Lady of the United States."

To diGenova's chagrin, on election day in 2000 the voters of New York State elected Hillary Rodham Clinton to the United States Senate. Whether she would assist Jonathan Pollard's efforts for freedom remained to be seen.

* * *

An enticing perspective on Pollard's case was contained in the writings of Milton Viorst, a Washington, DC journalist and author of *Sandcastles: The Arabs In Search of the Modern World.*

In an article entitled "Americans Deserve To Know Why Pollard Isn't Free," Viorst began by addressing a recent letter he had received from Avi Weiss, whom he characterized as "an activist rabbi known for his strident positions in behalf of Jewish causes."

"According to Weiss," Viorst wrote, "Pollard is the victim of anti-Semitism. He was arrested as an American...punished as a Jew and his case symbolizes the right of Jews to be judged by the same standards as other Americans."

To that claim, Viorst expounded, "Weiss offers no evidence whatever to support his allegations, and I find the tone of his [remarks] to be reprehensible. Like most Jews, I have no sympathy for Pollard, nor do I identify with the segment of my community that extols the purity of his motives. Since his imprisonment, furthermore, Pollard has come across in interviews as self-pitying and impenitent."

In view of those words, the logical transition was for Viorst to condemn even the slightest hint that Pollard should be freed. But his summation was surprising. He wrote, "And yet, as an American, I too have concerns about the sentence. The issue is not Jewish, it is one of elemental justice."

To reinforce his claim, Viorst cited the Sixth Amendment, which he said, "guarantees to any accused an open trial, a right designed to allow the citizenry to monitor the fairness of the judicial process. Lawyers acknowledge that the courts have never articulated a comparable doctrine for sentencing. Still, a sense of fairness strongly suggests that a person should not be committed to prison for life without the public knowing why." Summing up, Viorst wrote, "Surely no American should have to spend a life in prison on the basis of secret proceedings."

Speaking to President Clinton's refusal to grant clemency in 1999, due to the "enormity of Pollard's crime," Viorst suggested "Maybe so, but 'enormity' without evidence, is just a word."

Pollard allies were a varied group not bound by political beliefs, race, or ethnic background, but dissenters continued to oppose any relief for Pollard. Congressman Fred Upton, Republican representative from Michigan's Sixth District just across the border from South Bend, Indiana, where Dr. Morris Pollard resided, proclaimed in January 1999, "Jonathan Pollard is a traitor who deserves every day of his prison sentence. [His] name belongs alongside Benedict Arnold and Aldrich Ames. He must remain in prison, disgraced, and behind bars."

BOOK V

Chapter 20

POLLARD THE PARADOX

Israel used me and then threw me away…I am broken."

That lament was contained in a letter written by a bitter Jonathan Pollard, Federal prisoner #09815-016, to Nobel Peace Prize laureate Elie Wiesel.

Many believed Pollard was a whiner who blamed others for his woes. In effect, critics argued, he was his own worst enemy and had no one to blame but himself.

Assessing both sides of the argument was difficult, if not impossible, for any independent analysis indicated that the Pollard case was fraught with contradictions. Examples included:

• Media examination of Jonathan Pollard during his years at Stanford portrayed two different images. To opponents of the accused spy, he was an unstable youth prone to fantasy who was obsessed with war games, carried a gun on campus, and referred to himself as "Colonel Pollard." He called such accusations ludicrous, proclaiming that much of his behavior was humorous in nature and "no big deal." He defended his actions as those of a passionate young man who believed in the preservation of Israel and of his duty to stand up and be counted.

• Observations of those who knew Pollard during his six years (1979–85) at NIS *before* he began spying presented two opposite perspectives. Some thought he was a kook, an oddball, who attempted to impress everyone with a mystery side to his life. Others believed he was a competent analyst with a flair for intelligence. The commendations and promotions he received bolster the latter viewpoint.

• The spy the government portrayed in the media and in court documents was nothing short of a mercenary whose sole reason for betraying his country was the almighty dollar. Pollard defended those accusations by pointing out his belief that it was the United States government which was wrong and that he was true-blue Zionist spying for Israel and not against the United States.

• When it came to damage assessment, Pollard denied that any documents he provided the Israelis harmed the security of the United States or compromised any of their foreign agents. Secretary of Defense Caspar Weinberger, US Attorney Joseph diGenova, and other government officials denounced the denials, calling his efforts nothing short of treason and the damage caused "irrevocable."

• To hear Jonathan Pollard explain it, his lawyer Richard Hibey was incompetent and "sold him out." Joseph diGenova said Hibey was one of the best criminal attorneys in the country and that Pollard had only himself to blame for defying the plea agreement that Hibey had negotiated.

• Pollard accused diGenova and other government prosecutors of forcing him to plead guilty for fear his wife Anne would not receive adequate medical treatment. DiGenova labeled those accusations absurd, arguing that the evidence was so overwhelming against the spy that he had no alternative than to strike a deal in hopes of receiving a "substantial sentence" for his illegal acts.

• Government officials charged that Pollard violated terms of the plea agreement by not cooperating with them in their investigation. Pollard boasted that he passed several lie detector tests regarding the information provided and that he cooperated to the fullest extent possible. Confirming that is impossible since the test results disappeared before sentencing.

• Prosecutor diGenova swore that the Israelis imposed no conditions on documents they provided that confirmed Pollard was a spy. The Knesset report declared the documents had been supplied under the condition that they would not be used against the spy.

• Caspar Weinberger told the *Jewish Week* he filed his memorandum and letter regarding Pollard's conduct and damage to United States security at the behest of Judge Aubrey Robinson. Joseph diGenova called Weinberger a liar, recalling that it was he who requested that the secretary of defense file the documents.

- Supporters of Pollard contended that neither he nor his lawyers had access to classified documents prior to sentencing. DiGenova insisted that the spy and his attorneys had full access to every government document pertinent to the prosecution.

- Pollard attorneys denounced assistant US Attorneys Leeper and Geneson for chastising the spy at the sentencing hearing for violating the plea agreement by authorizing interviews with journalist Wolf Blitzer. DiGenova swears the violation did occur even though prison officials permitted the interviews since the secretary of the Navy was not notified.

- Appellate attorneys argued that lawyer Richard Hibey's admissions at sentencing that Pollard did not consult him about the Blitzer interviews violated the attorney-client privilege. Government officials point out that Hibey had no other choice when Judge Robinson questioned him about the matter.

- Anne Pollard swore that she had an agreement with *Sixty Minutes* to not telecast her interview until *after* the date of the sentencing. DiGenova says interviewer Mike Wallace told him that it was the Pollards who called and demanded that the interview be aired *prior* to the sentencing.

- Alan Dershowitz swore in a court affidavit that former Supreme Court Justice Arthur Goldberg told him that Judge Robinson admitted being biased by information concerning a connection between Pollard and the South African government. DiGenova called Dershowitz a baldfaced liar and "walking legal graffiti" while lambasting him for quoting a man who is dead and cannot be cross-examined.

- Pollard and his supporters criticized assistant United States Attorneys Leeper and Geneson for arguing for a life sentence in front of Judge Robinson in violation of the plea agreement. DiGenova replied that the argument while "tough" was warranted in view of the spy's irreverent conduct both before and after his arrest.

- Supporters for Pollard screamed foul since Pollard was sentenced to "life without parole." DiGenova pointed out that the claim is false since that sentence did not exist at that time and that Pollard was indeed eligible for parole in 1995, though he chose to ignore it so that executive clemency is the sole option for release.

These conflicting viewpoints cloud the Pollard case like no espionage case before it, or since. Two other controverisal issues cause even more confusion among those attempting to decide whether Pollard deserved life imprisonment as a lowlife spy or was the victim of government persecution.

The first involved the argument that Pollard was singled out and unfairly prosecuted because he is Jewish. Government officials have long denied that accusation despite the contrary viewpoint of Pollard supporters such as Professor Kenneth Lasson.

The allegation was intended to rally Jewish groups against what many considered to be an ethnic injustice, but efforts to produce actual evidence of bigotry appeared to be lacking. Other than Secretary of Defense Caspar Weinberger's apparent disgust toward the Israelis, a reflection Pollard supporters swore was evidence of his ill-feeling toward Jews, there did not seem to be adequate evidence to support the charge that the spy was a victim of discrimination because of his heritage.

Many Zionists were proponents of that theory, but Abraham Foxman, director of the powerful Anti-Defamation League, reported that he investigated Pollard's case and uncovered no evidence of anti-Semitism. As a result of his comments, Foxman discovered what it was like to be on what was perceived to be the wrong side of the case. "The only time I have ever been called a Nazi by Jews was by the people who supported Jonathan Pollard," he told the *Washington Post Magazine*. "Because I found no evidence of anti-Semitism, I was accused of being indifferent, insensitive, and having blood on my hands."

In 1988, an investigation led by Phil Baum, executive director of the American Jewish Congress, considered the facts surrounding the Pollard case. "We made an independent effort," Baum reported, "and we could not document any charges of anti-Semitism, no evidence that he was treated differently."

A second note of contention about the Pollard case related to supporters who labeled the case "Dreyfus, American style." That convenient label inflamed those who were familiar with the troubling facts in the French case. For Pollard allies, the comparison was a rallying point.

To opponents it made no sense. Their main argument was that Pollard admitted guilt as a spy, while Alfred Dreyfus, the obscure French captain, was innocent. Pollard supporters discounted that theory, believing that Jonathan was innocent of being a traitor, the label most linked with him.

Close examination of the two cases reveals certain similarities. That is obvious when matters involving background, actual criminal charges alleged, behavior of government prosecutors and judges, length of imposed sentence, and the media are considered.

Dreyfus's heritage traced back to a Jewish family that had emigrated from their native Alsace for Paris when Germany annexed the province in 1871. A quiet man who intended to be career military, he carried out his duties without a blemish to his record as the only Jew serving on the French Army general staff.

In late September 1894, the Army's Intelligence Bureau intercepted a letter (the bordereau). The letter provided the Germans with certain classified documents pinpointing French defenses. Written on a cream-colored slip of lightweight paper that was stamped with squares like graph paper, it contained, in part the following: "…I am sending you some interesting information—1. A note on the hydraulic brake of the 120 mm. gun and on the way it was found to work, 2. A note on the supporting troops… 3. A note on the modification of artillery formations.…"

Purportedly discovered in a wastebasket, the communiqué was addressed to von Schwartzkoppen, the German military attaché in Paris. Disturbed by the revelation, a full-scale investigation was initiated by the minister of war, General Mercier, since it appeared that a member of the French military had become a spy.

To bolster their case, two handwriting experts, Charavay and Teysonnières were summoned. When they alleged that Dreyfus was the culprit, he was arrested and transported in chains to the Cherche-Midi military prison in Paris.

Leading the barrage against Dreyfus was Colonel Jean-Conrad Sandherr, head of the Statistical Section that dealt with counterespionage. An Alsatian like Dreyfus, he was known to be anti-Semitic. When a fellow officer named Major Hubert Henry, who played a significant role in the case later, informed Sandherr about his suspicions of Dreyfus, the colonel yelled, "I should have thought of it," a reference to Dreyfus being Jewish.

On November 1, 1894, the accused spy, the traitor, was first mentioned in the press when government officials leaked his name to *La Libre Parole*. Soon Dreyfus was being bombarded from every direction. *Le Petit Journal* reported that "Had war broken out, Dreyfus would have been a trusted man of the Ministry. He might have sent his comrades to their deaths with his connivance."

Soon, every act of treason in memory was being attributed to Dreyfus. He was accused by one newspaper of having "Russian ties," and that he had been seen in St. Petersburg associating with German officials. In fact, Dreyfus had never been there.

Le Temps and *Le Matin*, two important French dailies, brought romance into the arena by alleging that Captain Dreyfus had an Italian sweetheart stowed away in Nice, and that she was the influence behind his spying actions. In effect, a new Dreyfus had been created, one who looked more guilty. To that end, three newspapers called for the "agent of international Jewry" to be put to death.

On 3 November, the military governor of Paris, General Saussier, ordered a judicial investigation to be headed by Major d'Ormescheville. A month and sixteen days following his appointment, the major prosecuted the case when Dreyfus's trial at the Rue Cherche-Midi, an eighteenth-century palace near the prison, began in secret proceedings. On the 22nd, based only on the handwriting sample analysis, and the testimony of a Major Henry, who swore under questioning from prosecutors and Dreyfus's appointed counsel Edgar Demange that Dreyfus was a traitor, the court-martial judges unanimously found the unlikely spy guilty as charged. Sentenced to life in prison, he was ordered "deported forthwith to a fortified place."

Later it was discovered that the judges were poisoned in their deliberations by having received illegally, according to French military law, a "secret file," or "memorandum." One was forwarded to the court at its request by General Mercier, who provided what will be described during a second look at the case as "documents overwhelmingly against Dreyfus." Neither the condemned man nor his counsel were provided opportunity to examine the Mercier transmission.

In order to further ridicule Dreyfus, he was subjected to a ceremony held in front of fellow military officers in the main courtyard of the École Militaire in Paris. As the convicted man stood before him, General Darras stated for all to hear, "Alfred Dreyfus, you are unworthy to bear arms. In the name of the French people, we degrade you!"

To this pronouncement, Dreyfus screamed, "Soldiers! An innocent man is being degraded! Soldiers! An innocent man is dishonored! Long live France—long live the Army!" Undeterred, an army senior noncommissioned officer ripped off Dreyfus's buttons, badges, and the insignia on his uniform. To emphasize the disgust for the traitor who stood erect and stoic, the officer removed Dreyfus's sword, glared at him, and then broke the sword across his knee.

The degradation continued as Dreyfus was marched before the soldiers shouting, "I am innocent! I am innocent!" Outside the walls, protesters heard the disgraced man's pleas only to whistle and shout, "Death to Dreyfus! Death to the Jew!"

A day later, Dreyfus' family was horrified to read in the French afternoon newspapers that the former captain had confessed to Captain Lebrun-Renaud. On 17 January, the day Félix Faure was elected president of the republic, the convicted man was dragged in chains onto a boat for a voyage to French Guinea and then to his new home for life, the infamous hellhole penal colony Devil's Island off the coast of South America. Right-wing media such as the *La Libre Parole* continued to denounce Dreyfus, espousing his Jewish heritage as the basis for his treason. Believing the captain to be a traitor, one who had confessed, no Jewish resistance was noted, no rallies initiated, no protests lodged even though there appeared to be an anti-Semitic overtone pervading the entire affair.

Jewish nonreaction to the Dreyfus Affair received a tongue-lashing from Bernard Lazare, a Symbolist and writer. "[The lack of protest is] a deplorable habit from old persecutions—of receiving blows and not protesting," he wrote "of bending their backs, of waiting for the storm to pass and of playing dead so as to not attract the lightning." Later he added, "Because he was a Jew, [Dreyfus] was arrested, because he was a Jew he was convicted, because he was a Jew the voices of justice and of truth could not be heard in his favour."

For two years the innocent man suffered the anguish of confinement with the worst of humanity. Finally, in March 1896, a non-Jew, Lieutenant Colonel Georges Picquart, himself an admitted anti-Semite, became French chief of army intelligence. Picquart learned that a letter-telegram (later categorized as the *petit bleu*) had mysteriously appeared in the office of the Intelligence Bureau. This letter was written by Major Count Walsin-Esterhazy, commander of the French seventy-fourth Infantry and addressed to von Schwartzkoppen. Picquart reopened the investigation.

After reviewing the evidence, Picquart was convinced of Dreyfus's innocence, believing Esterhazy to be the guilty party. Though Picquart suffered for his gall in suggesting that the case be reviewed by the courts, his revelation spurred others into action. One was the revered French novelist Émile Zola, whose famous writing *J'Accuse* became the standard-bearer for the demand that Dreyfus be freed.

Zola was intrigued by the case at the insistence of Bernard-Lazare, but it was a conversation with Louis Leblois, the lawyer for the persecuted Picquart, who convinced Zola of the injustice by showing him documents that questioned Dreyfus's guilt.

Deciding to join the fray, Zola, author of such noted works as *L'Assommoir* (Drunkard), which chronicled the sufferings of the Parisian working-class and alcoholism, *Nana*, dealing with prostitution, and *Germinal*, a depiction of the mining industry, wrote his first article on the Dreyfus affair November 25, 1897. In *La Figaro*, he championed a call for what he labeled "a revision of Dreyfus's trial." When Esterhazy's name surfaced as a possible culprit in the case, Zola published two additional articles "The Syndicates" and "The Minutes," both crying out for a reopening of the Dreyfus case. Two more articles, "Letter to the Young People" and "Letter To France," followed before the calendar turned to 1898.

By January, enough suspicion had been cast on Esterhazy that he was ordered to stand trial in military court. When a stunning verdict of acquittal was announced on 11 January, a seething Zola decided to increase his efforts to call public attention to the Dreyfus case.

The result was a letter entitled *J'Accuse* (Georges Clemenceau, later to be president of France, suggested the name), to M. Felix Faure, president of the republic. It was published in *L'Aurore* on January 13, 1898.

After chastising the entire process surrounding the Dreyfus affair, Zola stated,

> Not for one minute do I despair that truth will triumph. I am confident and I repeat, more vehemently even than before, the truth is on the march and nothing shall stop it. The Affair is only just beginning, because only now have the positions become crystal clear: on the one hand, the guilty parties, who do not want the truth to be revealed; the defenders of justice, who will give their lives to see that justice is done. I have said it elsewhere and I will repeat it here: if the truth is buried underground, it swells and grows and becomes so explosive that the day it bursts, it blows everything wide open along with it. Time will tell; we shall see whether we have not prepared, for some later date, the most resounding disaster.

Aware that he was exposing himself to potential civil and perhaps even criminal charges, Zola then listed his accusations utilizing several paragraphs that began with *J'accuse*. There were eight in all, including accusations against: Paty de Clam for miscarriage of justice, General Mercier of being an accomplice, General Billot of suppressing evidence of Dreyfus's innocence, the three handwriting experts of fraud, the War Office of "conducting an abominable campaign in the press in order to cover up its misdeeds and lead public opinion astray," and both court-martial members of violations of law as a result of their finding guilty and sentencing Dreyfus based on secret evidence. Confronting his opponents, he then wrote, "I have but one goal: that light be shed, in the name of mankind which has suffered so much and has the right of happiness. Let them dare to summon me before a court of law! Let the inquiry be held in bright daylight."

Zola's bold comments sold three hundred thousand copies of *L'Aurore* on the Paris streets and his words became the rallying point for those who became known as "Dreyfusards." Riots erupted in Le Havre, Nancy, Bordeaux, Marseilles, and Rennes. Regardless of the outcry, Zola got his wish when both he and Perrenx, the manager of *L'Aurore*, were hauled into court charged with libel. From 7 February to 23 February, testimony rang out from the principal characters in the story. When it was his turn, Zola stated: "Dreyfus is innocent, I swear he is. I stake my life on that. I stake my honor on that." The court disagreed, finding both Perrenx and Zola guilty, with the novelist being sentenced to one year in prison plus a heavy fine.

Due to Zola's accusations and the disclosure that new forged documents had been added to Dreyfus's file by Colonel Hubert Henry, who later committed suicide, the Army examined the case once again. Another court-martial followed, but Dreyfus was found guilty and returned to Devil's Island.

Meanwhile, Zola had fled to England, believing he could do more as a free man to help Dreyfus. When his charges had been dismissed, he returned to his beloved France to renew the fight once again by continuing his parade of words about Dreyfus's innocence. On September 19, 1899, seven days after the article "The Fifth Act" appeared in *L'Aurore*, Alfred Dreyfus was pardoned by Émile Loubet, President of France. Zola died three years and two days later and was applauded by many, including Anatole France, who stated, "Let us envy him, his destiny and his heart reserved for him the most superb of fates: he was a moment in the conscience of mankind."

Twelve years after being convicted, Dreyfus, who had returned from Devil's Island white-haired, bony, and barely able to speak, was exonerated when the Chamber of Deputies overturned the verdict against him in 1906. Despite what the innocent man had endured, he returned to Army duty, was promoted to the rank of Major, and later received the Legion of Honor.

* * *

It is understandable why Pollard supporters align themselves with the Dreyfus case. Both Dreyfus and Pollard were labeled traitors when neither was guilty of that specific offense. Both suffered when the media reported facts that were not true, causing irreparable harm regarding their backgrounds and motives. Both were left to defend themselves without assistance from Jewish leaders, who turned the other way after the media and the government had theorized they were guilty.

In Dreyfus's case, he was accused of treason based on the acts of others, just as Pollard was bombarded with accusations of espionage later determined to have been committed by such individuals as Aldrich Ames. Once sentenced, each was then whisked away; Dreyfus to Devil's Island instead of New Caledonia, where French prisoners were normally sent, Pollard to the mental hospital at the Springfield prison instead of another venue. For all practical purposes both became incommunicado and unable to defend themselves against their harsh sentences.

Pollard supporters allege that just as Dreyfus was unfairly judged by his court-martial, one that utilized false facts contained in a pretrial document, Pollard was sentenced based on misleading and false information contained in the Weinberger memorandum and letter. They point out that Dreyfus's two main supporters were non-Jews, Picquart and Zola. In Pollard's case, the main defender of his rights in court was Appellate Court Judge Stephen Williams, who unlike his Jewish brethren Laurence Silberman and Ruth Bader Ginsburg cried foul for the admitted spy.

Supporters of Pollard insist that in order to investigate the level of impropriety involved with the "Pollard Affair," Émile Zola's passage in *J'Accuse*, "Let the inquiry be held in broad daylight," is warranted. To prove that the persecution of Pollard equates with that of Dreyfus, they demand that the United States government declassify documents and produce actual evidence against the spy that warranted a life sentence. Only then, they say, will the truth be revealed.

Chapter 21

POLLARD AND DUE PROCESS

W*ebster's Dictionary* provides several definitions of "justice" imperative to debating the Jonathan Pollard case. They include: "The quality of being just, moral, rightness," "The administration of what is just according to the law," "To act fairly toward," and "The administering of deserved punishment or reward."

Based on these definitions, the ultimate question arises: Has justice been served in the Pollard case, or has there been a miscarriage of justice?

Answering that question requires an independent examination, one separating fact from fiction. Doing so permits an evaluation of whether Jonathan Pollard's constitutional rights to due process have been violated. That is essential, since even Pollard, who admitted guilt, is guaranteed the same rights as the innocent.

Paramount to any debate regarding due process is an understanding of the motives behind Pollard's decision to spy. Comparisons with others who broke the law to further a political agenda is also beneficial, as is an assessment of the damage caused by Pollard's spying efforts. Once those facts have been evaluated, questions regarding the competence of Pollard's counsel, consideration of the government's conduct regarding the plea agreement, potential bias on the part of Judge Aubrey Robinson, and the appropriateness of the life sentence can be addressed.

Despite the enormous publicity surrounding the Pollard case, few have thoroughly researched his background in order to gain a clear understanding of *why he did what he did.* Clearly, the young boy who grew up to be arguably America's most controversial spy was a product of loving parents who impressed upon him the importance of the continued preservation of the State of Israel. At a very early age, based on his view that he was persecuted for being a Jew, he adopted an "Israel first" credo that affected every decision he made as an adult.

As fate would have it, Pollard, a devout Zionist, was elevated to a post at the NIS where access to the relationship between US intelligence interests and those of Israel were at a loggerhead. Despite its duty to do so, Pollard believed, the United States was withholding security data vital to Israel's survival.

Based on that frame of reference, Pollard was certain his spiritual homeland was in peril. Faced with a moral, ethical, and yes, legal dilemma as to whether to betray the nation of his birth, Pollard's heart won over his brain even though his conscience told him that he was breaking the law.

The government alleged that Pollard was nothing short of a mercenary, but that argument conflicts with evidence that the spy was quite concerned about Israel's plight. Though he accepted compensation, albeit it nominal, and expenses for two European trips, the Jonathan Pollard who spied appeared to do so out of the heartfelt belief that he was aiding the ally Israel while not harming US interests. This assertion seems valid, for even during the flurry of providing classified documents to his handlers, Pollard was steadfast in refusing their demand for information that would have compromised US interests.

Prosecutors must have been aware that Pollard, if he had chosen to, could have compromised American security and earned millions of dollars by serving foreign governments that were enemies of the United States. His refrain from doing so (at the time of his arrest, Pollard had no savings, was heavily in debt, and drove a five-year-old car) didn't excuse his illegal actions, but it was an indication of the straightforward allegiance the spy had for his beloved Israel.

Where Pollard made his mistake, one acknowledged by even his most fervent supporters, occurred when he accepted money for his spying duties. He recognized that as well in an August 1986 memorandum to the court. He wrote:

> In spite of this disquieting aspect of my case, I never considered myself to be a mercenary, no matter how corrosive the payments were on my sense of personal integrity. Luckily, my ideology prevented me from descending to a level where I would reflexively respond to Rafi Eitan's commands, like some type of Pavlovian dog. As I've previously mentioned, when he requested information which I considered to be incompatible with my objectives and intentions I simply did not pro-

vide the material. It might be instructive to remember that unlike most mercenaries, I had no blackmail threat which could be directed against me. In fact, the classical roles of compromised agent and manipulative handler were actually reversed in this affair and if any party were vulnerable to extortion, it was the Israeli Government, which politically had a great deal to lose if my activities were discovered. Therefore if I were simply motivated by greed, I should have exacted a King's ransom for my services each time a delivery was made to the Israelis. That I did not demand an increasing amount of money during this operation should indicate that my ideological convictions were fundamentally genuine.

When all is said and done though, I did accept money for my services. That fact has a way of suggesting the worst kind of motive in a spy, a species not generally well regarded to begin with. Yet even idealistically inclined spies cannot exist on altruism or sheer stamina for very long because of the rate at which they tend to deteriorate from fear, exhaustion, and a guilty conscience. Unlike an agent operating behind enemy lines, I knew what I was doing was wrong and constantly tried to keep my spirits up by reminding myself that the information I was providing Israel was essential to its survival. But in the absence of any conventional yardstick by which I could determine my absolute worth to the state, I accepted the payments as a reflection of how well I was doing my job....

Pollard's remarks rationalizing the remuneration he received revealed a confused state of mind, but not a warped one. Pollard, through both his actions and his inactions, proved that he was a spy with a conscience.

"I never acted like a vacuum cleaner," Pollard told journalist Elliot Goldenberg. "My tasking was quite precise—and always limited to that material which was either being denied Israel in violation of the bilateral intelligence-sharing agreement, or was in some way being distorted by the United States."

Pollard alleged he refused to provide any data regarding intelligence sources the United States utilized in Israel believing that would surely compromise security interests. He also said he refused to provide the Israelis with any US confirmation of their arms agreements with other nations, including China, and denied his handlers information concerning the US presence of Israeli operatives. In effect, Pollard was a "selective" spy, agreeing only to provide Israel with data that assisted them, but didn't harm US interests.

When considered objectively, the matter of motive seems clear. During the months that he committed espionage, Pollard was a dedicated spy whose primary intention was to arm Israel with intelligence information he believed critical to its very existence. Any other assessment of his motive, despite his having accepted compensation, appears to ignore the facts.

* * *

Evaluating Pollard's conduct and how it will be perceived in history requires examination of those who ignored the law to achieve what they believed to be the greater good. Two familiar names to be included in that category are Mahatma Gandhi, who said, "To forgive and accept injustice is cowardice," and Martin Luther King Jr., who believed protest was "a duty."

Daniel Ellsberg intended no harm to his country when he divulged the Pentagon Papers bearing the title, *US Decision Making In Vietnam, 1945–1968*. In fact, Ellsberg, who had served in the war, believed that exposure of the information was his duty. During an interview at the University of Berkeley dubbed, "Conversations with History," Ellsberg said, "I saw…a president [Johnson] making secret threats, almost sure to carry them out, and deceiving the public as to what he was doing."

While the Ellsberg case reflected the mind-set of one who believed that disobedience was paramount to disclosure of the truth, the case of that genre that most parallels Pollard's involved the American scientist Theodore Hall. As portrayed in the book, *Bombshell: The Secret Story of America's Unknown Atomic Spy Conspiracy*, by Joseph Albright and Marcia Kunstel, Hall was a idealist youngster and whiz-kid physicist at Harvard thrust into the production of the atomic bomb in the mid-1940s. Selected to work on what was dubbed the supersecret Manhattan Project ramrodded by J. Robert Oppenhemier, Hall's selection was surprising in view of his background.

Similarities between Hall and Pollard abound. Pollard was immersed in books about Israeli history at an early age, while Ted Hall told Albright and Kunstel that he was consumed with reading about "French and British appeasement of Hitler." He also stated, "There was a lot of argumentation in the literature. There were books written which seemed to show very convincingly that the Allied nations actually encouraged the development of German fascism." He added, "The books were around the house and I remember discussing them." Based on those assertions, the authors surmised that with Hall, "Seeds of doubt about the capitalist system [America] were strewn already at this early age."

Like Jonathan Pollard, Ted Hall was instilled with the belief that being Jewish was an impediment to attaining any sort of success. Just as Jonathan's father's brother had decided a change of name was in order for "business reasons," so did Ted's brother Ed. Ted Holtsberg, age eleven, thus became Ted Hall.

The rebelliousness that pervaded Ted Hall's persona as a teenager was akin to that of Pollard. Just as Jonathan had been irritated with a rabbi who didn't care for the particulars of a speech he prepared in anticipation of his Bar Mitzvah, Ted Hall experienced ridicule when he produced a draft of his Bar Mitzvah speech for his rabbi. It professed the dangers of fascism in America and, according to authors Albright and Kunstel, was rejected for being "too polemical." To get even, Ted Hall and his brother played a practical joke on the rabbi and were reprimanded.

If the employment of Jonathan Pollard as an intelligence analyst appeared in hindsight ludicrous based on his Zionist views, then the selection of Ted Hall to be the youngest scientist working on the atomic bomb was even more so. Those who recruited Hall at age eighteen after his studies at Harvard failed to account for his anti-American views. A simple background check would have revealed his affinity for Russia, one symbolized by his writings in several right-wing publications and his membership in the local John Reed Society.

While Pollard became entrenched at Naval Intelligence in the 1980s, Ted Hall's sojourn to Los Alamos, New Mexico, in the mid-1940s catapulted him into the inner workings of the most important scientific experiment of the twentieth century. Working alongside revered scientists such as Edward Teller and Niels Bohr, Hall, a brilliant physicist, became knowledgeable regarding every aspect of the atomic bomb.

While Pollard believed that the United States was preventing Israel from securing important security information, Hall questioned the mass destructive capabilities of the bomb. As time progressed an inner voice told him that the world should share the secret. Otherwise, he felt that the United States could inflict great harm on its enemies and perhaps even its allies. One, Hall knew, was the Soviet Union, where distrust of Stalin by US leaders made their Allied partnership shaky at best. What if America turned the wrath of the bomb on Russia, Hall speculated? Or fell into a postwar depression and possessed an atomic monopoly?

Ted Hall decided that he must act to preserve a balance of atomic power in the world so that Russia would not be annihilated. To that end he requested a two-week leave from his duties at Los Alamos and traveled to New York City. Just as Pollard had met Colonel Sella, Hall made contact with a Soviet envoy and embarked on a clandestine mission to pass intricate details of the Manhattan Project to the Russians.

Both Pollard and Hall married strong women who accepted their revolutionary views as gospel. Joan Hall became fervent in the belief that her husband Ted was correct in aiding Russia's cause just as Anne Pollard supported Jonathan's allegiance to Israel.

Rationalization by Hall for his illegal behavior paralleled that of Pollard. Both asserted that they did not assist the enemy. Both believed that it would have been an act of cowardice if they had not taken action. Both acted, they said, out of passion and not for money, although Pollard's actions were clouded by money while Hall was indignant about accepting money and never did.

Inspection of the exact nature of documents passed by Hall to the Soviets produced another parallel between the two spies. While the government was pronounced in its assertion that Pollard stole secrets that jeapardized US interests, FBI agents investigating Hall charged that his actions could have amounted to absolute obliteration of America. If, they said, the secrets Hall passed to the Russians would have resulted in their creation of the atomic bomb first, the course of history could have been radically altered.

When Hall addressed his motives, it appeared that like Pollard, he was torn with dual loyalty. While he believed that the US had provided him with educational opportunities and the chance to succeed, he scorned government policies. His distrust of its allegiance to Russia as an ally, he said, propelled his belief that the Soviets must have access to the bomb. "…It seemed to me that an American monopoly was dangerous and should be prevented," he explained to authors Albright and Kunstel.

In effect, Hall's political philosophy had interjected into his frame of mind the absolute requirement that he commit espionage. Like Pollard, he was not a traitor in the true sense of the word, since Russia was an ally under siege from the Germans.

While Pollard was exposed in 1985, Ted Hall, due to investigative deficiencies, was never charged though several others were. He relocated to England where he spent his elder years teaching and fighting cancer.

Had Hall been apprehended, no doubt exists that a conviction would have resulted in a severe penalty, perhaps even death since public opinion at the time of his actions was clear. When Julius and Ethel Rosenberg were executed for aiding those spying for Russia, the populace accepted the punishment as just. Fifty years later, many question the wisdom of that sentence (as many do now regarding Pollard), wondering whether it was appropriate, for like Hall, the Rosenbergs were acting out of conscience, and at least in their mind, not to the detriment of US interests.

Based on investigation of the Hall case, authors Albright and Kunstel provided their view as to how to assess the conduct of those who decide that they are right and the law is wrong. In *Bombshell*, the authors wrote, "Ted Hall was not the first or last to break a law he thought was wrong. But the impact on a society is both explosive and unpredictable when people choose not to accept the rule of law…Civil disobedience has been a tool of dissent from Gandhi's India to Martin Luther King, Jr.'s South, a tool of people who have no choice but to break laws that crush their lives. But civil disobedience is a public protest by people whose commitment is defined by their willingness to go to prison." One might add, when discussing the Pollard case, "and for how long."

Authors Albright and Kunstel also observed, "The mix of morality and politics that make up Ted Hall's story is complicated and colored in a spectrum of varying shades, depending on the eyes of the viewer." The exchange of Jonathan Pollard's name for Hall's in that text is appropriate, providing a standard of measurement for both the conduct of Pollard and his punishment.

Chapter 22

DAMAGE ASSESSMENT

Did the actions of Jonathan Pollard jeopardize American national security and place US intelligence agents in harm's way? Answering that question depends on personal interpretation, for even those who have read court documents and other classified material regarding the extent of the spying disagree as to the long-term effects on both the United States and Israel. Those not privy to such documents and information can only speculate as to the damage. Early on, Pollard's appeal lawyers applied for the security clearance necessary to inspect the documents and information. Their request to do so was denied. That inflamed Representative Lee Hamilton of Indiana, who wrote to Dr. Pollard that "I agree with you that the Weinberger statement was a key document and that your lawyers shoud have had access to the document.... That would appear to be an extraordinary denial."

Confusing the issue is the fact that the damage assessment report (VIS) provided to Judge Aubrey Robinson was prepared with input from Caspar Weinberger. Not only was he indicted by a grand jury for obstruction of justice and several other crimes, but prosecutor Joseph diGenova, a defender of Weinberger's since the mid-1980s, said he was untruthful when the former secretary of defense alleged that he filed his Pollard memorandum and letter at the behest of Judge Aubrey Robinson.

Weinberger's credibility is further impacted by knowledge that he was opposed to providing Israel with security information despite the US-Israel Exchange of Information Agreement. His motives can be questioned because he believed Pollard had assisted in exposing the Iran-Contra Affair, which caused him to be indicted.

Besides Weinberger and diGenova, who prosecuted the spy, Pollard's most visible antagonist throughout the past decade was journalist Seymour Hersh. Without pause he continued to beat the drum against any reprieve for the convicted spy.

Hersh's 1991 book *The Samson Option*, which dealt with Israel's nuclear capability, charged that Pollard was responsible for the passing of more than five hundred thousand pages of classified documents to the Israelis. Included were, according to Hersh, "Top-secret American intelligence on the location of Soviet military targets, as well as specific data on the Soviet means for protecting those targets."

In 1999, Hersh chastised Pollard in a scathing article for the *New Yorker* entitled "The Traitor, The Case Against Jonathan Pollard." He suggested that Pollard had become a "cause célèbre in Israel and among Jewish groups in the United States" and pointed out that in Israel, "Pollard's release was initially championed by the right, but it has evolved into a mainstream political issue." Hersh wrote that "[American] officials told me [Pollard] had done far more damage to American national security than was ever made known to the public, for example, he betrayed elements of four major American intelligence systems."

Hersh further alleged, "In their eyes, there is no distinction between betraying secrets to an enemy, such as the Soviet Union, and betraying secrets to an ally....Many officials said they were convinced that information Pollard sold to the Israelis had ultimately wound up in the hands of the Soviet Union."

Regarding motive, Hersh wrote, "Pollard's argument that he acted solely from idealistic motives and provided Israel only with those documents which were needed for its defense was a sham designed to mask the fact that he was driven to spy by his chronic need for money." Hersh also noted that in his opinion the indictment against the spy would have been much more inclusive if not for the plea bargain agreement. "Before the plea bargain," Hersh wrote, "the government had been preparing a multi-count indictment that included—along with espionage, drug and tax-fraud charges—allegations that before his arrest Pollard had used classified documents in an unsuccessful attempt to persuade the governments of South Africa, Argentina, and Taiwan to participate in an arms deal for anti-Communist Afghan rebels who were then being covertly supported by the Reagan Administration."

Hersh's source for the allegations was journalist Kurt Lohbeck, whom Hersh admitted had a "checkered past." Nevertheless, the journalist furthered his allegations that Pollard was no better than a mercenary, quoting Lohbeck as saying, "I never heard anything political from Jay other than he tried to portray himself as a Reaganite. Not a word about Israel. Jay's sole interest was in making a lot of money."

Lohbeck, according to Hersh, labeled Pollard a drug addict, a charge Pollard denied. Nevertheless, Hersh quoted Lohbeck as saying, "Jay used cocaine heavily and he had no compunction about doing it in public. He'd just lay it in lines on the table."

Returning to the specificity of the spying allegations against Pollard, Hersh wrote, "Documents that Pollard turned over to Israel were not focused exclusively on the *product* of American intelligence—its analytical reports and estimates. They also revealed *how* America was able to learn what it did—a most sensitive area of intelligence systems and how they worked." As an example, Hersh alleged that "[Pollard] betrayed details of an exotic capability that American satellites have of taking off-axis photographs from high in space."

Regarding his long-held beliefs that the Israelis passed Pollard's documents to the Russians, Hersh explained, "One longtime CIA officer who worked as a station chief in the Middle East said he understood that 'certain elements in the Israeli military had used it'—Pollard's material—'to trade for people they wanted to get out' including Jewish scientists working in missile technology and on nuclear issues."

Journalist Hersh argued that Pollard had passed data contained in an in-house Navy document dubbed RASIN, an acronym for radio-signal notations. "The manual," Hersh wrote, "which is classified 'top-secret Umbra,' fills ten volumes, is constantly updated and lists the physical parameters of every known signal. Pollard took it all." Hersh further quoted an unidentified "former" communications-intelligence officer who observed, "It's the Bible. It tells how we collect signals anywhere in the world." Hersh then added, "The site, frequency, and significant features of Israeli communications—those that were known and targeted by the National Security Agency (NSA) were in the RASIN; so were all the known communications links used by the Soviet Union."

Hersh quoted another source as saying, "[RASIN] is a how-to-do-it book—the fireside cookbook of cryptology. Not only the analyses but the facts of how we derived the analyses. Whatever recipe you want."

Hersh concluded his diatribe against Pollard by alleging that he passed daily messages to the Israelis that detailed every movement in the Middle East as recorded by the NSA's most sensitive monitoring equipment. The information gathered was, Hersh reported, through his use of DIAL-COINS (Defense Intelligence Agency's Community On-Line Intelligence System), a computer that retrieved all intelligence reports filed by Navy, Marine, and Air Force personnel located in the Middle East. Hersh said Pollard utilized the SIGINT Requirements List, a top secret listing of requested intelligence coverage that could provide knowledge of anticipated aggression by the United States in a specific area of the world.

Pollard supporters believed that Hersh was an out-of-control journalist obsessed with the spy case. They charged that his research was faulty. Their position was bolstered in 1998 when one of Hersh's allegations was refuted.

That concerned Pollard's passage of RASIN documents and others of a security nature. That he did so appeared unlikely after ex-NSA senior cryptologic traffic analyst David Boone pled guilty to providing the Soviets with a four-hundred-page manual listing American reconnaissance programs and signal collection systems. Those illegal activities occurred in the mid-1980s when Pollard was awaiting sentencing by the court.

Regardless, Hersh, a Pulitzer Prize winner, wrote that he agreed with the assessment of a career intelligence officer familiar with the Pollard case. "He has come to view Pollard as a serial spy, the Ted Bundy of the intelligence world," Hersh said.

Combating Hersh's allegations were Pollard support groups such as the Zionist Organization of America (ZOA). They revealed that many of the journalist's sources were less than credible. ZOA referred to Ari Ben-Menashe, whom Hersh admitted was his source for the accusations that secrets passed to the Israelis by Pollard landed in the hands of the Soviet Union. The ZOA quoted a *Jerusalem Post* article labeling Ben-Menashe as a "notorious chronic liar." The ZOA also reported that *Newsweek*, which they said, "is hardly sympathetic to Israel," concluded that "Much of what Ben-Menashe says does not seem to check out."

Investigative journalist Steven Emerson provided his analysis of the Ben-Menashe matter. In a November 11, 1991, *Wall Street Journal* article, Emerson concluded, "Ben-Menashe has made numerous demonstrably false claims." Among them, the journalist wrote, was Ben-Menashe's claims that, "He was a commander of the Israeli raid to free hijacked airline passengers at Entebbe in 1976, that he planted a homing device in the Iraqi nuclear reactor at Osirak just before the Israeli attack in 1981,…and that he declined an offer to become head of the Mossad."

In 1990, Ben-Menashe was subjected to a lie detector test by ABC News. Producer Christopher Isham told *Newsweek* in a November 11, 1991, article that "he failed it."

Hersh's book *The Samson Option* had been criticized since its publication. *London Sunday Times* investigative reporter Peter Hounam told the *New Republic*, "It's a mystery to me that they went ahead and published that book, knowing that so much of the material is wrong." A *Jerusalem Post* article in 1991 called the *Samson Option* "unreliable" and a "sham." In March 1992 the *Washington Times* alleged, "Hersh's Israel-bashing is so egregious…it gives journalism a bad name."

After *The Samson Option* was published, Hersh, who burst into prominence in 1972 by breaking the My Lai massacre story, admitted that he had been duped by Joe Flynn, a principal source for the book. "Certainly being the victim of a hoax is not pleasant," he told the *Washington Times*.

Criticism regarding the former *New York Times* reporter's attention to accuracy was directed at his penning of biographies about former *Times* executive editor A. M. Rosenthal, and Henry Kissinger. In 1997, Hersh's reputation suffered during his penning of *The Dark Side of Camelot*, an expose on the Kennedy myth. Hersh boasted about the exploits of a handwriting expert whose opinion was prominently featured in the book. The author was embarrassed when ABC News exposed the source as a fraud.

* * *

To Seymour Hersh's charges, Jonathan Pollard long protested his innocence. Time and time again he reiterated his belief that the classified documents he stole were utilized to protect Israeli security interests and did not in any way harm the United States.

New York Senator Charles Schumer believes the damage done by Pollard to US interests was minimal. After having been privy to classified documents, he swore that based on his knowledge little validity could be given to the accusations that Pollard harmed his country to the extent the government alleged. His contention was that "the punishment should fit the crime" and that Pollard's sentence was "excessive."

Angelo Codevilla, a former senior staff member of the Senate Intelligence Committee and professor of international relations at Boston University, supported Jonathan Pollard's position. In an interview with the *Washington Weekly*, the conservative Republican stated, "Jonathan Pollard was a GS-12 intelligence analyst without access to vital secrets. That's someone who is making $40,000 a year with no access to vital secrets." Asked by reporter Wesley Phelan the exact nature of the documents, Codevilla replied, "He gave them part of the flow of US intelligence which they used to receive regularly, but which the US cut off after 1981. As you know, the US has a long-standing, mutually beneficial intelligence exchange relationship with Israel. We give Israel a lot of information. In 1981 Israel used some of that information to strike and destroy Iraq's nuclear reactor. Bobby Ray Inman, at the time Deputy Director of the CIA, was very angry, and cut off a good chunk of that information."

Codevilla claimed in his interview with Phelan to posess personal knowledge of the situation. "I was in the US Intelligence Committee hearing room when Inman came in and told us how outraged he was that Israel had destroyed Iraq's nuclear reactor," Codevilla said. "He told us that the US was engaged in a 'sophisticated and very successful effort' to turn Saddam Hussein into a pillar of American foreign policy in the Middle East. The Israelis, in their 'blundering ways,' as he put it, had misunderstood Saddam Hussein. They had figured this nuclear reactor posed a danger of Saddam building nuclear weapons. The CIA knew better than that, and was outraged that the Israelis had done this. As a result, Inman was unilaterally cutting off the flow of US intelligence to the Israelis."

In December 1994, Inman was denied an attempt to become Secretary of Defense. His chief antagonist, revered columnist William Safire, chastised him for his role in the Pollard case, alleging that "Inman's animus contributed to the excessive sentencing of Pollard." The columnist wrote that Inman was "solely responsible" for cutting off vital information to the Israelis. "As an executive, he's a flop, as a judge of character, he is a naïf, and as a taxpayer, he's a cheat." Inman, who believed Safire and William Casey conspired to block his advancement in the CIA, was charged by Safire as having planted a false story that Israel was the source of rumors that a Libyan "hit team" was intent on assaulting the United States.

Regarding Pollard's role, Angelo Codevilla explained, "[He] was a young, Jewish intelligence analyst in the Office of Naval Intelligence who wrongly took it upon himself to provide to Israel that which had been cut off. This consisted of intelligence 'products.' I emphasize the word products. It was satellite pictures, reports of all kinds, electronic directories, so on and so forth. Jonathan Pollard could not have provided codes because he did not have any access to codes. GS-12 analysts don't."

Queried as to whether Pollard could have transferred satellite photographs of US and Soviet nuclear installations, Codevilla said:

No, not US installations.…He gave them primarily Middle Eastern information. You must understand that from an intelligence point of view, the subject of a report, coming from any given source, is not nearly as important as the source. What intelligence people rightly worry about are what they call 'sources and methods.' This is what Pollard did not have access to. Compare what Pollard did—giving away satellite photographs—with what William Kampelis did in 1978. He sold the [Soviets] the operating manual for the KH-11, which is our picture taking satellite. This was a log book which told you how the satellite worked, how it operated, what its schedule was, etc. Kampelis was sentenced to forty years, but he was let out about five years ago, after serving fourteen years. Pollard, who never gave out any operating manual to any intelligence system, is in jail for life. What he gave out were satellite pictures.…The US was still giving Israel pictures of southern and western Syria. Pollard was giving them pictures of eastern Syria and Iraq. So in terms of satellite intelligence SOURCES, his impact was nonexistent.

When Phelan said, "Well, the news reports say that he [Pollard] gave a whole room full of documents to the Israelis," Codevilla offered, "That's a lie." When Phelan followed up by saying, "They say many cubic feet of documents," the professor replied,

> A lie is an untruth that is known to be an untruth. The intelligence people who say those things include all of the documents in the bibliographies and table of contents of the documents Pollard turned over. In other words, if Pollard turned over a book with bibliography containing 50 books, he was accused, unofficially, mind you, because a distinction must be made between what he has been unofficially accused of and actually punished for and what he was officially indicted for. If you add up all the bibliographies in all the documents he turned over, you might say that they would fill a small room. But what he actually gave away was seven briefcases full, neither more nor less. Seven briefcases do not a room fill, except in the imaginations of insincere people.

Pollard proponents contend that Hersh's claims and those of other government officials who continue to condemn Pollard's actions fifteen-plus years later are wrong. Those supporters maintain that the damage done by the spy was indeed minimal as substantiated by Schumer, Codevilla, and officials of the Israeli government.

Similar to Émile Zola's proclamation regarding the Dreyfus Affair, the *Washington Post* called for full disclosure in a January 25, 1999, editorial.

> As far as we are concerned, this man has earned no favor, no mercy, no benefit of any doubt. It would not surprise us to learn from the full dossier that he deserves the full sentence. But as a defendant in an American courtroom he should have the protections available to others on trial. Right now he is in the position of having his fate determined in part by materials to which he had no access and proceedings of which he was not a part. The requirement here is not for relief for a loathsome and guilty spy but for some degree of greater openness for the American people. Especially with the passage of time, cannot a way be found to pierce some of the secrecy and provide the public with a better means of judging whether fairness was achieved in this case?

Those searching for justice in the Pollard case believed the *Post's* position was valid. They pointed out that the two chief accusers of the spy were Caspar Weinberger, indicted for perjury and obstruction of justice, and Seymour Hersh, a journalist whose sources and research techniques were discredited.

Chapter 23

THE FATE OF JONATHAN POLLARD

Every American has the right to be represented by competent legal counsel. When that representation falls below certain standards, justice cannot prevail.

Review of the counsel provided in the initial stages of the Jonathan Pollard case requires an assessment of the conduct of Richard Hibey. To do so in hindsight, more than fifteen years after the representation of his most famous client, must be undertaken with great care. That since only Hibey knows the exact details that led to critical decisions he made on behalf of Pollard. Since he will not discuss the case, his side of the story is left untold.

Within days of Pollard's arrest, Richard Hibey was hired by Dr. Morris Pollard to represent his son. Hibey was a respected Washington, DC criminal defense attorney who had experience as a former assistant United States attorney. As such he was savvy to the federal court system and acquainted with the inner workings of Joseph diGenova's office.

Early on, Richard Hibey assessed the government's case against his client and decided that it was overwhelming. The Israelis had aided that effort by supplying documents stolen by Pollard. Against the weight of the evidence, Hibey held one trump card, which he never played. It involved recognition that the government avoided at all costs public trials which might compromise national security and embarrass certain government officials.

In 2001, attorneys for FBI agent Robert Hansen, charged with espionage for passing secrets to the Soviet Union, avoided the death penalty for their client by pressing for a trial. Why Hibey did not utilize a similar strategy only he may know.

Instead of standing firm, Hibey approached Joseph diGenova and his deputies regarding a plea bargain at his client's behest. That was contrary to Pollard's statement that he was forced to plead guilty because of concern over wife Anne's mental condition.

Attempts to uncover the truth produce a logjam. No one except Pollard and Richard Hibey know what occurred and neither will change their version of the story. What is clear is that plea bargain agreements were struck that both Pollards agreed to honor.

Richard Hibey's competence as Pollard's attorney must be assessed on the basis of that document and how the lawyer dealt with its provisions. Careful scrutiny reveals that it appeared open-ended with several details left unaccounted for. Joseph diGenova swore that it was "boilerplate," but with so much at stake in a high-profile case, it was unfortunate that the respective parties did not clarify the specifics so that each would be certain of their responsibilities.

After Pollard was sentenced, two critical provisions in the plea agreement warranted scrutiny. The first was the "media approval" clause.

Richard Hibey could not have foreseen that Pollard would fail to notify him of the interviews with journalist Wolf Blitzer. That infuriated Judge Robinson, a former trial lawyer who realized what insubordination meant to a lawyer.

When Hibey was asked in court if he had knowledge of the interviews, he had no alternative than to answer "no." Whether he should have embellished on the answer, perhaps by detailing miscommunication between attorney and client, to suffocate the damage appeared appropriate.

Richard Hibey possessed one alternative that he should have considered. That was to withdraw as Pollard's counsel after he learned of, and then read, the Blitzer interviews. At that point the bond of trust between attorney and client had been severed, and Hibey must have had reservations about representing a client who was rebellious. When he failed to withdraw, Pollard was represented by a lawyer who no longer supported him 100 percent.

Indicative of the rift between lawyer and client was an exchange at the sentencing hearing. When Judge Robinson, who didn't appear to have much sympathy for Anne Pollard's pain due to her stomach ailment, noted that Anne was moaning, he asked Richard Hibey, "You don't need another recess, do you?"

"No," Richard Hibey replied. "We are prepared to go forward."

Judge Robinson then noticed that Anne was crying. "Is she all right?" he asked.

"Yes, sir," Hibey said.

Jonathan Pollard, who was staring at his wife in disbelief, then shouted "No!" while noting that Anne was now cradling her stomach with her arms.

For a split second, Richard Hibey's and Jonathan Pollard's eyes locked. Pollard's anger was apparent, and Hibey turned his head and said, "May we have a break, Your Honor?"

Richard Hibey's overall demeanor at the sentencing hearing disturbed Pollard supporters. According to those in attendance he appeared less than enthusiastic when arguing for his client. When Caspar Weinberger's letter criticizing Pollard was revealed by the judge and Hibey perused it, the lawyer appeared shaken by its contents. Nevertheless, he did not ask for a continuance or attempt to counter Weinberger's accusations with a strong rebuttal. Instead he retired to his seat at counsel table with the appearance of an attorney who realized the inevitable and was powerless to alter its course.

Regardless of Richard Hibey's performance, Pollard loyalists believed it was clear that the government acted in bad faith regarding the media clause. Despite Pollard's nondisclosure to his attorney, and diGenova's proclamation that the secretary of the Navy had to be advised of the Blitzer interviews and was not, the government, they alleged, acted wrongfully. That since Pollard had received permission from prison officials who were present at the time Blitzer conducted not one, but two interviews, with the spy after receiving written approval.

What effect the Blitzer media interviews had on Judge Robinson's mind-set and the ultimate sentence is speculative. According to those present in court, he appeared quite upset with the development, and with that of Anne Pollard's *Sixty Minutes* interview.

Richard Hibey's efforts regarding a second provision in the plea agreement drew fire from Pollard supporters and his appellate attorneys. It concerned the degree of cooperation his client provided the government. Without specific guidelines as to what the cooperation amounted to, both sides were left to their own interpretation. Joseph diGenova and his deputies believed that Pollard was untruthful, and nothing Richard Hibey said convinced the judge otherwise.

Pollard allies claimed that no matter what had been agreed to in the plea bargain, prosecutors had no intention of honoring any of the conditions contained in the agreement. Joseph diGenova disputed that argument and Richard Hibey won't comment.

* * *

When considering the *Webster's Dictionary* definition of "justice" that requires "The administering of deserved punishment or reward," multiple factors enter into the equation.

In evaluating the prison term to be imposed on Jonathan Pollard, Judge Robinson, like any judge in any criminal case, compiled a file that listed information regarding background, criminal record (Jonathan had none), motives for committing the crime, impact of the crime on the victim, in this case the United States government, chances of recidivism, and the likelihood of rehabilitation.

That completed, Judge Robinson factored affidavits of character witnesses supporting the defendant as well as affidavits of those chastising his behavior. He also considered the degree of cooperation by the defendant, or lack thereof, and any other points of mitigation made aware to the court.

All this tallied, the sentencing judge consulted sentencing guidelines and considered the recommendation of the prosecution in accordance with any plea bargain agreement. He researched comparable sentences imposed on defendants who had committed similar crimes.

If Judge Robinson adhered to this procedure, and there is no evidence to prove otherwise, he knew that he could sentence Pollard to any number of years to and including life imprisonment. He also knew that the government was requesting a "substantial sentence," whatever that was.

One such case Judge Robinson would have considered (see Appendix for chart listing similar sentences), involved Ensign Stephen Baba, who pled guilty in 1982 to passing documents relating to electronic warfare secrets and indices of code words to officials at the South African embassy. He was court-martialed and sentenced to eight years at hard labor. He served only two.

In 1985, Samuel Morison, a naval employee and coworker of Pollard's, sold a classified satellite photograph to *Jane's Defense Weekly*, a British publication, and received two years in prison. That despite allegations that the disclosure provided the Soviets with far more capability to understand United States satellite operations. A year later, CIA employee Sharon Scranage was convicted of revealing CIA operatives in Ghana to her boyfriend, a Ghana national. She was sentenced to five years in prison, later reduced to two.

When sentences relating to those spying for an enemy of the United States were considered, David Barnett was sent to prison in 1981 for eighteen years due to his disclosure to the Soviets of dozens of US operatives. In other cases, William Holden Bell, who provided a Polish agent with classified information on antitank missiles and radar technology, received eight years, Ernst Forbirch received fifteen years from a Florida judge for purchasing of US military secrets with the intention of passing them to East Germany, and Svetlana Ogorodnikova, a Soviet émigré, was sentenced to eighteen years for conspiring with an American, Richard Miller, to pass classified documents to the Russians.

While those cases occurred prior to Pollard's, an analysis of spies sentenced since provides comparisons that are also worthy. *New York Daily News* columnist Sydney Zion had particular interest in the case involving Michael Schwartz, a Navy lieutenant commander who passed military secrets to Saudi Arabia from 1991 to 1994. Zion wrote, "Schwartz got the kid glove treatment from the Navy; he pleaded guilty on a couple of charges lesser than espionage and was set free with nothing more than a 'less than dishonorable' discharge." He then added, "His arrest, his plea, his sentence went virtually unnoticed by the media and brought forth no attacks on the Saudis from any corner, including the White House, the State Department, the CIA, the Congress, and the Jewish establishment [whereas] Pollard became an overnight villain, a synonym for 'dual loyalty,' the bugaboo that has shivered American Jews since the advent of the State of Israel. The difference? Schwartz, despite his name, is a gentile, Pollard is a Jew…"

Significanct to those who believe Pollard's sentence to be disproportionate is the five-year sentence meted out to Abdelkaer Helmy, an Egyptian-born American citizen. While working at a weapons plant in California in 1988, he exported to Egypt 420 pounds of materials used in the manufacture of stealth aircraft, missiles, and rockets. Those weapons were being developed by Egypt in tandem with Iraq.

To Pollard's allies, evaluation as to whether his sentence was appropriate required comparison with similar penalties imposed on infamous spies John Walker, Jr., and Aldrich Ames. Walker provided, among other things, the Soviet Uniton with the ability to decipher intelligence information translated through coding machines. That provided the Soviets with an indefinable advantage in dealing with US intelligence.

The acts of Aldrich Ames were even worse. Over a nine-year period (1985–1994), he provided the Soviets with the existence of fifty intelligence operations and the identities of thirty-four US agents stationed there. Those disclosures resulted in the capture and death of twelve agents. Ames's actions permitted the Soviets to provide false intelligence information through the agents they turned.

Ames's exploits affected the Pollard case, since he avoided detection by alleging that Pollard was the source of classified information being passed to the Soviets. That based on the theory that documents Pollard passed to the Israelis were then provided to the KGB by spies within the Israeli government. Pollard was later cleared of those charges, but the stain of this association contributed to his lengthy imprisonment.

Both Walker and Ames, who spied for enemies, unlike Pollard, who spied for an ally, were given life sentences. Pollard supporters alleged that close inspection of the acts of the three men clearly indicated that Pollard's betrayal of his country pales in comparison to the other two. Should each have received the same penalty, they asked, when Pollard's crime involved espionage with a close ally of the United States that had no intention, as the Soviets did, of harming US interests?

Three additional cases bear mentioning when assessing the appropriateness of Pollard's sentence. The first involved former NSA analyst Ronald Pelton. Exposed for selling the Soviets information regarding American attempts to tap secret data from undersea cables utilized by the Soviets, Pelton was permitted to plead guilty in return for a forty-year sentence.

The second related to David Boone, the NSA senior cryptologic traffic analyst who, as previously mentioned, supplied the Soviets with vital information about US reconnaissance programs and signal collection systems. Exposed in 1998, Boone, whose crimes had been attributed to Pollard by journalist Seymour Hersh, was sentenced to twenty-four years in prison.

In 2001, spy Robert Hansen was permitted to plead guilty to espionage. Despite government charges that he passed secrets to the Russians for 15 years and was responsible for the deaths of two double agents, Hansen was sentenced to life imprisonment like Pollard.

Since comparisons of cases both before and after Pollard's indicate that his sentence was extraordinary in length (life), assessment is required as to the motives behind Judge Robinson's decision. While it seems evident that he found the actions of the spy and his wife to be despicable, there is supposition that the court considered another factor when deciding Pollard's fate. It relates to Judge Robinson's intent on punishing the State of Israel, Pollard's coconspirator, for its betrayal.

Pollard spoke of that possibility when he answered charges concerning the passage to the Israelis of documents outlining Iraq's completion of chemical warfare facilities that were under construction in the mid-1980s. In a 1989 letter penned from his prison cell, he stated, "In retrospect, perhaps one of the most damaging things that the Reagan administration did to Israel during the course of our trial was that it purposely distorted the nature of my activities in such a way so as to leave the impression that Israel had become a threat to the national security of this country. So by intent, the subsequent sentence I received was an arrow aimed directly at the heart of the US—Israel's special relationship.'"

If true, then Jonathan Pollard was given a heavier than normal sentence for spying for an *ally* of the United States than he would have if he had spied for an *enemy*. Certainly the attitudes of State Department officials and Caspar Weinberger toward the Jewish state alerted Judge Robinson to their disdain for that country's participation in the spy scheme. If so, then the judge was left with an indelible impression: A person spying for an ally of the US was even more culpable than one spying for an enemy, since spying was expected by enemies of the US, but not of allies.

That meant when Jonathan Pollard stood in front of Judge Robinson and was sentenced to life imprisonment, it was actually Israel that was being condemned and punished. And taught a very significant lesson: Don't ever again employ a mole to spy against your closest ally.

B'nai B'rith former president Seymour Reich's assessment bolstered that belief and took it one step further. He told the *Washington Post Magazine* that the defense establishment was "Trying to teach Israel a lesson, trying to teach American Jews a lesson, or trying to teach American Jews in government a lesson." If that was the motive, then government officials inflamed Judge Robinson with their rhetoric, portraying Pollard as an agent for Israel who must be punished to the full extent of the law.

Pollard's appeals lawyer Hamilton Fox, III believed that Israel's denial of its responsibility during the first few days after Pollard's arrest set the tone for a "let's show them" attitude in both the State and Defense Department. "The analogy I like to give is finding your wife in bed with your closest friend," Fox said. "It hurts more because it was your best friend. And Israel being one of the closest allies we have, it was a bit more. The American attitude was, 'We are going to send those bastards a message.'"

To do so, the government labeled Pollard a "traitor." Each time that occurred, either in the media or through Caspar Weinberger's memorandum, the word was further embedded into Judge Robinson's mind. That, the government must have hoped, would impede his ability to separate Pollard's actions for an ally from those who aided the enemy. If Judge Robinson's thinking was swayed in that direction, a life sentence for Pollard was much more probable.

Based on that contention, the Jonathan Pollard that stood before Judge Robinson on judgment day was 1) A spy for Israel, which had the audacity to betray its devoted ally, the United States, and 2) A "traitor" who should be treated like one who passed documents to the country's worst enemy. Combined with the judge's abhorrence for Pollard's conduct regarding the Wolf Blitzer interview, and his alleged noncooperation with the government, it was no surprise that the spy received the maximum possible punishment, life in prison.

* * *

Final analysis as to whether Jonathan Pollard's constitutional rights to due process were violated leading to a miscarriage of justice depends, of course, on the viewpoint of the beholder. At the least, concerns regarding his legal representation, the validity of evidence used against him in the damage assessment report, the prosecutor's conduct regarding Pollard's interviews with Wolf Blitzer, and the longevity of the sentence pronounced indicate that the Pollard case is indeed fraught with more questions than answers.

That is evident when focusing on the most glaring aspect of the Pollard case, the prison sentence imposed. With that in mind, Pollard supporters believe the case cries out for a resolution permitting the spy to be released and deported to Israel. Opposition to that potential centers on the belief by Pollard opponents that fifteen-plus years later, the spy remains a threat to US national security.

That argument is often proposed by the government, but no better version outlines their position than a 1995 letter from United States Attorney Eric Holder. It was written to John R. Simpson, regional commissioner for the United States Parole Commission.

Addressing Jonathan Pollard's suitability for parole, Holder urged the commission to "read the unclassified supplemental affidavit submitted by Secretary of Defense Caspar Weinberger which summarizes the damage to the national security of the United States caused by Pollard." Holder then attempted to persuade the commission to buy his argument stating, "Pollard's conduct since his sentencing demonstrates that he remains a threat to the security of the United States of America."

To bolster its position the government submitted portions of a letter sent by Pollard to the *Jerusalem Post*. Among other things, he was quoted as saying, "If it's true that I have indeed enhanced Israel's military capabilities to the point where it bothers Secretary Weinberger's Saudi paymasters, then I'm quite satisfied what I did was right…"

Summing up, Holder wrote, "If Pollard's lack of remorse for a crime which compromised the national security of the United States is not enough to assure that he should not be paroled, his steadfast refusal to comply with nondisclosure agreements even after his conviction and sentencing demonstrate that Pollard's parole would pose a continuing risk to the national security of the United States." In a footnote, he added, "The United States Intelligence Community is providing an independent statement of its reasons for opposing Pollard's parole. In that statement, Pollard's continuing violations of his nondisclosure agreements with the United States are summarized."

Holder's allegations aside, government officials' attempts to allege that Pollard has knowledge of critical US secrets is dubious, since he has been in prison for fifteen-plus years. Whether he remains a security threat must thus be assessed on what he knew at the time of his arrest. How that information can be relevant as the twenty-first century dawns is difficult to comprehend.

Until proof is offered that Pollard is indeed a threat to US security, one fact is known for certain: no spy *ever* aiding an ally of the United States has been sentenced to more than fourteen years. Even William Kampelis, who spied for an enemy, the Soviet Union, in the late 1980s, received forty years in prison. He was released after being incarcerated for nineteen years.

If justice requires that the punishment fit the crime, then there is adequate basis for concluding that Pollard's sentence should not exceed Kampelis's. That term of imprisonment, forty years, would appear to satisfy the government's goal of punishing Pollard while deterring others who might consider spying for Israel.

In a January 2001 interview, Pollard prosecutor Joseph diGenova altered his position regarding Pollard's penalty by stating that he did not disagree with a forty-year sentence. "I would have been pleased with that," he stated in reference to the original sentence imposed by Judge Robinson.

If one of Pollard's most vitriolic critics believes a substantially lesser sentence was appropriate, then the case demands extensive review. Only then will there be the opportunity to right a wrong and correct any semblance of a miscarriage of justice.

POSTSCRIPT

Besides one's health, freedom is the most precious commodity a human being possesses. Since 1985, Jonathan Pollard has been denied that freedom.

In the Butner, North Carolina federal penitentiary, Pollard occupies a cell smaller than most people's bathroom. His world is literally and figuratively constricted. He is told what to do and when to do it. He cannot walk across the street, attend the synagogue of his choice, or talk to any outsider without permission. Life for him is an endless string of cloudy days even when the sun shines brightly on the vast expanse of empty fields adjacent to the prison.

During his years of incarceration, he has endured the horror of a mental hospital where mentally ill people nearly drove him insane, solitary confinement three stories below ground where his only companions were rats and cockroaches, and isolation in a cell while he was verbally abused and threatened for his political beliefs and because he is Jewish.

Without doubt, the spy has experienced the mental anguish of never knowing quite what to think of events affecting his case outside the prison walls. Several times it appeared that he might be released. Then those hopes were dashed. How his psyche was affected by individuals who promised to assist him, then reneged, cannot ever be imagined.

Pollard also has experienced the collapse of his storybook marriage to Anne, and suffered the guilt of having been responsible for her imprisonment. The spy's family unit has disintegrated to the point where he has no contact with his father, mother, or sister. Unless he is released soon, he will never be united with his parents, since their health is failing due to interminable anguish over his imprisonment.

Jonathan's health is deteriorating as well. Those who have visited him report he suffers from depression, high blood pressure, chronic arthritis, and diabetes. "He is pale, swollen and his immune system is crippled," says Esther Zeitz-Pollard.

Based on all aspects of Pollard's punishment, when is enough enough? When has the point been reached where even those who have called for a pound of flesh, believing that the spy got what he deserved and should not be the recipient of sympathy, will be satisfied that he has suffered beyond their cruelest expectations? When will government officials or Pollard's enemies admit, based on an independent evaluation of the facts, that the time has come to end this man's nightmare?

To provide perspective, saviors for Pollard scream from the mountaintops that no one has proven Jonathan is a cold-blooded murderer, a child molester, a rapist, or a bunko artist who scammed elderly investors out of their life savings. To the contrary, it appears, his actions portray an individual who did not jeopardize American lives, but saved countless Israelis and others through his efforts.

One who could have balanced the scales of justice and restored his freedom was the president of the United States, Bill Clinton. Even though he had declined to do so at the Wye River Summit, another chance existed prior to his leaving office.

Joseph diGenova believed the president would free Pollard. In October 2000, he told this author, "According to people who know very, very well, this deal has been set up by Charles Ruff [former White House counsel]. It was Ruff who negotiated clemency for the Puerto Rican terrorists. In that case, there was no communication with the victims of the slaughter including the police officers and the individuals who were maimed for life. He did not consult with the Justice Department. We have been informed that Mr. Ruff has done the same thing in the Pollard case, and that the nature of the agreement, if the President chooses to do it, is that Mr. Pollard would be granted clemency but would not be released until after Mr. Clinton leaves office."

Attempts to confirm diGenova's claims regarding the participation of Charles Ruff became impossible when he died of a heart attack days following the 2000 presidental election. If a deal was brewing, there was no evidence of it when the Pollard case once again made headlines in December 2000. In a *New York Times* article titled "Pressure Is Again Emerging To Free Jonathan Pollard," reporter David Johnston wrote,

"Government officials said that the White House had given no indication that Mr. Clinton planned to reopen the Pollard case." DiGenova embraced that choice, stating, "This is a decision of such gravity that it will taint the president's legacy forever. It is absolutely indefensible from either a legal or humanitarian standpoint to grant clemency to this American citizen who had done the gravest kind of damage to the United States."

Opposing that view was the *Jewish Week*, which featured an article entitled, "Lame-Duck Push For Pollard." Urging President Clinton to free the spy, Rabbi David Saperstein said, "Clinton's lame-duck status gives him an opportunity to reconsider the situation free of external influences, and make a decision of what's appropriate and fair." Attorney Kenneth Lasson added, "Right now Clinton has nothing to lose."

On December 3, 2000, Jonathan Pollard penned a one-page letter from his prison cell that began with the salutation, "Dear Mr. President." The tone of the letter was remorseful, echoing personal thoughts that Pollard hoped would persuade President Clinton to provide clemency by January 20, 2001, his final day in office. In paragraph two, Pollard wrote, "I am writing to you personally, Mr. President, to express my deep regret for what I did." Three paragraphs later, he added, "I fully appreciate that what I did was wrong. Grievously wrong. My intent was to help Israel, but I had no right to violate the laws of this country or the trust placed in me. I had no right to place myself above the law."

Regarding the effect of his conduct on others, Pollard wrote, "For the rest of my life, I will have to live with what I did, as well as with the pain I caused my family, the American Jewish community, and this great nation." He closed by saying, "I know you are a man of great humanity and compassion. I ask, most respectfully Mr. President, that you accept this personal expression of profound remorse, and ask from the bottom of my heart that you grant me clemency and commute my sentence, so that together with my wife I can rebuild my life and leave a better legacy than the one I currently have."

To this painfully poignant letter, there was no White House response. As January 20, 2001, neared, millions of Pollard supporters world-wide hoped for a last-second reprieve, but none came.

That despite Clinton's pardon and commutations of sentences of more than 140 individuals during his final days in office. They included high-profile figures such as former Congressman Daniel Rostenkowski, half-brother Roger Clinton, Whitewater figure Susan McDougal, former CIA director John Deutch, ex-Housing Secretary Henry Cisneros, and SLA kidnap victim Patty Hearst. All were pardoned.

Among those imprisoned whose sentences were commuted was Kemba Niambi Smith, convicted of conspiracy to distribute and possess cocaine and conspiracy to engage in money laundering. Another was Bobby Franklin Griffin, incarcerated for bribery and mail fraud.

President Clinton drew the ire of many when he pardoned sixty-six-year-old billionaire fugitive financier Marc Rich, who fled the country to avoid fifty-one counts of tax evasion, racketeering, and conspiracy. Rich, whose former wife Denise was a heavy financial contributor to both Clinton and wife Hillary, was also accused of "trading with the enemy" after purchasing more than $200 million worth of oil from Iran despite President Jimmy Carter's ban on trade with that country during the hostage crisis.

New York Times journalist William Safire, in a February 1, 2001, column titled "Isn't It Rich?" noted a difference between Marc Rich and Jonathan Pollard. "Rich's former wife contributed over $1 million to Democratic campaigns," Safire wrote, "while Rich's direction of some ill-gotten gains to charities induced Israel's Ehud Barak to use up his one big pardon favor with Clinton, dooming the unrich Jonathan Pollard to a life in jail."

Doomed was right, for it appeared that Clinton had decided to pardon either Pollard or Rich, but not both. When Barak touted Rich and not Pollard, the spy was truly left out in the cold. Pollard supporters were incensed when they heard that Jewish leader and ADL head Abraham Foxman wrote a letter in behalf of Marc Rich. He even acknowledged that the idea to seek a pardon was his. That occurred shortly after Rich contributed $100,000 to the ADL in early 2000.

Pollard loyalists and countless other Americans were livid at the president's actions. The *Justice4JonathanPollard* website pointed out that while Clinton had "abandoned" Pollard, he had awarded pardons to, among others: "Murderers, kidnappers, armed banked robbers, burglars, crack cocaine dealers, racketeers, extortioners, money launderers, embezzlers, and those convicted of bank fraud." Unlike Pollard, deprived of every civil right, these individuals had theirs restored, meaning that they could vote, carry firearms, and have their record cleansed of any felonies.

Additional insight into the Marc Rich pardon was uncovered on 8 February when Indiana Representative Dan Burton convened hearings on the matter. Appearing as witnesses were Rich's attorney, former White House Counsel Jack Quinn and Deputy Attorney General Eric Holder.

Testimony revealed that Israeli Prime Minister Barak, instead of championing Pollard's cause for clemency, had "on several occasions" telephoned President Clinton begging for Rich's pardon. When Eric Holder told Clinton's White House counsel that he was "neutral, but leaning toward approval," based on Barak's plea, the President pardoned the fugitive.

Most disconcerting to Pollard supporters was the appearance of his prosecutor Joseph diGenova. He sat stone-faced in the row behind Quinn, who had retained him as personal counsel. To Pollard loyalists, that meant that while diGenova condemned Pollard, and fought with his every breath to keep him incarcerated, he believed that a pardon was proper for a fugitive of justice who betrayed the United States by dealing with enemies.

Why clemency or a pardon for Pollard did not occur was left to conjecture. Supporters contended that the President "did not want to upset the new President and others in his administration" by releasing the spy. Continued unrest in the Middle East between Israel and the Palestinians during the month before Clinton left office could have weighed in. Or perhaps release of Pollard was too big a political risk for the president.

Details regarding the behind-the-scenes maneuvering during Clinton's final hours in office were revealed in the June 2001 issue of *Vanity Fair.* Journalist Maureen Orth wrote, "The greatest electoral gift Clinton could have bestowed on Barak—probably over the dead body of US intelligence—was a pardon of convicted Israeli spy Jonathan Pollard, who is a cause célèbre in Israel."

Of the strategy employed by Quinn and former Israeli intelligence officer Avner Azulay, head of the Rich Foundation in Tel Aviv, Orth alleged, "Azulay and Quinn cleverly planted the seed in Clinton's mind that if he couldn't give the Israelis Pollard, he should give them Marc Rich." The journalist then quoted an e-mail Quinn typed after a discussion with White House counsel Beth Nolan. It read, "Lastly, I told her that, if they do hot pardon JP, then they should pardon MR."

Sixteen days before the President's final day in office, Azulay, working from inside Israel, the country Pollard had given up his freedom for, commented on the pardon matter again. According to Orth, he wrote, "I am convinced that the President is aware releasing JP will be a big problem with the intelligence community and Mr. R can be included in this since less attention will be paid to him.... If he [President Clinton] says no to JP, then this is another reason to say yes to Mr. R."

What Orth and the Burton Committee did not realize is that while influence was being sought at the highest levels of government for Marc Rich, the savvy attorney Quinn knew that not only was Deputy Attorney General Eric Holder a good friend easily influenced, but that Holder was a strong opponent of Pollard's release. The attorney held a trump card no one was aware of since, if Holder were forced to choose between Rich and Pollard, the fugitive would win out.

When Holder was informed that Barak was backing Rich in his telephone conversations with the President, that made it easy for him to cast his vote for Rich since he knew that meant any pardon for Pollard was dead. Orth, the Burton Committee, and the media's failure to question Holder about his anti-Pollard stance was unfortunate since it was critical to understanding why Marc Rich was pardoned and Pollard was not.

Surfacing in Orth's article was the allegation by Pollard's sister Carol that she was "solicited for a million dollars for a pardon for her brother— 'no guarantees.'" Carol Pollard later told supporter Beverly Newman that while "I was dubious of the offer," the contact boasted that "if I raised the money, Jonathan would be out in twenty minutes."

Carol Pollard did not raise the required funds. Whether the offer was genuine remained a mystery.

President Clinton's failure to release Pollard left him only the immediate hope that the courts would save him. If they denied his motions for sentence review, the spy faced the prospect of a continued lengthy incarceration. That since it appeared unlikely he would be released during the administration of President George W. Bush and Vice President Dick Cheney, an outspoken Pollard critic. CIA Director George Tenet, who had threatened to resign if President Clinton acted, continued his post under George W. Bush.

When Pollard learned the news that Clinton had declined to provide clemency, it must have been the darkest of all dark days. His hopes had been quashed, and the man who had viewed international events such as the election of three presidents of the United States, a war in the Gulf, four Olympic games, and the dissolution of the Soviet Union through prison bars had to believe that he would never leave his prison cell.

If Clinton wouldn't step forward, and President Bush was disinclined to do so, who would be the paladin for Pollard? Perhaps it would be a congressman or senator deciding to convene hearings regarding Pollard's plight or demand his immediate release, a leader in the American Jewish community dedicated to saving Pollard, or a high-level Israel official determined to free the spy his country abandoned. Perhaps Ted Olson, the new solicitor general, might pursue an investigation of his former client's case.

If Israel, at some point during its political dealings with the United States, stood firm and issued an edict that unless Pollard was released, it would not accede to whatever the US requested, then the spy had a chance to win his freedom. The Israelis had come close once, during the Wye River peace talks, but folded when President Clinton changed his mind. Whether they could muster the proper means to force the United States to act remained to be seen as the George W. Bush administration took charge.

To stand strong, perhaps the Israeli government should consider what would have occurred to the precious Jewish homeland if Pollard had *not* acted as he did. Without his efforts, perhaps Israel would have suffered from not only being denied the security information withheld, but from the misinformation being passed along. Either way, it appears that the State of Israel owes Jonathan Pollard a great debt of gratitude. The only way to repay him is through gaining his freedom.

Israel's first contact with President George W. Bush accomplished nothing toward speeding the release of Pollard. At a summit in early 2001, new Prime Minister Ariel Sharon barely mentioned the spy's name, if at all. In June 2001, he embraced peace efforts spearheaded by CIA director George Tenet, a staunch Pollard critic who upset the Jewish community by praising Yasser Arafat.

Pollard's most powerful ally should be the Jewish community, but it has failed to win his release. Besides strong rhetoric, their most potent weapon is money and votes, primary needs for any political candidate. During national elections,, Jews who back Pollard must stand united and firm and demand his guaranteed release as a prerequisite for their support.

Loyal supporters will continue to fight the fight for a man they perceive is a true guardian of Israel. They vow that those who have denied Pollard justice will be punished in accordance with the Bible verse that reads, "Israel is the Lord's hallowed portion, They that devour him shall be held guilty, Evil shall come upon them."

Meanwhile, until Pollard's Émile Zola appears, the Zionist whose case symbolizes a black mark on American jurisprudence will sit in his dank prison cell pondering why the United States government, as Joseph diGenova so chillingly stated, never wants him "to see the light of day." Will a prison guard will ever stand outside his cell and say, "Jonathan, you are going home"?

BIBLIOGRAPHY

Bombshell: The Secret Story of America's Unknown Atomic Spy Conspiracy, Joseph Albright and Marcia Kunstel, Random House, 1997.

Captain Dreyfus, Nicholas Halasz, Simon and Schuster, New York, 1955.

The Dreyfus Affair, J'Accuse and other Writings, Alain Pagès, Yale University Press, New Haven and London, 1966.

Firewall: The Iran-Contra Conspiracy and Cover-Up, Lawrence Walsh, W. W. Norton, New York, 1997.

A History of the Jews, Paul Johnson, Harper & Row, New York, 1987.

The Hunting Horse: The Truth Behind the Jonathan Pollard Spy Case, Prometheus Books, New York, 2000.

Oral History Project Document, The Historical Society of the District of Columbia Circuit, 1992.

Pollard: The Spy's Story, Bernard Henderson, Alpha Books, New York, 1988.

The Secret War Against the Jews, John Loftus and Mark Aarons, St. Martin's Press, New York, 1994.

Shadow: Five Presidents and the Legacy of Watergate, Bob Woodward, Simon and Schuster, 1999.

Spider's Web: The Secret History of How the White House Illegally Armed Iraq, Alan Friedman, Doubleday, 1993.

The Spy Who Knew Too Much, Elliot Goldenberg, S.P.I. Books, New York, 1993.

The Spy Who's Been Left In The Cold, Peter Perl, *Washington Post Magazine*, Washington, DC, July 1998.

Territory of Lies, Wolf Blitzer, Harper & Row, New York, 1985.

APPENDIX
Photo Gallery

Jonathan Pollard on the cello at age 13

Johnathan Pollard at age 16

Jonathan with his parents, Mollie and Dr. Morris Pollard

Jonathan Pollard at age 18

Jonathan Pollard in Washington, DC

Jonathan and Anne Pollard in 1984

Colonel Aviem Sella
Israeli war hero and Pollard's contact

AP/Wide World Photos

GlobalSacan International

AP/Wide World Photos

Raphael "Rafi" Eitan, an intelligence
branch officer in Israel's Defense Ministry

Jonathan Pollard being transported
in 1985

AP/Wide World Photos

US Attorney, Jospeh diGenova,
Federal Prosecutor

Former US Secretary of Defense,
Caspar Weinberger

Jonathan Pollard in Springfield, Missouri prison in 1987

Jonathan Pollard with his sister Carol, visiting
him in prison in 1986

*The Federal Correction Complex, in Butner, N.C., where
Jonathan Pollard was sent to serve a life sentence for spying*

*Esther Pollard holds her husband Jonathan Pollard's
Israeli passport during an interview with the
Associated Press in Jerusalem Tuesday, Oct. 28, 1997*

Pollard Chronology

08/07/1954	Jonathan Pollard is born in Texas.
05/01/1960	Anne Louise Henderson is born in New York.
08/1961	Pollard family moves to Indiana.
1970	Jonathan Pollard studies in Israel.
1972/1976	Pollard attends Stanford University and gains a B.A. in Political Science.
1977/1979	Pollard attends Fletcher School of Law and Diplomacy.
09/19/1979	Pollard is hired as a civilian Intelligence Research Specialist by the U.S. Navy.
1981/1982	Pollard and Henderson meet; they share an apartment in Washington, DC.
05/24/1984	Pollard and Israeli Colonel Aviem Sella have first telephone conversation.
05/29/1984	Pollard and Colonel Sella meet in Washington, DC.
07/07/1984	Pollard and Sella meet for the second time.
07/21/1984	Pollard and Sella meet for the third time; Anne Henderson and Colonel Sella's wife Yehudit, are present.
07/25/1984	Pollard accepts money for spying.
07/28/1984	Pollard delivers documents to the home of Ilan Ravid, a science counselor at the Israeli embassy. Colonel Sella tells Pollard he must return to Israel and cannot be his contact.
Fall/1984	Pollard is promoted to the Navy Anti-Terrorist Alert Center (ATAC).
Fall/1984	Pollard and Anne travel to Paris to meet Colonel Sella, Eitan, and Yagur. Pollards visit South of France, Italy, and Germany at Israeli expense.
07/1985	Pollard and Anne travel to Tel Aviv. Pollard is promised a Swiss bank account "retirement fund," which is never activated.
08/09/1985	Pollard and Anne are married in Venice, Italy.
11/18/1985	Federal agents intercept Pollard outside ATAC headquarters.
11/18/1985	Anne Pollard warns Colonel Sella. Sella flees country.
11/19/1985	Pollard is interrogated by federal agents. He does not expose Israel.
11/20/1985	Pollard is again interrogated. Later he telephones the Israeli embassy requesting sanctuary. He is told, "Jerusalem wants you to come in."
11/21/1985	Pollard accompanies Anne to physician; then drives to the Israeli embassy. When sanctuary is denied, Federal Agents immediately arrest Pollard.
11/22/1985	Anne and Dr. Pollard visit Pollard in the DC jail. Anne is arrested outside.
11/22/1985	Anne is held in isolated detention. It continues for 95 days.
11/27/1985	Anne and Pollard appear before the federal magistrate and are indicted on one count of transmitting classified information. Bail is denied.
05/26/1986	Anne and Pollard sign plea-bargain agreements.
06/04/1986	Judge Aubrey Robinson accepts guilty pleas from Anne and Pollard.
03/03/1987	Caspar Weinberger's secret memorandum is delivered to Judge Robinson.
03/04/1987	Pollard is sentenced to life imprisonment, Anne to five years.
1987/1988	Pollard is jailed at US Medical Center for Federal Prisoners, Springfield, MO.
02/1988	Pollard is transfered to Marion, IL federal prison.
03/31/1990	Anne Pollard released from prison.
03/20/1992	Federal Court of Appeals denies Pollard's appeal.
02/1994	Pollard is transferred to Federal Correction Complex, Butner, NC.
03/23/1994	President Clinton denies Pollard's request for clemency.
09/20/2000	Pollard lawyers file appeal based on incompetence of defense lawyer.
01/2001	Pollard begins his sixteenth year of incarceration.
01/20/2001	President Clinton denies pardon to Pollard; pardons wealthy fugitive Marc Rich.

TREATIES AND OTHER INTERNATIONAL ACTS SERIES 10617

DEFENSE
Security of Information

Agreement Between the
UNITED STATES OF AMERICA
and ISRAEL

Effected by Exchange of Notes
Signed at Tel Aviv and Jerusalem
July 30 and December 10, 1982

NOTE BY THE DEPARTMENT OF STATE

Pursuant to Public Law 89-497, approved
July 8, 1966 {80 Stat. 271 I. U.S.C. 113}—
"...the Treaties and Other International Acts Series issued
under the authority of the Secretary of State shall be completed
evidence...of the treaties, international agreements other than
treaties, and proclamations by the President of such treaties and
international agreements other than treaties, as the case may be,
therein contained, in all the courts of law and equity and of
maritime jurisdiction, and in all the tribunals and public offices
of the United States, and of the several States, without any further proof or authentication thereof."

ISRAEL

Defense: Security of Information

Agreement effected by exchange of notes
Signed at Tel Aviv and Jerusalem July 30 and December 1982;
Entered into force December 10, 1982.

EMBASSY OF THE
UNITED STATES OF AMERICA

Tel Aviv, July 30, 1982

No. 97

Excellency:

I have the honor to refer to the exchange of notes between the Honorable U. Alexis Johnson for the Secretary of State of the United States of America, and the Honorable Avraham Harman, Ambassador of Israel, signed on March 25, 1963, at the Department of State, Washington D.C., concerning the protection of classified information exchanged between our two governments.

The United States Government believes it is desirable to update and record the basic principals [sic.] which govern the exchange of such information. I have to honor to propose, therefore, a confiscation of the mutual understanding, that, with respect to the exchange of such classified information communicated between our two governments, the following principles will apply to information designated by the Government of the United States as "Confidential," "Secret" or "Top Secret" and to information designated by your Government as coming within the purview of this agreement.

His Excellency
Yitzhak Shamir
Minister of Foreign Affairs of Israel

GENERAL SECURITY OF INFORMATION AGREEMENT

"1. All classified information communicated directly or indirectly between our two governments shall be protected in accordance with the following principles:

a. the recipient government will not release the information to a third government of any other party without the approval of the releasing government;

b. the recipient government will afford the information a degree of protection equivalent to that afforded it by the releasing government;

c. the recipient government will not use the information for other than the purpose of which it was given; and

d. the recipient will respect private rights, such as patents, copyrights, or trade secrets which are involved in the information.

"2. Classified information and material shall be transferred only on a government-to-government basis and only to persons who have appropriate security clearance for access to it.

"3. For the purpose of this agreement classified information or material which is the interests of national security of the releasing government, and in accordance with applicable national laws and regulations, requires protection against unauthorized disclosure and which has been designated as classified by appropriate security authority. This includes any classified information, in any form, including written, oral or visual. Material may be any document, product or substance on, or in which information may be recorded or embodied. Material shall encompass everything regardless of its physical character or makeup including, but not limited to, documents, writing, hardware, equipment, machinery, apparatus, devices, models, photographs, recordings, reproductions, notes, sketches, plans, prototypes, designs, configurations, maps, and letters, as well as all other products, substances, or items from which information can be derived.

"4. Information classified by either of our two governments and furnished by either government to the other through government channels will be assigned a classification by appropriate authorities of the receiving government which will assure a degree of protection equivalent to that required by the government furnishing the information.

"5. This agreement shall apply to all exchanges of classified information between all agencies and authorized officials of our two governments. Details regarding channels of communication and the application of the foregoing principles shall be the subject of such technical arrangements (including an Industrial Security Agreement) as may be necessary between appropriate agencies of our respective governments.

"6. Each government will permit security experts of the other government to make periodic visits to its territory, when it is mutually convenient, to discuss with its security authorities its procedures and facilities for the protection of classified information furnished to it by the other government. Each government will assist such experts in determining whether such information provided to it by the other government is being adequately protected.

"7. The recipient government will investigate all cases in which it is known or there are grounds for suspecting that classified information from the originating government has been lost or disclosed to unauthorized persons. The recipient government shall also promptly and fully inform the originating government of the details of any such occurrences, and of the final results of the investigation and corrective action taken to preclude recurrences.

"8. a. In the event that either government or its contractors award a contract involving classified information for performance within the territory of the other governments, then the government of the country in which performance under the contract is taking place will assume responsibility for administering security measures within its own territory for the protection of such classified information in accordance with its own standards and requirements.

b. Prior to the release to a contractor or prospective contractor of any classified information received form the other government, the recipient government will:

(1) insure that such contractor or prospective contractor and his facility have the capability to protect the information adequately.

(2) grant to the facility an appropriate security clearance to this effect.

(3) grant appropriate security clearance for all personnel whose duties require access to the information.

(4) unsure that all persons having access to the information are informed of their responsibilities to protect the information in accordance with applicable laws.

(5) carry out periodic security inspections of cleared facilities

(6) assure that the access to the information is limited to those persons who have the need to know for official purposes. A request for authorization to visit a facility when access to the classified information is involved will be submitted to the appropriate department or agency of the government of the country where the facility is located by an agency designated for this purpose by the other government. For the United States, the request will be submitted through the U.S. Military Attaché in Tel Aviv; for Israel will be submitted through the Israeli Military Attaché or Procurement Mission to the U.S. as appropriate. The request will include a statement of the security clearance, the official status of the visitor and the reason for the visit. Blanket authorizations for visits over extended periods may be arranged. The government to which the request is submitted will be responsible for advising the contractor of the proposed visit and for authorizing the visit to be made.

"9. Costs incurred in conducting security investigations or inspections required hereunder will not be subject to reimbursement."

This understanding will apply to all exchanges of such information between all agencies and authorized officials of our two Governments, whether at the respective capitals of our two countries, at international conferences or elsewhere. Any other arrangements between our two Governments, or their respective agencies relating to the exchange of such information will, to the extent that they are not inconsistent with these principles, not be affected by this understanding. It is understood, however, that the foregoing does not commit either Government to the release to the other of any classified information or material.

If the foregoing is agreeable to your Government, I propose that this note and your reply to that effect, designating the types of information your Government wishes covered, shall supersede the March 25, 1963 agreement on this matter effective on the date of your reply.

Accept, Excellency the renewed assurances my highest consideration.

[Signed William A. Brown]
Charge d'Affaires, ad interim

Jerusalem, December 10, 1982

Mr. Ambassador,

I have the honor to acknowledge receipt of the note No. 97 of July 30, 1982 from Mr. W.A. Brown, Charge d'Affaires, ad interim, concerning the protection of classified information exchanged between our two governments.

In reply, I have the honour to inform you that the proposals made therein are acceptable by the Government of Israel who therefore agree that your Note and the present reply shall supersede the March 25, 1963, agreement on this matter, effective on the date of this reply.

The types of information designated by the Government of Israel to which the arrangements would apply are all information furnished by the Government of Israel and classified [Hebrew term omitted] (restricted or for official use only), "Confidential" [the equivalent in Hebrew omitted] or "Top Secret" [the equivalent in Hebrew omitted].

Accept, Mr. Ambassador, the assurances of my highest consideration.

Yitzhak Shamir

His Excellency
Mr. Samuel W. Lewis
Ambassador of the U.S.A.
in Israel

TIAS 10617

Spy Sentencing Comparison Chart

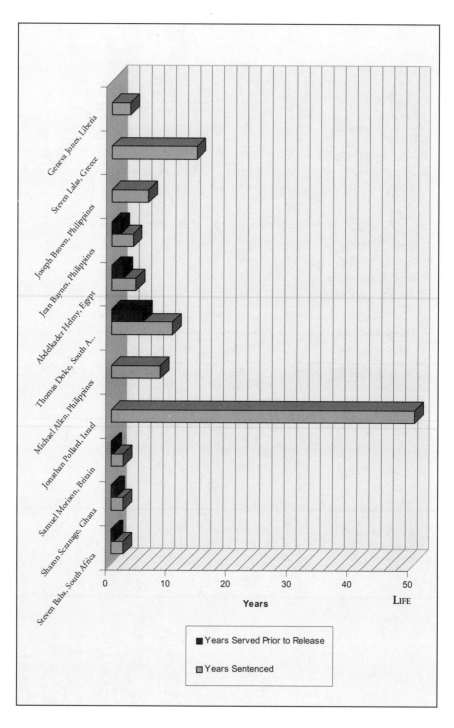

Spying For Allies of the United States

Name	Spied For	Punishment/Incarceration
Michael Allen	Philippines	8 years
Steven Baba	South Africa	8 years/2 years
Jean Baynes	Philippines	41 months/15 months
Joseph Brown	Philippines	6 years
Thomas Dolce	South Africa	10 years/5 years
Frederick Hamilton	Ecuador	37 months
Abdelkaer Helmy	Egypt	5 years/2 years
Geneva Jones	Liberia	37 months
Robert Kim	South Korea	9 years
Steven Lalas	Greece	14 years
Peter Lee	China	1 year
Samual Morrison	Great Britain	2 years/3 months
Jonathan Pollard	**Israel**	**Life**
Michael Schwartz	Saudi Arabia	Navy Discharge/no prison
Sharon Scranage	Ghana	5 years/8 months
Phillip Selden	El Salvador	2 years

Spying For Enemies of United States

Name	Spied For	Punishment/Incarceration
Aldrich Ames	Soviet Union	Life
David Barnett	Soviet Union	18 years
William Holden Bell	Soviet Union	8 years
David Boone	Soviet Union	24 years
Ernest Forbirch	East Germany	15 years
James Hall	Soviet Union/Germany	40 years
Robert Hanssen	Soviet Union	Life without parole
Ronald Humphrey	North Vietnam	15 years
Brian Horton	Soviet Union	6 years
William Kampelis	Soviet Union	40 years/19 years
Clayton Lonetree	Soviet Union	25 years/9 years
Richard Miller	Soviet Union	20 years
Edwin Moore	Soviet Union	15 years
Svetlana Ogordnikova	Soviet Union	18 years
Bruce Ott	Soviet Union	25 years
Ronald Pelton	Soviet Union	40 years
Francis Pizzo	Soviet Union	10 years
Roderick Ramsay	Hungary/Czechoslovakia	36 years
Daniel Richardson	Soviet Union	10 years
Amarylis Santos	Cuba	3 1/2 years
Kurt Allen Stand	East Germany	17 years
Michael Walker	Soviet Union	25 years
John Walker, Jr.	Soviet Union	Life
William Whalen	Soviet Union	15 years
Alfred Zoho	East Germany	8 years

Letter from the White House to Dr. Morris Pollard

THE WHITE HOUSE
WASHINGTON

May 6, 1994

Dear Professor Pollard:

Thank you for your letter to the President regarding your son's request for executive clemency. The President has asked me to respond on his behalf.

I regret that we were unable to schedule an appointment to discuss your son's case prior to the President's decision. Please be assured that the President had a great deal of information before him when he made this difficult decision. As you know, many concerned individuals and groups provided the President with information and opinions on Jonathan's behalf. This information was invaluable to the President in that it provided him with the full range of views concerning the case.

Thank you again for your letter.

Sincerely,

Lloyd N. Cutler
Special Counsel to the President

Professor Morris Pollard
Coleman Professor and Director
International Committee on Laboratory Animals
Lobund Laboratory
University of Notre Dame
Notre Dame, Indiana 46556

Letter from Celebrities to President Clinton

July 11, 1994

President William Clinton
The White House
1600 Pennsylvania Avenue
Washington, D.C. 20510

We, representing many people in the entertainment industry, were deeply disappointed by your recent decision not to grant clemency to Jonathan Pollard. The rejection of Mr. Pollard's petition undermines the fundamental principle of the American judicial system that people who commit similar crimes are supposed to receive reasonably similar punishments.

Jonathan Pollard has already served a longer sentence that any other American who passed classified data to an ally. Accordingly, every additional day that Jonathan Pollard is forced to remain in prison exacerbates the already gross injustice in this case.

We urge to reconsider your decision and demonstrate you commitment to the application of equal justice under the law by commuting Jonathan Pollard's sentence to the eight and a half years he has already served.

Sincerely,

Jon Voight
Jack Lemmon
Whoopi Goldberg
Gregory Peck
Barbara Horshey

Letter of Remorse from Jonathan Pollard to President Clinton

September 12, 1994

President Bill Clinton
The White House
1600 Pennsylvania Avenue
Washington, D.C. 20500

Dear President Clinton,

On the eve of this High Holiday Season. I want to extend my best wishes to you and your family for a healthy and happy New Year.

In one of the most poignant passages of the High Holiday services, we express our recognition that at this time of the year our judgment is being written and sealed. Who shall live and who shall die? Who will live out their full years and who will not? Who shall have tranquillity and who shall be afflicted? But the ultimate resolution of the passage is that, to a great extent, our individual and our collective fate is in our own hands.

I have expressed remorse for my actions on numerous occasions, both publicly and privately, and to myself, every day of my life behind these prison walls. I have been given the last nine years for reflection, and I realize and deeply regret that I did not find a legal means to transmit, what I thought to be, life saving information to Israel. I have always understood that I am not above the law and had to be punished for what I did.

Thanks to the tremendous efforts of my family and good friends, my case has galvanized Americans across the entire political spectrum, ranging from liberal Democrats such as Benjamin Hooks to conservative Republicans such as Pat Robertson. Resolutions and letters in support of the commutation of my sentence have been written by 41 members of Congress, State legislatures, the European Parliament, former Soviet Refuseniks, Nobel Peace Laureate Elie Wiesel and well-known Hollywood personalities such as Jack Lemmon, Gregory Peck, Jon Voight and Whoopi Goldberg. And the Government of Israel has made it abundantly clear that they strongly support the campaign to obtain my freedom.

I have spent half of my adult life in prison and have had many days to think about my actions. As I now ask G-d's forgiveness for transgressions, I am, at the same time, asking forgiveness from you and your help. Please commute my sentence now and allow me to become a productive member of our American society. Please bring an end to this case and the tragic consequences it has had for both my family and me.

May all of our wishes, dreams and aspirations for the New Year be granted.

Jonathan Pollard.

Letter to US President Clinton from 60 Senators

January 11, 1999

The Honorable William J. Clinton
President of the United States
The White House
Washington, D.C., 20500

Dear Mr. President:

We understand that during the course of the Wye talks you committed to review commuting the sentence of the convicted spy Jonathan Pollard. Therefore, you must now decide whether Jonathan Pollard should go free. We believe that he should not.

Because you have previously reviewed Mr. Pollard's case, we believe you are aware of the compelling reasons for his continued incarceration. We urge you to recall your latest denial of Pollard's request for commutation where you cited the "enormity of Pollard's offenses, his lack of remorse, the damage done to our national security, the need for general deterrence and the continuing threat to national security that he pose[s]." Mr. President, nothing has changed since that time. Any grant of clemency would not be viewed as an acquiescence to external political pressures and a vindication of Pollard's specious claims of unfairness and victimization. It would also establish two disturbing precedents.

First, a commutation of Mr. Pollard's life sentence would imply a condonation of spying against the United States by an ally. It would also give credence to the claim that espionage is somehow less serious when Americans spy on behalf of a friendly nation with which they sympathize. This would send the wrong signal to employees within the Intelligence Community. It is an inviolable principle that those entrusted with America's secrets must protect them, without exception, irrespective of their own personal views or sympathies.

Second, it undermines our ability to act as an honest broker throughout the world. We maintain relationships with many nations that are not necessarily complementary to one another. Those relationships depend upon our assurances of confidentiality. If you release Mr. Pollard, it will convey a message to our partners that we view secrets kept from our friends as less sacrosanct. They are not, and we must assure our partners that they are not.

You have stated that you will consider congressional views in your review of the Pollard case. We welcome your invitation and express our strongest opposition to any commutation of the life sentence given Jonathan Pollard for betraying our country. We urge you to deny clemency in the interest of justice and in the interest of national security.

Sincerely,

Richard C. Shelby
Chairman

J. Robert Kerrey
Vice Chairman

Bill Frist
Bob Graham
Bob Smith
Charles E. Grassley
Charles S. Robb
Christopher J. Dodd
Christopher S. Bond
Chuck Hagel
Conrad Burns
Craig Thomas
Daniel K. Akaka
Daniel K. Inouye
Diane Feinstein
Don Nickles
Ernest F. Hollings
Frank H. Murkowski
Frank R. Lautenberg
Fred Thompson
Herb Kohl
James M. Inhofe
James M. Jeffords
Jeff Sessions
Jesse Helms
Jim Bunning
John Ashcroft
John B. Breaux

John F. Kerry
John H. Chafee
John McCain
John W. Warner
Jon Kyl
Joseph I. Lieberman
Judd Gregg
Kay Bailey Hutchison
Kent Conrad
Larry E. Craig
Mary L. Landrieu
Max Baucus
Michael Enzi
Mike Crapo
Mike DeWine
Mitch McConnell
Pat Roberts
Patrick Leahy
Paul Coverdell
Pete V. Domenici
Phil Gramm
Richard G. Lugar
Richard H. Bryan
Robert C. Byrd
Robert F. Bennett
Rod Grams
Sam Brownback
Strom Thurmond
Thad Cochran
Tim Hutchinson
Trent Lott
Wayne Allard

INDEX

Beirut, 77

Bell, William Holden, 219

Ben-Menashe, Ari, 210–11

Benner, Harry, 89

Bennett, Bill, 177

Bennett, Robert, 131, 133

Berger, Samuel, 175

Bernard-Lazare, 193–94

Bialkin, Kenneth, 93

Bible, 70, 156, 232

Billot, General, 195

Black Muslims, 116

Black September Group, 59

Blake, George, 47

Blitzer, Wolf, xv, 18, 25, 26, 51, 52, 60, 63, 76, 77, 115–18, 127, 140, 142, 164, 170, 171, 189, 216, 217, 222, 223

Bloomfield, Douglas M., 114, 156–57

B'nai B'rith International, 92, 161, 222

Bohr, Niels, 203

Bombshell: The Secret Story of America's Unknown Atomic Spy Conspiracy, xix, 202, 205

Bonds, Israeli, 6

Boone, David, 210, 220–21

Boston Globe, 69

Boston University, 212

Brandeis, Louis, 55

Braun, Carol Mosely, 153

Brooke Army Medical Center, 46

Brookins, Gary, 164

Brown, Mrs., 53

Budlong, Morris, 113

Bundy, Ted, xv, 210

Bureau of Prisons, 148, 171, 180

Burton, Dan, 229

Burton Committee, 230

Bush, George H. W., 86, 129, 130, 132–33, 154, 158

Bush, George W., 86, 121, 163, 231, 232

Butner Federal Penitentiary, xx, 172, 225

Caesar, Julius, 61

Campbell Soup Company, 29

Camp David Accords, 41, 71

Camp David Summit, 179

Canadian Jewish News, 156

Caro, Laura, 77

Carter, Jimmy, 41, 62, 71, 228

Casey, William, 213

CBS, 141, 177

Chamber of Deputies, French, 196

Characters and Events in Roman History, 49

Charavay (handwriting expert), 191

Charney, Leon, 13, 15, 103, 105

Chelmno, 69

Chemical Specialties Manufacturers Association, 16

Cheney, Dick, 121, 231

Cherche-Midi military prison, 191, 192

China, 30, 103, 137, 201

Chinese embassy, 30, 91

Christian Broadcasting Network, 154

CIA (Central Intelligence Agency), xvii, 7, 8, 60, 62, 63–64, 75, 76, 85, 86, 87, 133, 134, 150, 169, 176, 209, 212, 213, 219, 228, 231, 232

Cisneros, Henry, 228

Clark School, 52, 53

Clemenceau, Georges, 195

Clinton, Bill, vii, xix, 86, 122, 129, 131, 132, 153, 154, 160, 175, 176, 177, 178, 179, 180–81, 182, 183, 226, 227–31

Clinton, Hillary Rodham, 179–80, 181–82, 228

Clinton, Roger, 228

CNN, xv, xviii

Codevilla, Angelo, 212, 213–14, 214

Coffee, Gordon, 89–90

Cohen, Danny, 21

Cohen, Lona. *See* Krogers

Cohen, Morris. *See* Krogers

Cohen, William, 176

Cohn, Robert, 134

Coleman, Sam, 178

CommCore, 30

Congress, US, 71, 87, 115, 130, 131, 133, 154, 163, 173, 219

Constitution, US, 128, 173

Fifth Amendment, v, xv, 114–15

Sixth Amendment, 182–83

Copacabana, 13

Cornell University, 5, 45, 111, 112, 125

Court of Appeals, US, viii, 113, 162, 164, 197

Crovitz, L. Gordon, 162

Cutler, Lloyd, 87

Dachau, 55–56, 178

Dan, Uri, 175, 176

Dark Side of Camelot, The, 211

Darras, General, 193

Dawson, Congressman, 112

De Clam, Paty, 195

DeConcini, Dennis, 148

Defense, US Department of, 66, 71, 97, 129, 169, 222

Defense Intelligence Agency, US (DIA), 6, 20, 28, 210

Defense Ministry, Israeli, 7, 100. *See also* LAKAM (Lishka le Kishrey Mada)

Demange, Edgar, 192

Depression, 42, 43, 44, 204

Dershowitz, Alan, 114, 122–24, 125, 159–60, 169, 189

Deutch, John, 228

Devil's Island, 193, 196, 197

DIAL-COINS (Defense Intelligence Agency's Community On-Line Intelligence System), 210

DiGenova, Joseph, xviii, xix, 86–87, 89, 91, 94, 95–96, 101–2, 104–5, 107, 113, 114, 117–18, 119, 125, 126, 127, 135,

140, 142, 143, 167, 169, 174, 176, 181–82, 188–90, 207, 215, 216, 217, 218, 224, 226, 227, 229, 232

District Court, US, 53, 56, 89, 90, 97, 106, 111, 112, 113–14, 121, 122, 137, 168, 169, 172

District of Columbia Circuit, Historical Society of, 111–12

D'Ormescheville, Major, 192

Down For The Count, xviii

Dreyfus, Alfred, xix, xx, 115, 190–97, 214

Drinan, Robert, 173

Dror, Annon, 155

Dryfus Affair, The, xix

Dub, Larry, 172

Due process, rights to, v, xv, xvi, xvii, xviii, 160, 180, 199–205, 223

Dumbarton Oaks, 9, 11

DuPlessis (South African naval officer), 75

East Germany, 31, 63–64, 219

Eban Committee, 101, 102

École Militaire, 193

Egypt, 60, 73, 220

Eichmann, Adolf, 7

Eitan, Rafael "Rafi," 7–8, 9, 12, 16, 17, 18, 19, 21, 24, 27, 36, 37, 95, 98, 200–201

"El-Abed" missile, 151

El Al, 61

Ellsberg, Daniel, 202

Emerson, Steven, 210–11

Emerson Preparatory School, 14

Enders, John Franklin, 5, 48, 84

Engineering and Mining Journal, 13

EPA (Environmental Protection Agency), 163

Erb, Irit, 12, 28, 29–30, 36, 95

Esfandiari, Babek, 32

Esfandiari, Christian, 32

ESPN, xviii

"Even Pollard Deserves Better Than Government Sandbagging," 162

Rabbinical Alliance of America, 160

Rabin, Yitzhak, 62, 96, 97

RASIN (radio-signal notations), 209, 210

Rauh, Carl, 133

Ravid, Ilan, 12, 36, 97

Reagan, Ronald, 25, 41, 66, 71, 72, 77, 83, 86, 96, 114, 116, 121, 129, 132, 147, 163, 208, 209, 221

Redford, Robert, 62

Reich, Seymour, 161, 222

Reno, Janet, 176, 180

Republican National Committee, 164

Rexin, Cecelia, xvii

Rice, Charles, 161, 169, 173

Rice University, 83

Rich, Denise, 228

Rich, Mark, vii, xix, 228, 229, 230

Robertson, Pat, 154

Robinson, Aubrey Eugene E., III, xvi, xviii, 18, 111–13, 115, 122, 123, 124–26, 127, 130, 135, 137–42, 143, 144, 147, 148, 153, 156, 161, 165, 167, 168, 169, 188, 189, 199, 207, 216, 217, 218, 221–22, 224

Robinson, Edward Jason, 172

Rogers, Bill, 131

Roosevelt, Franklin Delano, 69, 70

Roper, Elmo, 68

Rosenberg, Ethel, 127, 205

Rosenberg, Julius, 127, 205

Rosenne, Meir, 38

Rosenthal, A. M., 211

Rostenkowski, Daniel, 228

Rous, Peyton, 5

Rubinstein, Elyakim, 37, 38, 84

Ruff, Charles, 176, 226

Russert, Tim, 180, 181

Russia. *See* Soviet Union

Sabin, Albert, 48

Sadat, Anwar, 41, 71

Safire, William, vii, 212–13, 228

Salk, Jonas, 48

SAM missile, 75

Samson Option, The, 208, 211

Sandcastles: The Arabs In Search of the Modern World, 182

Sandherr, Jean-Conrad, 191

Saperstein, David, 227

Saudi Arabia, 219, 223

Saussier, General, 192

Schultz, George, 96, 100, 128, 129, 130, 131

Schumer, Charles, 212, 214

Schwartz, Michael, 219

Schwartzbar, Andre, 56

Scientific Liaison, Office of, 7

Scientology, Church of, 113

Scranage, Sharon, 219

Scud missiles, 151

Secord, Richard, 130

Secret War Against The Jews, The, 129

Select Committee on Intelligence, 130

Sella, Aviem, 2, 5–9, 11, 12–13, 16, 17, 19, 22, 24, 27, 29, 30, 31, 32–33, 34, 35, 80, 84, 88, 95, 101, 121, 127, 153, 204

Sella, Yehudit, 6, 11, 29, 33, 34, 93

Semmelman, Jacques, 169

Senate, US, 86, 176, 177, 179, 180, 182, 212

Serling, Rod, 90

Shadow: Five Presidents and the Legacy of Watergate, 87

Shamir, Yitzhak, 77, 96, 97

Shapiro, Sumner, 144

Sharon, Ariel, 175, 232

Shelby, Richard, 176

Shenon, Philip, 91–92, 96

Shope, Richard, 48

Siewert, Jake, 180

SIGINT Requirements List, 210

Silberman, Laurence, 162, 163–64, 197

Simpson, John R., 223

Simpson, O. J., xviii
Sinai Synagogue Hebrew School, 53–54
Six-Day War, 6, 54, 61–62, 65, 71
Sixty Minutes (TV program), 141, 142, 189, 217
SLA (Symbionese Liberation Army), 228
Smith, Kemba Niambi, 228
Sofaer, Abraham, 95
Soloveichik, Aaron, 154
Sorbonne, 44
South Africa, 75, 77, 79, 122, 123–26, 189, 208, 218
South Bend Riley High School, 53
Soviet Union, 70, 72, 75, 77, 92, 114, 128, 137, 139, 150, 203, 204–5, 208, 209, 210, 213, 215, 219, 220, 221, 224, 231
Specter, Arlen, 153–54
Spielberg, Steven, 93
Springfield Penitentiary, 147, 148–49, 197, 225
Spy Who Knew Too Much, The, xv
St. Louis Jewish Light, 10, 134
Stalin, Joseph, 204
Stanford, Leland, 59
Stanford University, 8, 59, 60, 61, 62, 187
Stanley, Wendell, 5
Starr, Ken, 131
State, US Department of, 66, 70, 71, 95, 96, 169, 219, 221, 222
Stern, Gustav, 5
Stern, Steven, 2, 5
"Stockholm syndrome," 155
Streisand, Barbra, 93
Supreme Court, Israel, 157
Supreme Court, US, 55, 112, 122, 162, 166, 189
"Syndicates, The," 194
Syria, 6, 29, 62, 72, 99, 128, 213

Taiwan, 208
Teamsters Union, 14

Tel Aviv University, 6
Teller, Edward, 203
Tel Nof Air Base, 121, 127
Temps, Le, 192
Tenet, George, xvii, 176, 231, 232
Territory of Lies, xv, 18, 51, 115, 117
Terrorists, Shi'ite, 77
Testament to Courage, xvii
Teysonnières (handwriting expert), 191
Thornburgh, Richard, 124
Three Days of the Condor (film), 62
Time magazine, 177
Tower Commission, 131
"Traitor: The Case Against Jonathan Pollard, The," 208
Triangle Shirtwaist Company, 43
Truman, Harry S, 70
Tufts University, 23, 63
TWA (Trans World Airlines), 83
Twentieth Century Fox, 177
Twilight Zone (TV series), 90
201st Fighter-Bomber Squadron, 6
Tyson, Mike, xviii, 115, 122

Under Fire, 133
United Nations, 70
University of Baltimore, 158
University of Berkeley, 202
University of Chicago, 59, 83
University of Maryland, 14
University of Notre Dame, xviii, 46, 47, 59, 60, 62–63, 83, 87, 88–89, 158, 161, 169
University of Texas, 46
University of Wisconsin, 59
Upton, Fred, 183
USA Today, xviii, 176
US Decision Making In Vietnam, 1945-1968, 202
US-Israel Exchange of Information Agreement, 1, 18, 72, 201, 207, 212